Global International Society

This ambitious book provides a new framework for analyzing global international society (GIS). In doing so, it also links the English School's approach more closely to classical sociology, constructivism, liberal institutionalism, realism and postcolonialism. It retells the story of the expansion of international society to explain why the differences amongst states are as important as their similarities in understanding the structure and dynamics of contemporary GIS. Drawing on differentiation theory, it sets out four ideal-type models for international society. These cover the 'like-units' of the classical English School, as well as differentiation by geography, hierarchy/privilege and function. These models offer a systematic way to integrate international and world society and to understand the relationship between the deep structure of primary institutions and the vast array of intergovernmental and international nongovernmental organizations. In this pioneering book, Buzan and Schouenborg present the reader with the first systematic attempt to define criteria for assessing whether international society is becoming stronger or weaker.

BARRY BUZAN is Emeritus Professor in the London School of Economics Department of International Relations; Honorary Professor at Copenhagen, Jilin and China Foreign Affairs universities; and a fellow of the British Academy. Amongst his twenty-six books are *From International to World Society? English School Theory and the Social Structure of Globalisation* (2004), *An Introduction to the English School of International Relations* (2014) and, with George Lawson, *The Global Transformation: History, Modernity and the Making of International Relations* (2015, winner of Francesco Guicciardini Prize for Best Book in Historical International Relations 2017).

LAUST SCHOUENBORG is Associate Professor of Global Studies in the Department of Social Sciences and Business at Roskilde University, Denmark. He has authored *The Scandinavian International Society: Primary Institutions and Binding Forces, 1815–2010* (2013) and *International Institutions in World History: Divorcing International Relations from the State and Stage Models* (2017) and contributed to *Guide to the English School in International Studies* (2014, eds. Navari and Green).

Global International Society

A New Framework for Analysis

Barry Buzan

London School of Economics and Political Science

Laust Schouenborg

Roskilde Universitet

CAMBRIDGE
UNIVERSITY PRESS

University Printing House, Cambridge CB2 8BS, United Kingdom

One Liberty Plaza, 20th Floor, New York, NY 10006, USA

477 Williamstown Road, Port Melbourne, VIC 3207, Australia

314–321, 3rd Floor, Plot 3, Splendor Forum, Jasola District Centre,
New Delhi – 110025, India

79 Anson Road, #06–04/06, Singapore 079906

Cambridge University Press is part of the University of Cambridge.

It furthers the University's mission by disseminating knowledge in the pursuit of
education, learning, and research at the highest international levels of excellence.

www.cambridge.org
Information on this title: www.cambridge.org/9781108427883
DOI: 10.1017/9781108628167

First published 2018

Printed and bound in Great Britain by Clays Ltd, Elcograf S.p.A.

A catalogue record for this publication is available from the British Library.

Library of Congress Cataloging-in-Publication Data
Names: Buzan, Barry, author. | Schouenborg, Laust., author.
Title: Global international society : a new framework for analysis / Barry Buzan
and Laust Schouenborg.
Description: Cambridge : Cambridge University Press, [2018] | Includes
bibliographical references and index.
Identifiers: LCCN 2018015814| ISBN 9781108427883 (hardback : alk. paper) |
ISBN 9781108448352 (pbk. : alk. paper)
Subjects: LCSH: International relations–Social aspects. | International
relations–Philosophy. | Political sociology.
Classification: LCC JZ1251 .B89 2018 | DDC 303.48/2–dc23
LC record available at https://lccn.loc.gov/2018015814

ISBN 978-1-108-42788-3 Hardback
ISBN 978-1-108-44835-2 Paperback

Contents

Contents

Preface

This project came out of the workshop on regional international society held in Roskilde in June 2015 that was organized by Laust Schouenborg and Morten Valbjørn. The link between the two of us goes back to 2007–10, when Schouenborg's PhD thesis was supervised by Buzan at the London School of Economics (LSE). The conversations in Roskilde inspired Buzan to pull together some longstanding, but not very coherent, ideas about the expansion and differentiation of global international society, and what it was we were talking about when we used terms such as 'global-level international society'. Schouenborg accepted this as the basis for a joint book project, and we began to write in July 2015. Our approach to coauthoring was that each of us took first responsibility for drafting specific chapters, with the other writing into them subsequently until we reached an agreed draft. Buzan took the lead on the Introduction, Chapters 1, 3, 6 and 7 and the first part of Chapter 2, and Schouenborg on Chapters 4, 5 and 8 and the second part of Chapter 2. But all have been jointly revised multiple times and are now agreed as coauthored.

We would like to thank the many colleagues at the University of Copenhagen who at a departmental seminar in November 2015 gave a lot of useful comments around an early version of Chapter 1. Ann Towns helped out by engaging in some stimulating discussions on how to place gender differentiation into the discussion of international society, and Mathias Albert likewise gave us guidance on functional differentiation. Thomas Diez, Knud-Erik Jorgensen, Shogo Suzuki and Yongjin Zhang read drafts of the first six chapters for the 2017 World International Studies Committee (WISC) conference and gave us very helpful feedback. We are grateful to all of these for both their collegiality and their high standards.

Acronyms

AOSIS	Alliance of Small Island States
AIIB	Asian Infrastructure Development Bank
ASEAN	Association of Southeast Asian Nations
BIS	Bank for International Settlements
CCP	Chinese Communist Party
CSCE	Conference on Security and Cooperation in Europe
CARE	Cooperative for Assistance and Relief Everywhere
ES	English School
EC	European Community
EU	European Union
FDM	functional differentiation model
GATT	General Agreement on Tariffs and Trade
GCS	global civil society
GG	global governance
GIS	global-level international society
GUS	global uncivil society
GPM	great power management
GDP	gross domestic product
HPM	hierarchy/privilege model
IPCC	Intergovernmental Panel on Climate Change
IAEA	International Atomic Energy Agency
ICAO	International Civil Aviation Organization
ICJ	International Court of Justice
ICC	International Criminal Court
FIDH	International Federation for Human Rights
ILO	International Labour Organization
IMF	International Monetary Fund
INGO	International Nongovernmental Organization
ISO	International Organization for Standardization
IPE	international political economy
IR	international relations (the academic discipline)
IUCN	International Union for Conservation of Nature

ICANN	Internet Corporation for Assigned Names and Numbers
IS	Islamic State
LUM	like-units model
MSF	Médecins Sans Frontières [Doctors Without Borders]
MNC	multinational corporation
NAM	Nonaligned Movement
NPT	Non-Proliferation Treaty
NSA	non-state actor
NAFTA	North American Free Trade Agreement
NATO	North Atlantic Treaty Organization
NEA	Nuclear Energy Agency
OECD	Organization for Economic Cooperation and Development
PI	primary institution
RSM	regions/subglobal model
R2P	Responsibility to Protect
SoC	standard of civilization
TNA	transnational actor
TNC	transnational corporation
UCD	uneven and combined development
UN	United Nations
UNCTAD	United Nations Conference on Trade and Development
UNCLOS	United Nations Convention on the Law of the Sea
UNEP	United Nations Environment Programme
UNGA	United Nations General Assembly
UNHCR	United Nations High Commissioner for Refugees
UDHR	Universal Declaration of Human Rights
WANO	World Association of Nuclear Operators
WHO	World Health Organization
WTO	World Trade Organization
WWF	World Wide Fund for Nature

Introduction

This Introduction starts by setting out the questions and rationale behind the writing of this book. The second section looks at the payoffs that we see our approach offering for both international relations (IR) theory generally, and English school theory in particular. The last section summarizes the rest of the chapters in the book.

1   Rationale

What exactly is meant by phrases such as 'international society at the global level' or 'global international society' (GIS)? The assumption and rationale of this book are that the answer to this question is far from clear. And without being able to specify the composition and characteristics of GIS in some concrete way, it is not really possible to answer questions either about how GIS was and is composed and whether it was and is getting stronger or weaker. The so-called English School (ES) of international relations can be said to have a de facto copyright to the term *international society*, but arguably this overall question about the composition of GIS is of importance to all other approaches to international relations, as well to other social science disciplines dealing with social relations at a planetary scale. Everyone needs to be able to specify what the 'whole' is that we attempt to discern when we adopt a global social perspective. That goes for ES scholars, globalization scholars, sociologists and the like. This is not to say that answers to this question are entirely missing at present, but that they are often vague, implicit and scattered. Let us begin by outlining the tentative ES perspective on GIS.

GIS comes about as the outcome of the ES's international society expansion story, whereby what starts as a European social form expands to global scale. It does so mainly through processes of colonization and decolonization (the Americas, Africa, South and Southeast Asia, Middle East), but also through socialization and competition (Russia, the Ottoman Empire) and encounter and reform (Japan, China, Iran). After the Second World War and the major round of decolonization that followed it, these processes resulted in a GIS based more or less on the European *Westphalian* model of sovereign equality amongst all states, albeit with the longstanding 'legalized hegemony' of the great powers still embodied in the P5 arrangement of the UN Security Council.

So far, so good. We find the basic force of the expansion story persuasive, and accept that its outcome was indeed a GIS that is a meaningful global social structure, and therefore an important part of the landscape of IR. But that is when the questions start. Mainstream ES writing tended to take this 'thin' GIS as given, and then worried about its cohesion (the 'revolt against the West' by the new third world members) and its normative evolution (mainly in terms of liberal political values such as democracy and human rights). The classical ES did not interest itself much in the possibility of regional international society, even though it grew up while two such examples were in plain sight. The Soviet challenge offered both an alternative regional form and a challenge to the Westphalian format on a global scale. And the European Community (EC) showed a clearly emergent regional differentiation. Neither did the ES pursue the idea strongly latent in 'the revolt against the West', and later in the postcolonial and *dependencia* literatures, that there were deep and significant differences of type amongst the states-members of GIS, and a clear continuation of the core-periphery structure set up during the colonial era. This latter blindness was intensified by the ES's disinclination to engage with the economic dimension of GIS, other than a rather vague commitment to the idea that development would even things out within some politically acceptable timescale. It was hard to avoid the conclusion that just as neorealism's concept of bipolarity served the interests of the two superpowers by privileging their position as an exclusive club of two, so GIS served the interests of the West by covering up both the violent and exploitative relationships of the colonial era that gave birth to it, and the ongoing inequalities that dominated much of its contemporary operation. Moreover, classical ES writers had no teleological view that GIS would inevitably get stronger. As mentioned previously, they feared that expansion/decolonization had weakened the cultural coherence of GIS by diluting the previously dominant Western element. But how could one assess the validity of this claim, or indeed, of its reverse? By what criteria could one understand whether GIS was getting stronger or weaker?

So the ES expansion story, to us, gives rise to a package of questions about the composition of GIS that includes the issues of the characteristics of units, hierarchy, spatial differentiation, strength/weakness and cultural coherence. Conveniently, these issues are also what animate key debates within other IR paradigms, as well debates within the other social sciences. IR realists are majorly concerned with states as core units, sociologists with hierarchy and the strength/weakness of society, anthropologists with cultural coherence and probably all three with spatial differentiation. And, of course, some of these interests overlap. It therefore seemed to us that this package of questions, and the ES angle, provided a useful starting point for an attempt to clarify how we can think about GIS or, if you prefer the noncopyright label, the 'social whole' from a global perspective.

At this stage, the reader is probably wondering what we can bring to the table, how we can leverage our previous research to help answer the overall question about the composition of GIS and whether it is getting stronger or weaker. Five strands of work are relevant in this respect.

The first strand is Buzan's work on interaction capacity (Buzan, Jones and Little, 1993; Buzan and Little, 2000). Interaction capacity is a way of looking at international systems in terms of their carrying capacity for information, goods and people, and the speed, range and cost with which these things can be done. Interaction capacity determines how loosely or tightly international systems are integrated, and consequently how weakly or strongly the neorealist logics of socialization and competition can work. This work was not initially inspired or framed by ES thinking about GIS. But eventually it led in that direction, and amongst other things it raised Buzan's consciousness about both how systems could be internally differentiated, and what the criteria might be for assessing whether a system was strong/thick or weak/thin, and indeed, whether strong/weak and thick/thin were the same, or different, or different but correlated.

The second strand is work on regional international societies. Buzan was already attuned to the regional level from his work on international security (Buzan and Wæver, 2003). From an early point in his late 1990s project to reconvene the ES, regional international society was a particular target. The most obvious opportunity was to build bridges between the ES and those studying the European Union (EU), for what was the EU if not an unfolding case study of the most solidarist international society ever attempted. Lacking the requisite knowledge himself, Buzan encouraged others to look into this (Diez and Whitman, 2002; Riemer and Stivachtis, 2002). And thinking that this was probably the most fruitful way of unpacking GIS, Buzan partnered with Ana Gonzalez-Pelaez (2009) and Yongjin Zhang (2014) to pull together in-depth studies of two other possible regional international societies: the Middle East and East Asia. Both of these cases proved to be more difficult and less conclusive than the EU one. The Middle Eastern study underlined the dramatic differences between the postcolonial weak states in that region and the strong states in the core. It showed some significant signs of a regional societal structure, but it was difficult to put clear boundaries around this. There were indeed several possible boundaries, and these were shaped as much by the transnational and interhuman domains as by the interstate one. The East Asian study underlined both the difficulty of putting boundaries around a regional international society and the powerful and pervasive influence of what were essentially core–periphery dynamics of how local states accepted or challenged the institutions of what Buzan and Zhang referred to as 'the Western-global international society'. These projects, and some others on Latin America (Merke, 2011), suggested that while there were indeed significant elements of international society on the regional level, this was not the only, or perhaps even the best, way of unpacking differentiation within GIS. An interest in regional international society is what initially brought the two of us together. As a history student at the University of Copenhagen in the early 2000s, Schouenborg had been drawn to Buzan's work and decided to pursue a doctorate at the London School of Economics (LSE) with a thesis exploring Scandinavia as a regional international society, which was later published by Routledge (Schouenborg, 2013). This work pushed the research agenda forwards by further investigating how regional international societies could be differentiated from the larger GIS, what constituted them, how they expanded and what held them together. A notable contribution was the first sustained empirical investigation of the concept of binding forces that Buzan had introduced in his 2004 book. This concept is discussed further later in this Introduction.

The third strand is Buzan's work on primary institutions (PIs) (Buzan, 2004a; 2014). By setting up primary institutions as a social structural way of analysing GIS, this work provided the tools for comparing and differentiating international societies across time and space. It was this toolkit that was applied to the regional case studies on the Middle East and East Asia. While discussion of primary institutions is well developed for the interstate domain, almost nothing has been done to think about how to identify social structures in the transnational and interhuman domains.[1] All of these concepts will also be more thoroughly explained later in this Introduction.

The fourth strand is Buzan's work on differentiation theory with Mathias Albert (Buzan and Albert, 2010; Albert and Buzan, 2011; Albert, Buzan and Zürn, 2013). This came about when Albert noticed

---

[1] For first attempts at doing this, see Davies (2017) and Buzan (2018a).

a potential isomorphism between what the Copenhagen School (Buzan, Wæver and de Wilde, 1998) was calling *sectors* and his interest in sociological theories of functional differentiation. Sectors were about analysing securitization logics within economic, political, military, societal (identity) and environmental domains. Functional differentiation, particularly in the work of Luhmann on which Albert was focused, had a seemingly parallel set of what it labelled *function systems.* Although not originally linked to Buzan's work on the ES, this work on differentiation theory opened his mind to thinking more deeply about the composition of social wholes, and the ways in which social structures could be both defined by, and compared on the basis of, how they were differentiated. Differentiation theory began to merge with his thinking about primary institutions, which also took sectoral/functional forms. Functional differentiation likewise had a major impact on Schouenborg's thinking about international society and primary institutions. Following Buzan's lead, he developed a functional typology for theoretically differentiating between primary institutions (Schouenborg, 2011; 2013). This typology was later refined and tested on a crosscultural and transhistorical sample of societies (Schouenborg, 2017). The guiding ambition was to allow for unbiased comparisons between modern international societies and international societies in the more distant past.

The fifth strand is Buzan's work on the expansion and evolutions stories (Buzan and Little, 2009; 2014; Buzan, 2010a; 2012; 2014). This work raised his consciousness not only about the processes by which contemporary GIS was formed, but also about the critical literature around the expansion story, and its Westcentric character. Amongst other things, this engagement led him to start thinking about the making of GIS in terms of two abstract models. The monocentric model, in which one subglobal international society overawes and absorbs the rest, points to a core–periphery legacy. The polycentric model, in which various subglobal international societies expand and interact until they form a global one, points towards regional differentiation.

These five strands of work have offered pathways into formulating the initial question about the composition of GIS, and they have also familiarized us with a diverse set of literatures that have bearing on this question. This book is mainly about pulling these literatures together to achieve a new synthesis, and in the process to think systematically through the issues in the previously outlined package of questions. That inevitably means that the literatures outside IR, with which we are only superficially familiar, receive more limited attention. However, we do consider it a distinct advantage to be able to clarify the ES and IR perspective on the composition of GIS, which can then act as a foundation for a more qualified crossdisciplinary dialogue. For there are, of course, partial answers outside IR to the what-is-GIS-question. A lot of this literature seems to have been partly inspired by the need to capture the contested phenomenon we today label globalization. Appadurai (1996: 33; see also 2013), for example, has introduced five different kinds of global flows: (a) ethnoscapes; (b) mediascapes; (c) technoscapes; (d) financescapes; and (e) ideoscapes. Similarly, political scientists Held et al. (1999: 16–17) have talked about flows and networks of interconnectedness. Castells' (1996; 1997; 1998) impressive work on a theory of the network society is in the same genre. The world society work of the so-called Stanford School (Meyer et al., 1997; Meyer, 2010; Navari, 2018) is another complementary perspective that moreover shares its core concept with the ES (although with a significantly different meaning). Going further back in time, Wallerstein (1974; see also Chase-Dunn and Hall, 1997; Hall et al., 2011) and Mann (1986; 1993; 2012; 2013) have also in their separate ways offered concepts suitable for capturing global social structure. These perspectives point in quite different directions from the ES's conception of global social structure, and none appears to directly address whether that structure, however defined, is getting stronger or weaker.

We believe it is a propitious time to reflect on the question of the composition of GIS. The ongoing shift in power and authority from the West to the rest, changes in the global political economy and what that will mean for the previously Western-dominated global institutions and indeed order have made the task of understanding the fundamental structure of GIS all the more urgent. While not always adopting this specific language, it appears to be a common preoccupation of policy makers and scholars (e.g., Acharya, 2014) to formulate opinions about the potential weakening or strengthening of GIS (the weakening camp seems to be in ascent). Much of this debate in IR is, however, implicitly or explicitly, framed in terms of hegemonic stability theory. In other words, it assumes that hegemons generate international orders, and that as hegemons decline so do the orders they create. Our approach is more in tune with Keohane's (1984) insight that social institutions have strength and staying power separate from hegemons. In other words, social orders have normative and institutional structures that can and should be assessed in their own terms. But how can this be settled? What should we look for and which criteria should be applied? This book is our contribution to putting this debate on a stronger footing.

2   Aims

Our general aim is to address all those in IR (and beyond) who are
interested in the composition and structure of the international system/
society. There is some tendency to differentiate the ES, on the one hand,
from realism and liberalism, on the other, by attaching an 'international
society' label to the former, and an 'international system' one to the latter
two. But while it is alluring in some ways to make the differentiation
between system (physical, mechanical) and society (social, and under
endless reproduction and reconstruction), this separation has always
been false. As Onuf (2002: 228) astutely pointed out, even for realists,
'sovereignty is the only rule that matters for the constitution of anarchy'.
Thus even realism depends on a social construction, for if the rule of
sovereignty was not there, the 'system' would not be anarchic. As Bull
(1977: 233–81) explained long ago, there are many other forms that
the world political system could take, and may take in the future. Both
the ES and constructivists (e.g., Wendt, 1999) have established that the
international system is an inescapably social structure, and that social
structure cannot exist apart from the mechanical interactions that define
systems. Within the ES, there is a substantial body of thought that rejects
the system/society distinction altogether, essentially seeing a range of
types of international society (for a summary of that debate, see Buzan,
2014: 171–2).

   If one accepts that system and society are two sides of the same coin,
then the enquiry we make here speaks to all those in IR who want to
understand the system/society nexus. In part, this is therefore a general
theoretical contribution applicable to all times and places where there is
'an international' to be studied.[2] But its main empirical focus is on the
formation and structure of the contemporary GIS. Once the conflation of
system and society is accepted, and sovereignty recognized as a social
institution rather than a permanent fixture, then the apparent perman-
ence of 'anarchy', so beloved by realists, evaporates. Sovereignty/anarchy
becomes just one social choice amongst many. On that basis, the key ES
question about how strong or weak an international society is, and in
which direction it is moving, ceases to be a concern only of those focused
on international society, and also becomes a central question for those
who prefer the 'international systems' label. Those primarily interested
in international systems have not paid much attention to the strength/
weakness of systems as such (Buzan and Little, 2000). They have focused

---

[2] On the concept of 'the international', see Rosenberg (2013; 2016).

on the distribution of power within the system, and the stabilities/instabilities of that, rather than on the underlying system itself, which is either taken as given or assumed to be a permanent condition.

The constructivist norms literature has also, somewhat surprisingly, not given much thought to what the social whole is that we encounter at the global level and the strength/weakness of this social structure. Wendt (1999) is more or less the only one who has adopted the holistic or global perspective with his ES-inspired discussion of different cultures of anarchy. There is an implication in Wendt that his Hobbesian, Lockean and Kantian types of international society represent a spectrum of weaker-to-stronger, but his thinking is so infused with normative preferences for more liberal values that it is difficult to disentangle the two lines of thought. The early constructivist scholars who focused on the development and spread of norms (e.g., Finnemore and Sikkink, 1998; Keck and Sikkink, 1998; Risse et al., 1999) were generally not concerned about the social whole, but sought to explicate how, mostly 'nice' (meaning Western and progressive), norms were successfully promoted by activist 'norm entrepreneurs' and gradually internalized by states. When later work put an emphasis on norm contestation (Wiener, 2004; 2014), selective and mediated adoption of norms by states in non-Western regions (Acharya, 2004; 2011) and direct opposition in the form of 'norm antipreneurs' (Bloomfield, 2016; Bloomfield and Scott, 2017), there was still little in the way of sustained reflection on what the aggregate social formation was/is and whether contestation led to its weakening or strengthening. At most, this literature appeared to talk about antagonistic normative communities (Bloomfield, 2016: 320, 331), without sufficiently specifying the boundaries, conceptual and geographical, of these phenomena.

Liberal institutionalist approaches view GIS much more in terms of secondary institutions (regimes and intergovernmental organizations [IGOs]) than primary ones. Like constructivist approaches, they are also infused with preferences for liberal/Western values, and in addition carry the burden that they are often highly US-centric in their concerns. Liberal institutionalists seem more worried about the impact of US decline on a US-centred world order, and the consequences for the US of it disengaging from supporting that order, than they are about GIS itself. This attitude is very clear in recent works such as Ikenberry (2009) and Brooks, Ikenberry and Wohlforth (2012–13), which seem to be aimed mainly at keeping the United States in play as the leader of a liberal world order, not least by pointing out all of the advantages that it accrues from being leader. In an earlier round of declinism, Keohane's (1984) classic *After Hegemony* could be interpreted as saying that world order was stronger with a hegemon in play, but once established, might survive as a system of rules even after the hegemon had declined. This literature reflects the influence of hegemonic stability theory (Gilpin, 1981; 1987), and carries the implicit hypothesis that GIS is stronger with a hegemon than without, though disentangling this from the particular interests of the hegemon itself, in this case the United States, is not easy.

But while mainstream liberal institutionalism offers only thin insights into the structure of GIS, there is a promising literature emerging on thinking about the linkages between primary and secondary institutions (Spandler, 2015; Navari, 2016).[3] Here the main focus is on how to think about primary and secondary institutions together, with each constituted by and constitutive of, the other. Primary institutions set the framework for secondary ones, but secondary institutions are not just expressions of primary ones. They are also places where primary institutions are reproduced and practiced, and where their meanings and practices are developed and evolved. Few secondary institutions would be structured as they are without the primary institution of sovereignty, and primary institutions such as development, the market and environmental stewardship would not mean what they now do without the extensive debates and negotiations around them that took place in secondary institutions. Exploration of this theme is still at an early stage, but its development seems very likely to throw useful light on how we understand the structure and evolution of GIS.

With all of this in mind, our main aims for this book are to contribute to IR theory along the following lines.

- We want to add to the consciousness within IR that much of its theory is abstracted from (mainly Western) history, and that IR theory and world history are in important ways co-constitutive (Buzan and Lawson, 2018). We do this by relating the ES's historical analysis, particularly its expansion story (Bull and Watson, 1984a; Buzan and Little, 2014; Dunne and Reus-Smit, 2017) to its structural one. Linking these two shows how the process of formation that led to the contemporary GIS has led to a variety of structural legacies both for the states forged in this process and for GIS as a whole. These legacies drive a set of significant differentiations of state type and of geography, status and function within GIS, that are important components of any structural understanding of GIS.

---

[3] Tonny Brems Knudsen and Cornelia Navari are also working on a book on this topic: *International Organization in the Anarchical Society.*

- These differentiations provide specific taxonomical tools for assessing the strengths and weaknesses of GIS, and indeed international society at any level, which has become an urgent issue as the West loses the dominant global position it has enjoyed over the past two centuries, both in its ability to generate and exercise power and authority and in its control over the agenda setting and rule making for GIS. As the West goes into relative decline, it will become increasingly important to be able to understand how and why GIS is getting stronger or weaker. To do this, we take a close look at the composition and structure of the contemporary GIS, developing four ideal-type models of it: *like-units*, *regional/subglobal*, *hierarchy/privilege* and *functional differentiation*. We assess how well or badly these models capture the units, structures and binding forces of GIS.
- Through these models, we provide links to the literatures in both the ES and IR more generally, about both hierarchy and hegemony and functional differentiation within the anarchical society. Amongst other things, we cast some light on how to link the transnational and interhuman domains to the interstate one, and for the ES and IR theory, how to relate the ES's core concept of primary institutions to the IR 'institutionalism' that focuses on secondary institutions (intergovernmental and nongovernmental organizations and regimes).
- We aim also to provide a wider range of systematic criteria for comparative and evolutionary studies of international societies.

Our focus in this book is on social structures. We do not cover the dramatic increases in the physical interaction capacity of the international system that have been extensively documented elsewhere (Buzan and Little, 2000; Buzan and Lawson, 2015a).

It is also a book prioritizing the analytical over the normative. As ES scholars, we represent a marginal position in this respect. Most writers in this tradition, past and present, have had a normative focus, often inspired by political theory. Generally, they have concerned themselves with the 'is' as a bridge to reflect on the 'ought': how to achieve a better international society or how to move beyond it to a better alternative. We, by contrast, are only focused on the 'is'. This is emphatically not because we conceive the analytical and the normative to represent two fundamentally incompatible intellectual projects. Rather, we see them as highly complementary. Clarifying what 'is', to us, seems to be an indispensable move in contemplating what 'ought' to be and how best to get there. With this book, we do not claim that a strong international society is necessarily normatively better than a weak one; we aim for as detached and analytical a perspective as possible. But for those mainly interested in the normative project of promoting a better and stronger international society (or, like the Brexiteers, a 'better' but weaker one), we think that such a project would be greatly enhanced by being able to first specify what comprises international society and how to assess whether it is getting stronger or weaker. We see better/worse as a distinct, though sometimes overlapping, question from weaker/stronger. By focusing on the latter question, we hope to deliver one possible point of departure for those interested in more normative projects. Buzan's 2004 revision of ES theory and the normative/analytical distinction was already 'rather radical', according to his own assessment as well as that of others (Buzan, 2004a: 228; Williams, 2011: 1237), and in this book Schouenborg may have radicalized Buzan even further! However, in one sense, at least, our project does stay true to the heritage of one of the ES 'founding fathers'. Hedley Bull also had a penchant for going back to first principles to rethink and shed new light on the complex problems thrown up by contemporary world politics (Howard, 2008: 127), and in this book we fiercely pursue that agenda. Last but not least, in the course of our argument, we also engage the traditional ES debate between solidarists and pluralists, and we believe we offer several novel additions and clarifications to it.

3   Summary of Contents

Chapter 1 argues that international society at the global level is inadequately theorized. It sets up a differentiation approach as a way to rectify this shortcoming and applies that both to the units that comprise the membership of GIS and to the structures of GIS itself. It also considers how to theorize the binding forces that hold social structures together. This two-level framework of differentiation – of the types of members, and of the substructures – of GIS, alongside the issue of binding forces, forms the basic approach of the book.

Chapter 2 focuses on how the formative process of GIS over the past few centuries explains the differentiation we find both among states and within GIS. The formative process is framed in the form of two general models: *polycentric* (where several separate civilizational cores merge into a single international society) and *monocentric* (where one local civilizational core rises to dominate all the others). The monocentric model is the one that fits most closely with the expansion story, and the chapter explores four submodels within that of how both the states and some of the other substructures of GIS came into being: *unbroken creation, repopulation, colonization/decolonization* and *encounter/reform*. The analysis concentrates on how these models generated marked differentiations amongst the types of states that became members of contemporary GIS and sometimes distributed these differences in patterned ways.

Chapters 3 through 6 build on the theory and history in the first two chapters to set up four ideal-type models of contemporary GIS: 'like-units', regional/subglobal, hierarchy/privilege and functional differentiation. Each of these chapters sets out the assumptions of the model and gives a short sketch of how the world looks through the lens of the model. This is done in both static (what the GIS looks like now) and dynamic (how has history unfolded to bring us to where we are) modes. On this basis, we set out the criteria within the model by which one might judge whether an international society viewed in these terms is getting weaker or stronger. The chapters then turn to a critical assessment of the model, asking how well or badly it captures the units, the structures, and the binding forces of GIS.

Chapter 7 combines these four ideal-type models into an attempted representation of the contemporary GIS in all of its complexity and contradiction. It starts by attempting to allocate the relative weight of the four component models across four historical eras from classical times to the present. It then turns to the question of whether, and in what ways, GIS is getting stronger or weaker. This is done by aggregating the criteria for this identified in the four models and asking how this complex and often messy GIS is evolving, and how its different layers play into each other in co-constituting ways.

Chapter 8 explores the implications of this framework for both English School and IR theory and reviews how well or badly we fulfilled our opening aims and why, and what research agenda thereby unfolds.

Part I

Theory

1 Theorizing International Society

The English School (ES) has made quite a lot of progress in setting out a structural approach to the analysis of international society. The main concepts for this have been *primary institutions* (which identify the deep structure of international society) and the differentiation into three domains defined by the type of actor dominant within them (interstate, transnational and interhuman) (Buzan, 2004a; 2018a). Nevertheless, this chapter argues that the structure of global-level international society (GIS) remains inadequately theorized. We retain the approach to GIS through primary institutions and domains but add to it a differentiation theory borrowed from sociology as a way to rectify this shortcoming. We apply this differentiation theory both to the units that comprise the membership of GIS and to the structures of GIS itself. We also bring in Wendt's (1999) ideas about the binding forces that hold social structures together as part of the framework.

1 The Inadequate Theorization of the Global Level in English School Theory

Most of the ES's work on international society focuses either implicitly or explicitly on the global level. The school's main historical story is about how the form of international society that developed in Europe from the fifteenth century eventually expanded to global scale on the back of European power (Bull and Watson, 1984a; Keene, 2002; Buzan and Little, 2014; Dunne and Reus-Smit, 2017). The expansion story privileges the global level in two ways: first, by focusing on the making of a global-scale international society; and second, by focusing on how that society has evolved as a global social structure. This privileging of the global level has been to some extent reinforced by the normative concern about universal values within the ES, where the universalist perspective easily elides with global scale. The form of international society that emerged in Europe is often labelled *Westphalian*, linking it to the key

IR benchmark date of 1648, which is commonly, though arguably,[1] used to symbolize the rise of the sovereign, territorial state as the prime unit of the international system/society. The essential features of Westphalian international society are sovereign, territorial states relating to each other as legal equals and 'like-units' and not acknowledging any higher secular authority.

There is much contestation about the details of the expansion story. These issues are dealt with elsewhere in the ES literature,[2] and will not be specifically discussed here other than where they impact on our core theme. The main debates (and our position on them) are as follows:

• Was the European development pristine, or somehow related to wider Eurasian and global dynamics? (Our position: the latter.)
• Did Europe expand into a kind of sociopolitical void, or did it have a series of interactive encounters with other forms of international society? (Our position: the latter.)
• Was the process of European expansion to global scale a fairly steady process starting from the voyages of exploration in the late fifteenth century, or was it episodic, with the relatively easy takeover of the Americas in the fifteenth and sixteenth centuries, contrasting with much slower and more contested dynamics in Africa and Asia, in most of which the Europeans did not become dominant until the nineteenth century? (Our position: the latter.)
• In this expansion process, what was the balance between coercive imposition by the strong over the weak versus consensual acceptance by 'less advanced' cultures of the forms and values of the 'more advanced cultures'? (Our position: a mix, but with a lot of coercion, both applied and latent.)

Regardless of these controversies, there is a general consensus that during the nineteenth century the Westphalian form of international society, or at least the core set of mainly Western states representing it, became globally dominant. The revolutions of modernity for the first time enabled a relatively small group of states to dominate the rest on a global scale (Buzan and Lawson, 2015a). Since the middle of the nineteenth century, by which time the last great holdouts of the classical world, China and Japan, had been 'opened', there is not much dispute that an international society on a global scale has been in existence. It is that understanding that provides the starting point for our enquiry.

---

[1] See discussion of this debate in Buzan and Lawson (2015a: 48–50).
[2] See Buzan and Little (2014) for a survey.

Within this general understanding lie very different views of what that GIS looks like. Building on Buzan and Zhang (2014: 5–6), we can provide a useful, if rather grandly simplified, characterization of the ends of the spectrum:

- The *globalization view* perhaps represents the orthodox, Western and mainly liberal understanding of GIS. It sees GIS as fairly evenly, if thinly, spread on a global scale. The foundation of this view is the widespread acceptance by nearly all states and peoples of the basic Westphalian institutions of sovereignty and nonintervention (and sovereign equality), territoriality, diplomacy, international law, great power management and restraints on war. Nationalism, human equality and the market are also seen as enjoying relatively wide and consensual acceptance by states and peoples. A common, but by no means universal, assumption in this view is that the global level will tend to get stronger in relation to the regional one, because international society is becoming more homogenized as a result of the operation of global economic, cultural and political forces (also known as global capitalism). This view has a lot of room for world society because both liberal states and advances in communication technology have facilitated the rise of an organized global civil (and uncivil) society. The globalization view mainly anticipates either a triumph of liberal Western hegemony or a kind of compromise in which some non-Western elements are woven into the Western framing. This view tends to downplay or discount both the coercive history behind the construction of GIS and the rather considerable differences that lurk within both the category of 'state' and the idea of GIS itself.

At the other end of the spectrum is the following view:

- The *postcolonial view* represents the perspective from the other side: those who came out second best in the encounter with an expanding West empowered by the revolutions of modernity. It sees international society as an imposed and uneven core–periphery structure in which the West still has a privileged, but partly contested, hegemonic role, and non-Western regions are in varying degree subordinate to Western power and values. The emphasis is on the coercive imposition of GIS, the large inequalities within it, and the differences in the types of state that compose it. The ongoing hegemonism of the Western core is expressed in its promotion of 'universal' liberal values such as human rights, democracy and the market, and universal shared-fate values, particularly environmentalism, that are contested by significant parts of the periphery (and indeed some within the core, though in the case of liberal values many fewer than before the end of the Cold War). Here the main assumption, and for some, hope, is that as the Western vanguard declines relative to the rise of non-Western powers such as China, India, Russia, Turkey and Brazil, the global level of international society in its current form will weaken. A widespread antipathy to hegemonism will add to this weakening. It is less clear what then follows: perhaps a relative strengthening of regional international societies as non-Western cultures seek to reassert their own values and resist (at least some of) those coming from the Western core; perhaps a reformed, more multicultural and probably pluralist GIS; perhaps just a general weakening of social order at the global level.

These two views suggest a broad spectrum of possibilities both for how to understand GIS and how to assess in what direction it is evolving. Combinations of features are possible, and there is a lot of scope for messy mixtures in the middle of the spectrum.

Our purpose in this book is to enquire into the form and nature of the GIS, and to do so not just in a static, snapshot way, but also in a dynamic way to show how it has evolved and where it might be heading. We are interested in engaging with the debates about how the contemporary GIS was made, but mainly in terms of how the process of making affects the structure and dynamics of the 'whole' that came into being during the nineteenth century and has been evolving ever since. The formative process shapes not only the types of state that become members of GIS, and when and under what circumstances they become members, but also what primary institutions become dominant. The formative process equally shapes the substructures of the GIS, whether those be geographical (regional, subglobal), egalitarian (sovereign equality), hierarchical (core–periphery, states over non-state actors), functional differentiation (sectors) or all four together. How the GIS was made thus affects powerfully the nature of the global whole that it produces, and the legacies of the formative process are not short lived, but often enduring. This shaping effect is strongly hinted at, though not much explored, in the classical ES's concern with whether the major expansion of international society that took place with decolonization after 1945 weakened the cohesion of GIS by diluting its cultural coherence (Bull and Watson, 1984a; Watson, 1992; Buzan, 2010).

Raising the question of structural inequity and differences of position poses the problem of how weak or strong GIS is and in which direction it is moving on that spectrum. The ES generally does not have a teleological view of international society, allowing that it might be weaker or stronger in different times and different places, and might be moving in either direction, according to how its member states both define their identities and construct their behaviour. But within that, the ES has not thought much about what the criteria might be for designating any international society as weaker or stronger. By implication, the main element at stake is the range and extent of shared values amongst states that enable them to construct the institutions of international society, both primary and secondary. To the extent that states share values, they can build primary institutions such as sovereignty, nationalism, the balance of power and such. This view was what led to a certain pessimism amongst the first generation of ES writers, many of whom worried about the effect of decolonization in diluting the shared values available to support GIS. Even when values are shared in a broad sense, as with sovereignty, there may be differences of interpretation and practice within that, with some taking a quite hard, absolute view of sovereignty, as China famously does, and others taking a softer, more conditional view, like that within the EU. And then there is the issue of why states share values: through belief, through calculation or through coercion (Wendt, 1999).

These thoughts open the door to the more general question of how international society is internally differentiated: along what lines, and at what depths, does such differentiation take place; and how do the particular forms of differentiation play into, and define, what GIS actually means? How much is actually shared at the global level, how much contested, and by whom? Is what is contested, or simply different, actually threatening to the cohesion of GIS, or might some forms of differentiation be neutral towards, or even complementary with, GIS? Functional differentiation into, say, economic, political, nuclear, and environmental international societies, might work in this way.[3] Does the differentiation within GIS itself have structural patterns, and are these patterns relatively stable or visibly in transition?

The argument we are making is that to understand the GIS, one needs to know not only what are the common elements that define it, but also how it is differentiated. And both of these elements need to be understood not just as static structures but as dynamic processes of construction, evolution and obsolescence. The ES has made some progress in charting the globally shared elements in this dynamic way (Mayall, 1990; Buzan, 2004a, 2014a; Holsti, 2004), but relatively little in exploring differentiation and its dynamics even within the interstate

---

[3] The idea of 'sectoral' international societies is suggested by Stroikos (2015), who makes a preliminary case for a nuclear international society.

domain, let alone the transnational and interhuman ones (also known as 'world society' in ES jargon). Both historical observation (for example, of colonial international society) and contemporary empirical analysis (for example, of the different types of states in play within GIS, of core–periphery structures and of regional international societies such as the EU) suggest that differentiation is a substantial feature of GIS, both in terms of geography and hierarchy. There is certainly significant substance to the idea that 'like-units' share sufficient primary and secondary institutions (these concepts are defined later in this chapter) to comprise an international social order at the global level. But there is likewise a lot of evidence suggesting that to think of GIS as a homogeneous construction composed of 'like', sovereign states sharing a set of values and institutions is at best dangerously oversimplified and at worst seriously misleading.

2   Constructing a Differentiation Approach to the GIS

To answer these questions requires constructing a differentiation approach to GIS. In what ways can an international society possess sufficient homogeneity to count as a society in a significant way, yet still be internally differentiated in ways that significantly affect its operation and structure? Our foundation for this construction is the application to IR of differentiation theory from sociology and anthropology proposed by Buzan and Albert (2010). They set out a simple scheme based on three basic types of differentiation: segmentary, stratificatory and functional.

- *Segmentary* (or *egalitarian*) differentiation is where every social subsystem is the equal of, and functionally similar to, every other social subsystem. In anthropology and sociology, this points to families, bands, clans and tribes.[4] In IR, it points to anarchic systems of sovereign states as 'like-units'. Segmentation is the simplest form of social differentiation, though that does not mean that societies of this type are in any general sense simple. A segmentary form of differentiation is the one most prone to be organized in terms of territorial delimitations, although this is not necessarily so. The obvious fit with IR is in terms of sovereign territorial states as 'like-units'.

---

[4] See Schouenborg (2017) for an extensive critique of the theoretical construction of these specific unit concepts and their ties to stage models of development across the social sciences. However, note that Schouenborg does not dispute the idea of segmentary differentiation as an organizing principle.

- *Stratificatory* differentiation is where some persons, groups or units raise themselves above others, creating a hierarchical social order. Stratificatory differentiation covers a wide range of possibilities and can be further subdivided into rank and class forms distinguished by whether or not there is significant inequality not just in status (rank) but in access to basic resources (class). Stratification can occur in many dimensions: coercive capability, access to resources, authority, status. In IR, it points to the many forms of hierarchy: conquest and empire; hegemony; a privileged position for great powers; a division of the world into core and periphery, or first and third worlds; and the primacy of states over non-state actors (NSAs).

- *Functional* differentiation is where the subsystems are defined by the coherence of particular types of activity and their differentiation from other types of activity, and these differences do not stem simply from rank. The idea was initially drawn from biological metaphors about the different subsystems that compose living organisms. This form of differentiation is closely related to the division of labour into specialized skills, which creates powerful structures of interdependence within a population. It is generally thought of as the essential characteristic of modernity. It points to the increasing division of society into legal, political, military, economic, scientific, religious and suchlike distinct and specialized subsystems or sectors of activity, often with distinctive institutions and actors. In IR functional differentiation points, *inter alia*, to international political economy (IPE), international law, world (or global civil) society, transnational actors and the debates about deterritorialization, a set of elements that have so far lacked a unifying concept in IR theory debates other than the extremely loose one of 'globalization'.

If seen as abstract ideal-types, these three forms of differentiation each represent a profoundly different organizing principle. If seen as a grand scheme for representing human history, then these forms define the dominant organizing principle for a particular historical era: segmentary defines hunter-gatherer societies, stratificatory defines the structures of agrarian societies and functional defines the societies of industrial modernity. There may be other types of social differentiation, but so far nobody has come up with anything convincing outside these three.

There is some sense of historical sequence based on these three types, an evolution in which more complex forms grow out of the simpler ones that precede them: segmentary hunter-gatherer bands preceded the stratified city states and empires of ancient and classical times, which preceded the functionally differentiated societies characteristic of modernity.[5] That said, there is no teleology of progress about this: higher forms can revert to lower ones. It is also not the case that one form eliminates the others. Instead, one form becomes the dominant one, containing and framing the others, or possibly two or more forms coexist without either being obviously dominant. This co-presence is immediately apparent in contemporary modern societies and states, where it is easy to identify all three types of differentiation in simultaneous operation. The contemporary GIS also contains all three forms, with the dominant segmentary one (territorial states, sovereign equality, anarchy) being questioned by both stratificatory elements (the return of empire, great powers, hegemony, core–periphery, the dominance of states over non-state actors) and functional ones (globalization, deterritorialization, transnational actors, an increasingly autonomous global economy and international law).

This scheme was designed for analysing the first order, unit-level societies studied by anthropologists and sociologists, in which the members are individual human beings. Transposing it to IR generates a two-level problem in which both the units and the international system/society are themselves differentiated, creating a considerably more complicated picture. International societies are second-order ones, not a society of individuals, but a society of societies. If there are two levels in play in IR, one needs to apply the structural questions of differentiation to both, asking not just how the individual units are differentiated internally, but also how GIS as a whole is differentiated. Standard answers to these questions might be that the leading states display quite advanced degrees of functional differentiation, while the interstate domain remains a mixture of segmentary (sovereign equality) and stratificatory differentiation (hegemony). States retain a formal primacy over NSAs both domestically and within GIS, but this is being challenged at both levels, and both formally and informally, from the transnational and interhuman domains.

A two-level framing of differentiation in IR means that segmentary differentiation has to be reconsidered. In an IR perspective, segmentary differentiation at the system level can become much more sophisticated because the 'like-units' that compose it may themselves have very complex and sophisticated modes of differentiation within them. A segmentary differentiation of the system based on units that are functionally differentiated internally is neither simple nor primitive.

---

[5] Again, see Schouenborg (2017) for an extensive critique of the stage models of development often assumed in such evolutionary stories across different disciplines. However, at the same time he does not dispute idea that societies have generally become more stratified and functionally differentiated over time.

In a second-order society, the question is how the different modes of differentiation, both within states and within GIS, play into the rise, evolution and obsolescence of the institutions of international society studied by Mayall (1990), Holsti (2004) and Buzan (2004a; 2014a). Specifically, if great powers are the key generators of such institutions, can one link the nature of their own internal differentiation to the specific types of institutions that they promote and support? The suggestive evidence for such a link is strong. Colonialism and great power management surely link to stratificatory differentiation, sovereign equality and nationalism to segmentary differentiation and the market and international law to functional differentiation.

Our general approach to differentiating GIS therefore has three basic types, or forms, of differentiation operating in potentially quite complex ways across two levels: the units that compose GIS and the structure of GIS. Cutting across and through this formation are the three domains: interstate, transnational and interhuman.[6]

3   Differentiation at the Unit Level

The classical Westphalian model of the ES puts a lot of emphasis on the members being 'like–units' in terms of the particular set of forms and institutions that define the modern state. States then formally recognize each other on the basis of this similarity and thus lay the foundations for a society of states. Down this path, the membership of GIS is uniform in the sense that all members have to meet a set of criteria that define them as the same type of entity. Other types of entity, such as firms or international nongovernmental organizations (INGOs), are only allowed to play, and indeed exist, within the rules set by states. This classical, state-centric model defines an international society in which the dominant differentiation is segmentary (sovereign equality), albeit with significant elements of stratificatory differentiation in the form of both hegemony and special rights for great powers within the society of states (Simpson, 2004) and the dominance of the state form of organization over all other civic NSAs.

Because this model depends on the 'like-units' assumption, it has not encouraged enquiry into how the state members of international society might nevertheless differ significantly from each other within the broad parameters that make them 'like-units'. Our scheme suggests that 'like-units' might be quite radically different from each other, and that this might be quite consequential for the functioning of international society. Most obviously, the internal structure of some units might be

---

[6] For discussion of the three domains, see Buzan (2004a: 118–38), and Buzan (2018a).

dominated by functional differentiation, whereas that of others might be dominated by stratificatory differentiation. Advanced, 'postmodern', liberal capitalist societies suggest functional differentiation, whereas authoritarian states and absolutist monarchies suggest that stratification is still dominant. The very nature of the modern state in concentrating sovereignty centrally perhaps makes a segmentary state difficult to conceptualize. But loose forms of federalism, such as in Switzerland, and 'failed states', such as Somalia or Afghanistan in which local warlords hold sway over patches on the internal territory, come close.

The question of how different the state members of international society can be within the framing of 'like-units' is a basic taxonomical question similar to many other questions of classification. For example, the category 'fruit' identifies a subset of 'like-units' within the larger category of plant life and provides criteria for differentiating fruits from vegetables. But fruit is still a pretty broad category, containing everything from tomatoes and oranges, through bananas and pineapples, to apples, figs and durian. Narrower categories tighten the criteria for membership in the group: for example, apples. But within the apples category, there is also a large scope for differentiation into subtypes, such as Bramley, Cox's, Golden Delicious and several thousand others. There is a certain fractal quality to the classification process of 'like-units' in which every subgroup can itself be further disaggregated. In the end, because no two members of any group are ever going to be absolutely identical, it can be carried to the technically true, but analytically counterproductive, extreme of claiming that everything is unique. On this spectrum, the category of 'state' is probably something like 'apples'. It has fairly tight criteria for defining membership of a set of 'like-units', but, as witnessed by vast literatures on levels of development, type of politics, differences of culture, amounts of wealth and power and such, also a lot of scope for differentiation within the set. Similar scope for differentiation within a set exists for religions (the many branches of Christianity, Islam and Buddhism) and ideologies (the many types of Marxism), both of which are famously fissiparous. Above the category of state is the more fruitlike category of *polities* (Ferguson and Mansbach, 1996; Schouenborg, 2017), which might include such things as empires, tribes and confederations. So even the 'like-units' idea of Westphalian international society contains a lot of scope for differentiation amongst the membership.[7]

---

[7] Schouenborg (2017) has argued that the 'state' should be abandoned as an abstract social science concept applicable to all times and all places throughout history. However, this does not rule out operating with the concept of states as a more narrowly defined type of polity in the post-1648 era, characterized by fairly stable and identifiable properties.

But international societies do not have to be confined to a single type of member. The solidarist wing of the ES has for long argued that GIS should be, and up to a point already is de facto, composed of multiple types of unit, not just states, but also multinational corporations (MNCs), INGOs and even individuals (Buzan, 2004a). It argues that up to a point these units already have autonomous standing in international (or world) society, and that they can and should have such status. When that is the case, the membership of international society is formally differentiated right from the beginning, and the 'like-units' assumption about international society falls. In international societies with multiple types of legitimate member, recognition is based not on likeness, but on an acknowledged position within a division of labour: states govern, firms do business, INGOs lobby. Waltz (1979) famously argued that functional differentiation of units along these lines necessarily indicated a hierarchical (i.e., stratified) structure, but while this might be the case it is difficult to see why it has to be so. Under functional differentiation, a division of labour can be constructed consensually without any one unit having to be dominant overall. In international societies with multiple types of member, there will again be scope for differentiation within each of the allowed types of legitimate member, e.g., states, MNCs, INGOs.

Chapter 2 will explore in more detail differentiation at the unit level with a view not only to sketching the range, depth, origins and character of the differences, but also to opening up thinking about how such differences might play into the nature and cohesion of international society.

4   Differentiation at the Level of GIS

When we move up to the system level, all three basic forms of differentiation become available. The conventional IR wisdom, as noted previously, is that the international system/society is dominantly segmentary based on states as 'like-units'. But it is easily possible to imagine it as stratificatory using images of a world empire, a world federation or a core–periphery structure. There are plenty of views from postcolonial core–periphery to American hegemony that support such an analysis. A little less easily, because it brings the primacy of states into question, is imagining the international system/society as dominated by functional differentiation. Few think this to be the case yet, but some globalization enthusiasts see it as trending in this direction.

The English School has not so far thought much in terms of this kind of differentiation theory. Within ES theory, the principal marker for social structure is primary institutions, though there is an increasing sense that the interplay between primary and secondary institutions needs to be understood more deeply, so that secondary institutions can be brought into this picture as well (Spandler, 2015; Navari, 2016). The ES uses this institutional approach not only to define the boundaries and character of particular international societies, but also to compare international societies across space and time, and to differentiate regional level international societies from the global one. Buzan (2014: 16–17) defines primary and secondary institutions as follows:

- *Primary institutions* are those mainly talked about by the English School. They are deep and relatively durable social practices in the sense of being evolved more than designed. These practices must not only be shared amongst the members of international society, but also be seen amongst them as legitimate behaviour. Primary institutions are thus about the shared identity of the members of international society. They are constitutive of both states and international society in that they define not only the basic character of states but also their patterns of legitimate behaviour in relation to each other, and the criteria for membership of international society. The classical 'Westphalian' set includes sovereignty, territoriality, the balance of power, war, diplomacy, international law and great power management, to which could be added nationalism, human equality and, more recently and controversially, the market. But primary institutions can be found across history wherever polities have formed an international society. Buzan (2018a) has recently argued for two additional primary institutions in world society: *collective identity* in the interhuman domain, and *advocacy* in the transnational domain.
- *Secondary institutions* are those mainly talked about in regime theory and by liberal institutionalists. They are the products of certain types of international society (most obviously liberal, but possibly other types as well) and are for the most part intergovernmental arrangements consciously designed by states to serve specific functional purposes. They include the United Nations (UN), the World Bank, the World Trade Organization (WTO) and the nuclear nonproliferation regime. Secondary institutions are a relatively recent invention, first appearing as part of industrial modernity in the later decades of the nineteenth century.

Both types of institution can be used to track the shape of social structure at both the global and subglobal levels. For example, primary institutions such as sovereignty, diplomacy and international law, and secondary ones such as the UN and the WTO, clearly operate globally, but primary institutions such as human rights or democracy, or secondary ones such as the EU or Association of Southeast Asian Nations (ASEAN), clearly do not operate globally. Human rights and democracy are contested at the global level but strong subglobally, and the EU and ASEAN are clearly regional structures. Many substructures are not regional, but simply subglobal, such as the Organization for Economic Cooperation and Development (OECD) or the North Atlantic Treaty Organization (NATO). Many primary institutions (e.g., international law, diplomacy, the market, balance of power) and secondary institutions (the International Atomic Energy Agency [IAEA], the WTO, the World Health Organization [WHO]) suggest functional differentiation, though the ES has not much considered them from this perspective. There is also a distinction within primary institutions between 'master' or 'foundational' institutions and 'derivative' ones (Buzan, 2004a: 176–90). This distinction carries an implicit implication that some primary institutions are more important, or more basic, than others, and to the extent that is true, then that carries implications for how one assesses the strength or weakness of international society. If its master institutions are in trouble, that might signify a deeper weakness than if only derivative institutions are under question.

This understanding of institutions relates mainly to the interstate domain, but thinking about GIS in a comprehensive theoretical way requires also that one bring in the transnational and interhuman domains. Buzan (2004a: 118–28, 257–61) argues that there are three types of actor in play within the contemporary GIS: states, transnational actors (TNAs, or NSAs as they are conventionally known) and individual human beings. These types of actors, and the interactions amongst the actors of each type, define three theoretically pure domains within GIS: interstate (state-to-state interaction), transnational (TNA-to-TNA interaction), and interhuman (individual-to-individual interaction mainly in the form of shared identities). The interhuman domain is the closest to the traditional sociological understanding of society as being composed of individual human beings. As the ES's discussions of 'the great society of humankind' indicate, no such society exists at the global level in practice, and its main function in the ES has been as a moral referent against which to judge interstate society. The main practical manifestation of interhuman society within GIS is in terms of large, but mainly subglobal, identity groupings. Interstate and transnational societies are *second-order* societies in which the members are not individual human beings, but organized collectivities of people (states and the various types of NSAs).

Nothing forbids these three domains from overlapping (e.g., state-to-TNA, etc.). In theory and in practice, all sorts of mixtures are possible.

But the ES has not yet thought through how its institutional approach relates to the transnational and interhuman domains. Primary and secondary institutions thus speak mainly to the interstate domain. One possibility is that a single set of primary and secondary institutions operates for all three domains. Thus individuals would accept things such as nationalism, sovereignty, territoriality and human equality, and TNAs would accept sovereignty, international law, diplomacy, etc. Individuals and TNAs would thus become part of the social processes that reproduce and legitimize these institutions. This would certainly be the simplest solution, requiring only that the role of the transnational and interhuman domains in the institutional structures of international society be made explicit. Clark (2007) has made a useful start on this. Another possibility is that each domain has its own primary and secondary institutions. This is easier to think about in the transnational domain, where it is common practice for TNAs at least to generate their own secondary institutions to coordinate activity at the global level. It is more problematic at the interhuman level, because secondary institutions would push things into the transnational domain, but it is not inconceivable that there could be distinctive primary institutions within the interhuman domain (Buzan, 2018a). Again, these are not mutually exclusive propositions: both can be in play at the same time.

Buzan and Zhang (2014: 6–7) provide a detailed picture of how the ES uses its institutional approach to think about social structure at both the global and regional levels:

The idea of a global level international society clearly has considerable substance in terms of shared commitments to a range of key primary institutions, several of which have become effectively naturalised across many populations. Even values that were originally carried outward by the force of Western military superiority during the 19th and 20th centuries have, over time, become internalised by those states and up to a point peoples on whom they were originally imposed. At the level of state elites, sovereignty, territoriality, non-intervention, diplomacy, international law, great power management, nationalism, self-determination (not all versions), popular sovereignty, progress, equality of people(s), and up to a point the market (more for trade and production than finance) are all pretty deeply internalised and not contested as principles. Particular instances or applications may excite controversy, but the basic institutions of a pluralist, coexistence, interstate society have wide support among states, and pretty wide support amongst peoples and transnational actors. Most liberation movements seek sovereignty. Most peoples feel comfortable with nationalism, territoriality, sovereignty and the idea of progress. Most transnational actors want and need a stable legal framework. Thus, even as Western power declines, it does not seem unreasonable to think that most of these pluralist institutions will remain in place (Keohane, 1984; Ikenberry, 2009; 2011), as too might the modest, and hopefully increasing, level of commitment to environmental stewardship (Falkner and

Buzan, 2017). A mixture of coercion and copying and persuasion meant that Western institutions became widespread, running in close parallel to Waltz's (1979: 74–7) idea that anarchy generates 'like units' through processes of 'socialization and competition' . . .

But while the 'like units' formulation carries some truth, it also deceives in various ways. Other primary institutions such as human rights, non-intervention, democracy, environmental stewardship, war, balance of power and hegemony are contested, and therefore need to be part of what is problematised in thinking about GIS and how it might be differentiated. As well as contestations over primary institutions, variations in the practices associated with them are quite easy to find. Non-intervention is relatively strong in East Asia, and relatively weak in South Asia (Paul, 2010: 3–5) and the Middle East. Human rights are relatively strong in the EU, much less so in most other places. Peaceful settlement of disputes is relatively strong in Latin America and the EU, much less so in South Asia, the Middle East and East Asia. Thus while the degree of homogeneity at the global level is impressive and significant, it is far from universal or uniform. To find differentiation between international society at the global and regional levels one can track the differences in their primary institutions, which are the building blocks of international societies and which define their social structure.

How, then, can we combine the ES's approach to differentiation through primary and secondary institutions, and the three domains, with the more sociological approach based on segmentary, stratificatory and functional differentiation? In the preceding discussion, we identified four empirical forms of differentiation that seem relevant to thinking about the structure of GIS: like-units, regional/subglobal, core–periphery and functional differentiation. Functional differentiation is the same in both schemes and is therefore not conceptually problematic. The problem is one of empirical application, which, apart from like-units, the ES has not yet really attempted in any systematic way, but which has to some extent been explored in the globalization literature. For example Held et al. (1999: 23), in their much cited book on globalization, explore the global flows and interconnectedness of a set of functionally defined activities: political, military, economic, cultural, migratory and environmental. Regional differentiation fits quite comfortably under the segmentary type. It is basically a territorial differentiation on a scale between the state and the GIS. Hierarchical differentiation, such as core–periphery, is primarily stratificatory. Neither core nor periphery are defined primarily by geographic location, and there is a clear understanding of the core being in a dominant position within GIS. Subglobal differentiation is a bit more difficult to pin down. In cases such as the primary institutions of democracy, or secondary institutions such as the G20, the OECD or the Alliance of Small Island States (AOSIS), this kind of differentiation is territorial in the sense that it is composed of states, but not geographically coherent because the members of such groups may be scattered all over the system. Some instances of subglobal differentiation might be mainly segmentary (AOSIS, the Islamic Conference, the Commonwealth, the Community of Portuguese Language Countries), but they could equally well be elements of a stratificatory structure (G20, OECD), or possibly part of a functional differentiation (North American Free Trade Agreement [NAFTA]).

The 'like-units' understanding, which has dominated ES thinking about GIS, privileges global homogeneity, and thereby sets the target against which differentiation approaches to GIS take aim. We need to look more closely at the four empirical forms of differentiation: regional, subglobal (both geographical), hierarchy (stratification) and functional.

Regional

Regional differentiation is about geographically coherent, and therefore primarily segmentary, differentiation. One key idea behind the growing interest in regional international society is that culture and history still matter, and that regional differentiation within a globalized international society is therefore hardly surprising. Another is that the different formative processes and histories that brought different regions into GIS might also generate a certain local coherence different in some key respects from that of the core at the global level. This is discussed in more detail in Chapter 2. As the period of intense Western hegemony begins to draw to a close, one might reasonably expect the regional level to become more prominent and more differentiated, perhaps making connections to some of the international societies that were submerged and transformed, but by no means completely destroyed, by the Western expansion and overlay (Watson, 1992; Suzuki, Zhang and Quirk, 2014).

Until recently, the English School showed little interest in the idea of regional international societies. A good example of this neglect was Hurrell (1995) who, when writing on theoretical perspectives on regionalism did not mention the English School (see also Bull, 1977: 279–81; Vincent, 1986: 101, 105).[8] Watson (1992) gave a lot of coverage to premodern international societies. But these were not strictly speaking regional because there was not yet a GIS for them to be subsystems within. Rather, they were, like Europe, quasi-autonomous, subglobal societies, for the most part thinly connected to each other, with each thinking of

---

[8] Hurrell corrected this in later work on 'one world and many worlds' (Hurrell, 2007a; 2007b: 239–61).

itself in universalist terms. Only when there was a GIS could regional international societies exist within it, which in practice means that regions within a global international society have only been possible since the middle of the nineteenth century. The expansion story largely dominated the ES's perspective on world history, fixing its focus firmly on the teleology towards a GIS. Given that the school grew up during the depths of the Cold War, regional international societies might also have seemed necessarily divisive and conflictual. The Cold War, after all, is easy to reconstruct as a zero-sum competition between two subglobal international societies competing to see which would dominate at the global level. In that perspective, any regional developments might well have been seen as dividing and weakening GIS. Yet the European Union (EU) constitutes a powerful and quite solidarist regional international society that arguably complements rather than threatens the GIS. To the extent that there is a distinctive regional international society in Latin America, the same may apply. Indeed, where regions are sufficiently institutionalized to have actor quality in their own right, such as the EU, there is the potential for them to become a new kind of member of GIS.

As Buzan (2004a: 205–27) argues, regional developments *may* lead to conflict over who dominates at the global level, but there is nothing determined about this. Regional international societies may equally well evolve in relative harmony with the global level, as the EU has done (Diez and Whitman, 2002: 45). The EU is an ongoing experiment in the difficulties and limits of constructing advanced solidarism across a substantial group of states and societies. More generally, other authors argue that the expansion of European international society beyond its home culture to global scale almost necessarily generated regional international societies with greater cultural homogeneity than those at the global level (Riemer and Stivachtis, 2002: 21–2). There is growing interest (especially in East Asia) not only in recovering the regional-level stories (Ayoob, 1999; Zhang, 2001; Buzan and Gonzalez-Pelaez, 2009; Suzuki, 2009; Zhang, 2009; Quayle, 2013; Schouenborg, 2013; Buzan and Zhang, 2014; Suzuki, Zhang and Quirk, 2014), but also in the prospect of a more region-centric structure for international society as the likely future (Kupchan, 1998; 2002; 2012; Buzan, 2010; Acharya, 2014; Womack, 2014; Buzan and Lawson, 2015a). Others, using both historical and contemporary cases, argue for the regional distinctiveness and differentiation of international society even if they do not necessarily see higher solidarity in the regions than in the core (Hurrell, 2007a; 2007b; Wang, 2007; Stivachtis, 2010; Merke, 2011; Schouenborg, 2012). Jackson (2000: 128) also supports the view that the English School should take a more regionally differentiated view of contemporary international society, seeing it as 'of mixed character and uneven depth from one global region to the next', and more solidarist in Europe/the West than elsewhere.

Subglobal

As noted, subglobal differentiation is a diverse phenomenon. Different instances of it seem to fit under all three of the basic types of differentiation in our model. We will deal with this pragmatically in the rest of this book, assigning empirical instances to the categories that they seem to fit best. It is worth noting that subglobal differentiation can become extremely important when the GIS itself is contested. One example of this is the fascist international society amongst Germany, Italy and Japan explored by Schouenborg (2012). Another would be the Cold War, which, as previously noted, can be understood as a conflict between two quite radically different types of international society for global dominance. Neither the Western world nor the Soviet bloc were regions in the normal sense, though the Soviet bloc came closer to that form.

Hierarchy/Privilege

A differentiation on the basis of hierarchy or privilege is quite clearly primarily stratificatory. It could have a geographical element, such as if the core in a core–periphery structure was all in one region, but its primary characteristic is a hierarchical relationship between a dominant core and a subordinate periphery. For this purpose, the core and the periphery might well be geographically scattered. The sense of a core–periphery structure rose early in the ES, though not using that terminology. Bull's (1984) worry about 'the revolt against the West' by the newly decolonized members of GIS suggests at the very least that the GIS had taken a hierarchical form in which periphery states shared some practices, norms and primary institutions with the core, but contested others. More recently, Buzan and Zhang (2014) have reinforced this core–periphery view by characterizing the contemporary GIS as 'Western-global international society'. Buzan and Lawson (2015a) have built on this by proposing three stages in the evolution of GIS: 'Western-colonial' up to 1945; 'Western-global' from 1945 to circa 2008; and now moving into what they call 'decentred globalism'. A better label for this emergent structure might be 'deep', or 'embedded', pluralism, signifying not only a wide enough distribution of wealth and power to make it impossible for any state to become a superpower, but also a wider array of cultural resources able to sustain legitimacy claims within GIS (Acharya and

Buzan, 2019). As these labels imply, the potential variance in the form of a core–periphery substructure of GIS can be quite large. A strong form would be as in Western-colonial international society up to 1945, in which sovereignty was divided and unevenly distributed, and the periphery was effectively excluded from GIS by the power and the 'standard of civilization' of the core. A medium form would be as in the contemporary Western-global international society between 1945 and the early twenty-first century, in which the mainly Western core was still dominant, but without empire, and with the periphery having obtained sovereign equality and membership in GIS. A mild form would be as in something like now, or where we seem to be headed, where there is still a core, but it is getting bigger and more inclusive as former periphery countries such as China and India join in. The periphery becomes increasingly residual, and the dynamics of international society become more about the politics of the expanded core than about core–periphery relations (Buzan and Lawson, 2015a).

Functional

As noted, functional differentiation has not been much explored in relation to the differentiation of international society. Indeed, although functional differentiation is strongly implicit in IR more generally – as indicated by the use of terms such as 'international society', 'world society', 'international political economy', 'international law', 'globalization' and the 'global environment' – it has not yet been made an explicit form of mainstream IR analysis (Buzan and Albert, 2010). Albert and Buzan (2011) characterize it as follows:

'Functional differentiation' in general refers to the fact that it is a prime characteristic of modern society that functional specification plays an important role in structuring social relations. 'Functional specification' means basically that in modernity, politics, the economy, law, art, science etc. emerge as relatively autonomous realms of society and that this specification over time becomes more important than specifications according to status (as in stratified societies) or place (as in segmented ones) . . . views on functional differentiation vary according to what is conceived as the basic 'unit' of the social. On the one hand, and in various forms and intensities, are those which basically start with people. Functional differentiation can then in the end be seen as a form of role differentiation. On the other hand are those which start with communication. Functional differentiation then means that communication always refers to some basal, functionally specific code in order to generate meaning. While the latter position is again most prominently occupied by Luhmann, Parsons and Habermas lean strongly towards the first, but then at times seem to hover back and forth between the two.

Regardless of whether the starting point is the actor- or the systems/ communication-based view, there is agreement on two shared aspects about functional differentiation:

First, in modernity a differentiation between functionally defined realms of society has overall become more important than a differentiation according to status and rank (stratification) or location (segmentation). Thus, for example, an issue is first and foremost observed to be a political, an economic, a legal issue etc. before it is observed to be a German, a Welsh, a working class or an upper class issue. Other forms of differentiation persist, but are usually secondary to functional differentiation. *Second*, functionally differentiated realms enjoy a certain degree of autonomy, each operating according to its own 'logic'. Thus, the economic system makes sense of things in economic terms, the scientific system does so in scientific terms, etc.

In the domestic realm, there is a big debate about whether functional differentiation breaks up a society previously integrated by tradition, shared values and culture, or itself comprises a new, modern form of emergent society. This, however, is not relevant to international society because there is no traditional *Gemeinschaft* society in place at that level to be threatened (Albert and Buzan, 2011). In the ES perspective, international society is necessarily emergent, and if functional differentiation is becoming a feature at the global (or indeed regional or sub-global) levels, then it will be part of what constitutes that emergent GIS. The question to look at would be the interplay between increasing functional differentiation in the GIS on the one hand, and the existing segmentary and stratificatory differentiations within the GIS on the other. As Albert, Buzan and Zürn (2013) argue, at present, all three forms of differentiation are in play within GIS, and stratificatory and functional differentiation are in play within states. Those states that have strong functional differentiation within them project this outward into international society, and when such states are great powers, this can be threatening to states that are internally dominated by stratification. Similarly, powerful states that are internally stratificatory threaten states that are more functionally differentiated internally. This goes a long way towards explaining why the United States on the one hand, and China and Russia on the other, find each other threatening. We look at this more closely in Chapter 6.

As previously noted, the standard ES presentation of primary institutions is already suggestive of significant functional differentiation in GIS. International law, the market, diplomacy, nationalism, war, sovereignty, etc., all speak to functional differentiation. The classical institutions of Westphalian international society were in good harmony with the segmentary differentiation of the society of states despite this functional leaning.

As Mayall (2000) argues, and also much of the globalization and deterritorializing literature, newer institutions, the market particularly, also nationalism, and perhaps increasingly environmental stewardship, proffer many disturbances to segmentary differentiation.

Conclusions

This discussion of the types and forms of differentiation in the structure of international society points towards two possible applications. First, it suggests useful theoretical and empirical foundations on which comparative studies of international societies might be based. The three basic types of differentiation – segmentary, stratificatory and functional – generate quite different models of international society. In principle, these are universal models for all times and all places, though in practice, much of international history will be dominated by segmentary and stratificatory differentiation, with functional differentiation being a relatively recent arrival.

Second, these types and forms of differentiation provide useful tools for addressing the question of how weak or strong we deem an international society to be. If GIS is conceived as being essentially a homogeneous entity, then weakness/strength is relatively easy to gauge on the basis of the number and depth of the shared values and institutions that comprise it. But if, as seems certainly to be the case with contemporary GIS, it is uneven, and significantly differentiated internally, then whether that unevenness weakens or strengthens GIS becomes an important and rather complicated question. In the classical 'anarchical society' argument, segmentary differentiation is both the necessary condition for GIS and the major problem to be overcome. If segmentary differentiation is too strong, GIS will be weak or absent. There has to be a shared desire for order, and some common perception of *raison de système*, defined as 'the belief that it pays to make the system work' (Watson, 1992: 14). If we see regional international societies as forms of segmentary differentiation, these might strengthen or weaken GIS. They could be basically in harmony with it, but embody a deeper development, as might be argued of the EU. Or, if constructed as a way of dropping out of GIS, and pursuing a different set of values and institutions, they could be seen as weakening it, as was the case with the Soviet challenge. Stratificatory differentiation divides opinion. Those leaning towards the necessity for hegemony, or for a political vanguard, to get things done will argue that it strengthens GIS. Those with a more postcolonial view are likely to see stratification as weakening GIS by focusing periphery opposition onto the privileges, injustices and inequities of the core. Functional differentiation might likewise cut both ways. In one view, a move towards functional differentiation necessarily begins to compose a new form of international society based on the interdependence and division of labour amongst function systems. In another, functional differentiation will corrode both segmentary and stratificatory differentiation, weakening the existing foundations of GIS before it provides anything robust enough to put in their place.

If we are moving towards a world order defined by embedded pluralism, then, after two centuries of Western cultural, political, military and economic domination, the need to understand more accurately the multiple elements of differentiation in play in the composition of contemporary GIS is becoming rather urgent.

5   What Holds Societies Together?

The discussion so far has concentrated on what the social structures are that comprise GIS, not just the types of unit that compose its membership, but also the substructures that differentiate it, and indeed the structure of GIS itself. But one more element is needed to complete the picture, and that is the one about the mechanisms that regulate behaviour and thereby hold any social order together. Discussion about this is littered all through the literature of international relations and international law. Within international law, the question is why actors obey the law (when they do): Because they think the law is right? Because they calculate the costs and benefits of reciprocal actions? Or because they fear punishments? In IR, perhaps the key approach to it is the differentiation between the 'logic of consequences', essentially rationalist calculation, and the 'logic of appropriateness', essentially constructivist, hinging on belief about what is right/wrong, good/bad, introduced into IR from organization theory by March and Olsen (1998). This differentiation has become deeply institutionalized into the discipline as the marker separating rationalist and reflectivist approaches. In addition, IR's extensive discussion of deterrence and compellence as strategic logics has had a great deal to say about how the threat and use of force shapes behaviour. Although this is perhaps not normally thought of as social structure, it is beyond doubt that a good deal of political order, both domestically and internationally, rests on coercion. That coercion is not an efficient (in terms of resource expenditure) way of maintaining social order is evident from the experience of dictatorships that mainly depend on it. But it is a factor in almost all social orders, and in some, such as empires, and the domains of warlords or mafias, the dominant one, and therefore has to count amongst the binding forces of society. The identification of what provides the cohesion underpinning any form of social structure has a major bearing on the question of how weak or strong any international society is, and also provides another useful criterion for comparing international societies across space and time.

Our approach to this is through the work of Alex Wendt (1999: 266–73), who nicely clarifies the discussion by separating out the essential mechanisms in play. According to Wendt, institutions can be held in place mainly by belief (i.e., they are internalized to a consensual logic of appropriateness), mainly by calculation (a logic of consequences) and/or mainly by coercion (a logic of deterrence/compellence). This framing neatly teases apart the different logics of rational calculation with and without the element of coercion. It can be applied to any kind of social structure. In principle, pure forms are possible. One would expect, for example, that some religious communities would come close to a model of pure belief, and that regimes imposed by invaders, warlords and religions of the sword would come close to a model of pure coercion. The logic of corporate behaviour in the business world might come close to a model of pure calculation. In practice, however, nearly all social structures will be held in place by some mixture. Dictatorships might look mainly coercive, but they generally benefit from some elements of consensual support and belief, and from quite a lot of calculated quiescence. Democracies might look mainly consensual, but they still require significant internal police and security forces. In some places, religions are backed up by state laws forbidding people to convert to other religions or no religion. Even so basic a social unit as the family will generally display all three binding logics in varying proportions.

The same logic also applies to the ES's primary institutions. Some of these, most obviously sovereignty and nationalism, are broadly consensual and based on belief. Both of these have been deeply internalized in populations all over the world. Others, most obviously the market, reflect a mixture of all three of these binding forces, with different mixes in different places. For example, in the United States, the market is widely accepted as generally the best way of organizing the economy, whatever differences there may be about the best way to implement this. Since China is still ruled by a communist party, it is hard to imagine that the market is internalized in the same way. Deng Xiaoping's reforms starting in the late 1970s were mainly an instrumental calculation: China needed to acquire wealth and power as quickly as possible, and Deng rightly worked out that the market was the best, and perhaps the only, way to do this, and that global conditions were benign enough to allow China – and the Chinese Communist Party – to expose itself in this way. While the Chinese Communist Party thus abandoned the totem of the command economy, that does not mean that it actually believes in the market as the preferred form of political economy. Historically, market norms have often been coercively imposed, as they were during the Western-colonial period, and still are, albeit in more subtle ways such as International Monetary Fund (IMF) and EU 'conditionality', on many weaker states in the third world. As Simpson (2004) argues, the institution of great power management is partly imposed by the great powers, but also partly accepted consensually by lesser states as necessary for international order.

The mechanisms that hold institutions in place are thus an observable marker by which international societies can be internally differentiated and compared (see Buzan, 2004a; Schouenborg, 2013). Implicit in this scheme, there is also an insight into the strength and weakness of any social structure. A social structure held together mainly by coercion will quickly disintegrate once the coercion is reduced or removed. The Soviet Union and its empire imploded once it became clear that the government was not going to use force to prevent that, and a similar fate attended many classical empires, such as the Assyrian and Mongol. Coercion is a costly way to achieve social cohesion and thus inherently inefficient. Social structures in which the principal binding force is coercion might thus be considered weak. At the other end of the spectrum, social structures held together by belief are exceptionally durable and efficient. The Orthodox religion, for example, survived seven decades of severe repression in the officially atheist Soviet Union and quickly bounced back once the repression was removed. In China similarly, Mao Zedong's attempt to sweep away traditional Chinese culture did not work, and since his death the Chinese Communist Party has increasingly cultivated Confucianism as a means to bolster its legitimacy. In between these two lies the logic of calculation. By definition, this logic is conditional on circumstances. Support for the social structure will be maintained so long as it delivers benefits and will fade when the calculations turn negative. The market is perhaps the clearest example of this, with a lot of support swinging depending on whether the market mechanism is delivering wealth or delivering crisis, recession and extreme inequality. How efficient the binding forces of calculation are depends on how sustainable they are, but the likely range lies between the extremes of inefficient coercion and efficient belief.

We can posit as a marker, therefore, that the more a social structure is held together by coercion, the weaker it is, and the more it is held together by belief, the stronger it is, with calculation somewhere in the middle and contingent on specific circumstances.

With this theoretical framing in mind, we now turn to a historical perspective on how the contemporary GIS was formed, and how that process of formation plays into the structures of differentiation and binding forces that we see before us.

2 The Making of Contemporary Global International Society
How Do International Societies Grow/Expand?

One way of understanding the patterns of differentiation that mark the contemporary GIS is to track the processes by which they came into being. Both the members and the substructures of the GIS are products of a very particular process of formation. This chapter sets out two general ideal-type models of how a GIS can be created: *polycentric* and *monocentric*. It argues that the monocentric model is the one closest to what actually happened in the world over the last millennium, but that aspects of the polycentric model also apply in some places. On this basis, it sets out four abstract ideal-type submodels of how both the members and the geopolitical substructures of contemporary GIS were brought into GIS: unbroken creation, repopulation, colonization/decolonization and encounter/reform. A fifth model, engagement between equals, is suggested but not developed. The chapter then shows how these variations underpin and explain the differentiation of states into the many significantly different types that now compose GIS.

1   Polycentric and Monocentric Models of GIS Formation

There is plenty of evidence from the English School's historical wing that international society goes back a long way, being more or less coterminous with the history of civilization (Wight, 1977; Watson, 1992; Zhang, Y, 2001; Zhang, F, 2009; Zhang and Buzan, 2012; Suzuki, Zhang and Quirk, 2014; Schouenborg, 2017). The general picture of the world before the contemporary GIS is one in which the various cores of agrarian civilization generated their own forms of international society. The driving logic behind this development is captured by the much-cited quote from Wight (1977: 33, see also Buzan, 2010; Linklater, 2016) that: 'We must assume that a states-system will not come into being without a degree of cultural unity among its members.' Thus prior to the European expansion, one can find a variety of subglobal international societies scattered around the planet. Most of these were 'regional' in the sense of being geographically concentrated in what we would now think of as a region, but not regional in the sense of being a subdivision of a global-scale international society. Until the world became permanently interconnected by transoceanic shipping during the sixteenth century, there was no global international society for regions to be part of. The exception to this 'regional' scale rule was the Islamic world, which, as indicated by the travels of Ibn Battuta, stretched across large parts of Asia and Africa a form of world society (Mackintosh-Smith, 2002), operating more in the transnational (NSAs) and interhuman (shared identity) domains than in the interstate one. It was this politically, socially and culturally variegated world, containing everything from small-scale hunter-gatherer bands, through middle-scale chiefdoms, city-states and kingdoms, to large-scale, sophisticated, urbanized agrarian empires, into which Europe expanded from the fifteenth century onwards (Buzan and Little, 2000; Suzuki, Zhang and Quirk, 2014).

On this basis, Buzan (2014: 60–1) argues the case for the polycentric and monocentric models as follows:

In principle, a global international society could have come about in one of two basic ways. One way would have been for the various civilizational cores of the ancient and classical world to have expanded into increased contact with each other, so requiring that they develop rules of the game to mediate their relations: a *polycentric* system of systems. In such a case, global international society would have developed on the basis of cultural diversity and fusion. The other way is closer to what actually happened, namely the takeover of the whole system by one of the civilizational cores, and the absorption of all the others into its particular rules, norms, and institutions. This *monocentric* model necessarily starts from relations of inequality, and highlights 'the standard of civilization' as the key criterion for non-Western societies to gain membership (Buzan, 2010). This model sets up tensions over how such a society is now to evolve as the distribution of power reverts from the extreme concentration that allowed its creation in the first place, to something of the more even distribution (the rise of China, India, and other non-Western powers) that marked the ancient and classical world. Thus, although there are even and uneven routes to a global international society, and they end up in the same place, the monocentric model ends up there with a very different set of dynamics and problems than would have been the case if we had got here by the polycentric route.

These two models open up a wealth of possible research projects to explore historical cases of how international societies grow and expand. There are at least three clear cases for observing the polycentric model in action between two civilizational cores: the encounter between Christianity and Islam, between Islam and the Hindu world and between Buddhism and Confucianism. The encounter between Christianity and Islam dates back to the rise and rapid expansion of Islam from the seventh century onwards. It has often been violent, and the fortunes of the two sides have fluctuated markedly, with sometimes one side being the stronger and more expansionary (e.g., Islam's opening conquests of the eastern and southern coasts of the Mediterranean plus Spain, and the later Ottoman conquests in the Balkans and around the Black Sea), and sometimes the other (the Crusades and Europe's erosion and penetration of the Ottoman Empire during the nineteenth century). The encounter between Islam and the Hindu world was also mainly violent, and took the form of repeated Muslim invasions of the Indian subcontinent and the steady establishment of Muslim rulers and Muslim populations in that area starting in the eighth century, but mainly between the twelfth and sixteenth centuries. This was mainly one-way traffic, but the Indian subcontinent was in itself a major civilizational core, did put up significant resistance (Watson, 1964) and did have its own history of expansion, mainly to the north and east. The encounter between Buddhism and Confucianism was mainly carried along the Silk Road trading routes connecting China and South Asia by land and by sea from around the first century AD. Again, this was mainly one-way traffic, with Buddhism penetrating China, Korea and Japan, but Confucianism remaining largely in East Asia. Unlike the other two polycentric encounters, this one did not involve clashing armies. It was a movement of ideas and people (traders, monks, converts) between two civilizational cores. It was not without violence, because sometimes Buddhism was actively suppressed in China, but it was not delivered, or imposed, by violence. The encounter between Christianity and Islam involved all three domains: interstate (various kingdoms and empires), transnational (the Roman church) and interhuman (religious identities). That between Islam and the Hindu world was perhaps mainly interstate, with less action in the other two domains. That between Buddhism and the Confucian world was mainly in the transnational (traders, monks) and interhuman domains and not much about state-to-state relations.

The expansion of Europe is probably not the only example of the monocentric model, though it is certainly the most important for contemporary GIS and will receive more detailed attention in this book. Other cases that might fit here are the expansion of Islam, Hinduism and Buddhism into Southeast Asia. Here civilizational cores projected their culture into what might be called 'less developed' areas. This was one-way traffic, and more carried by traders and missionaries than by armies – though since most traders in those days went armed, the distinction between peaceful and coercive interaction was blurred. It might also be possible to look at the expansion of China from its original core around the Yellow River to its present extent using this model. Sometimes China was encountering and absorbing tribal peoples; sometimes it was encountering people with a high culture of their own, as in Tibet, and along the

Silk Road to Central Asia; and sometimes it was encountering nomadic 'barbarian' empires that could not compete with its high culture, but which could and often did defeat it militarily.

Both polycentric and monocentric models can range across the spectrum from mainly violent and coercive, in which transformation is achieved by occupation or pressure (much of the Western expansion, the encounter between Christianity and Islam, the Islamic occupation of India), to relatively peaceful and consensual expansion along trade routes (the expansion of Buddhism and Hinduism, the expansion of Islam into Southeast Asia). As a rule, the expansion involves all three domains, but there is a lot of variation in this, especially as to whether the interstate domain is the dominant one or not. Expansion of international society certainly does not require that the interstate sector be the leading one.

If we start now to think about the European case of monocentric expansion to global scale, things start to get complicated. For most of the five centuries during which the process took place, the world was a very big place (given the available technologies, interaction capacity was low, and it would take more than a year to get from one side to the other and back), and extremely diverse in terms of culture and levels of development. The Europeans encountered a huge variety of races, cultures and polities, and often did so at the end of very long and tenuous sea lines of communication. Sometimes they encountered peoples they could subdue very easily, both because of their susceptibility to Eurasian diseases and their technological backwardness: what Jared Diamond (1998) colourfully called 'Guns, Germs and Steel'. Elsewhere, they encountered either well-organized and powerful societies that they had to deal with as equals (or sometimes even accept a subordinate position), most obviously China and Japan, or environments hostile to European health, as in sub-Saharan Africa (Headrick, 2010).

There is no doubt that brute force was the principal engine of the European expansion, but coercion was not the only binding force in the making of GIS. Even though often backed by force, trade was also a factor in its own right, both in terms of driving European motives and in generating a calculation dynamic of mutual interest. The same can be said for belief and the power of European ideas. Initially, this element was largely about Christianity, which until at least the seventeenth century was principally how Europe defined its civilization. In some places, such as sub-Saharan Africa, and up to a point Northeast Asia, this made a big impact, whereas in others it was strongly and successfully opposed, as in the Islamic and Hindu worlds. During the nineteenth century, however, the main power of ideas shifted to industrial modernity, and the huge attraction of modern science and its products from medical to military. In the later stages of its expansion, Europe and Japan thus confronted the rest of the world with a dual challenge. First, they had to deal with the overt power of both modernizing states, which was ruthlessly deployed against them, and of NSAs that penetrated their societies in all kinds of ways. Second, and in some ways the greater challenge, they had also to deal with the existential threat posed by industrial modernity to the whole ideational and social structure of agrarian societies. This was a test that Japan passed at about the same time as Italy and Russia, but for a century it was the only non-Western country to do so, making it the first mover in what is now labelled 'the rise of the rest' (Zakaria, 2009). How to find stable political and social and economic forms in a highly unequal encounter against this dual challenge was the problem posed for the rest of the world by the monocentric expansion of Europe (Buzan and Lawson, 2015a).

From its position of strength, the modern core imposed itself on the rest of the world in a great variety of ways and across the whole spectrum of domains. In the interhuman domain, there was large-scale replacement of populations, as in the Americas and Australia. There was also absorption of foreign peoples directly into their own state by metropolitan powers, for example, France and Algeria, Russia and Central Asia, Japan and Korea and Britain and Ireland. In the transnational domain, large numbers of newly empowered NSAs, most notably Christian churches and private business firms, penetrated deeply into the non-Western world, challenging the economic, political and social structures they found there. In the process, they often dragged their home states after them by demanding protection. In the interstate domain, many peoples were occupied and taken under the unconditional sovereignty of the metropole. This was the case for much of Africa, the Middle East and South and Southeast Asia. Beyond that were peoples who were colonized but retained or won elements of independence within a European empire, for example a variety of protectorates, the British dominions, the League of Nations mandates and perhaps the Japanese in Manchuria. Some countries could be described as semicolonized, notionally independent but heavily penetrated and influenced by metropolitan powers. This was the eventual fate of the Ottoman Empire, China, Central America and perhaps also places discussed under the heading 'informal empire', such as Argentina in the nineteenth century. On the lightest end of the interstate encounter were countries that were not even semicolonized, but nonetheless subjected to considerable outside pressure to reform themselves in ways that conformed to the Western 'standard of civilization'. The principal example of this is Japan (Suzuki, 2009).

Keeping all of this complexity in mind, it is possible to generate a set of ideal-type models that together cover the main forms and dynamics of how the contemporary GIS was made.

2   Four Submodels of GIS Formation

Four ideal-type models can easily be drawn empirically from the mono-centric case of European expansion.[1] In brief, they are the following:

- *Unbroken creation*, in which the formation of states (or polities), and a matching international society, is largely independent and uninter-rupted by foreign domination. This model is likely to identify the vanguard of the monocentric process, which in the case of the current GIS is Europe.
- *Repopulation*, in which the vanguard intentionally or unintentionally displaces or destroys most or all of the indigenous population and replaces it with its own people and/or people from other regions. In the case of the current GIS, the main examples here are the Americas and Australia, with South Africa, New Zealand and Israel as more partial cases.
- *Colonization/decolonization*, in which the vanguard conquers and rules other populations for a period, leaving them more or less *in situ*, but imposing its own rules, and up to a point culture, on them before withdrawing to leave behind a variety of postcolonial states. In the case of the current GIS, the lead examples here are Africa; the Middle East; South, Central and Southeast Asia; and Korea.
- *Encounter/reform*, in which the vanguard penetrates and influences other populations, but does not take on direct rule. Instead, the penetrated state and population are pressured to conform to the prac-tices of the vanguard before they are given full entry to international society. The lead examples here are Japan and China, but also Russia, and for a time the Ottoman Empire.

It could be argued that these models are not just specific to the European case, but might stand as a general set for any form of monocentric creation of a GIS. Up to a point they also cover a lot of what might happen in a polycentric model, though perhaps then a fifth model, *engagements among equals*, would need to be added in order to cover the spectrum of possibilities. The preceding four models all reflect an unequal encounter between a dominant core and a weaker periphery. But in a polycentric

---

[1] This section builds on Buzan (2012: 26–35).

model, the expectation would be that most of the original cores survive, and that the encounter process would be marked more by engagements among equals than between stronger and weaker. The obvious example here is the long and ongoing encounter between Christianity and Islam. Unlike in the encounter between Islam and the Hindu world, where Islam dominated militarily, at least up until the nineteenth century neither side won, nor consistently dominated, the encounter between Christianity and Islam. This meant that both were shaped in a sustained way by the more or less permanent conflict between them. Whether this pattern is still ongoing, with the latest round being defined by transnational terrorism emanating from the Islamic world, or whether the Western domination from the nineteenth century onwards constitutes a decisive shift to colonization/decolonization is an interesting point for discussion. This fifth model thus blends aspects of unbroken creation with aspects of encounter/reform. We will not develop this fifth model separately here because it is not relevant to understanding the formative process of contemporary GIS. But we return to it in the conclusion to this chapter as a possible way of thinking ahead.

We should, however, note that the first four models oversimplify things. In particular, they risk taking out of the picture the often significant learning processes that occurred in both directions during the encounters that made the contemporary GIS. As shown in the following subsections, many elements that went into the making of modernity in Europe were imported from its encounters with the rest of the world.

Unbroken Creation

Because Europe was the vanguard that remade the rest of the world, only it can claim an unbroken formative process. There was for a long time prior to the nineteenth century an element of engagement with equals in its encounter with Islam, and more remotely with its encounters in South and East Asia. But in a broad sense, both state formation and the making of a distinctive international society unfolded without foreign intervention into Europe being a major shaping or imposing force. Other regions, most conspicuously in Asia, certainly had long histories of unbroken creation as international societies before their encounter with the Europeans. But all of these societies were in one way or another broken by that encounter, sometimes leaving little legacy to the modern regions that emerged with decolonization. More on this later in this chapter.

To say that Europe's formative process was unbroken is not to say that it was pristine and self-contained. Some accounts of Europe's rise from mediaeval to modern easily give the impression that it was pristine, but this is misleading. There is no historical case of pristine unbroken creation. Europe's formation was independent in the sense that Europe was never occupied or subordinated by outside powers. But it was far from being pristine in the sense of wholly self-contained. To make only the most obvious points, many technological and social ideas filtered into mediaeval and early-modern Europe from what were then the considerably more advanced civilizations elsewhere in Eurasia: China, South Asia and the Middle East (Bentley, 1993; Lach, 1965; 1970; 1993; Hobson, 2004; Buzan and Lawson, 2015a: 26, 37–8). In addition, as the buffer of a declining Byzantine Empire slowly decayed, developing Europe was in continuous economic, military and political encounter with the Islamic world to its south and southeast. From the long Moorish occupation of Spain starting in the seventh century, through the Crusades, to Europe's rivalry with the Ottoman Empire from the fifteenth century, Europe was deeply challenged, but not overwhelmed, by what was until the seventeenth century a more advanced and powerful neighbouring civilization. That encounter played powerfully into the formative process of Europe in terms of transfers of knowledge, the development of 'Westphalian' international society and the creation of a hostile Other (Wight, 1991: 52; Yurdusev, 2009: 70–9).

Thus, while Europe's development as a region was unbroken, it was also syncretic, being influenced by encounters with other Eurasian civilizations from an early stage. Wight (1991: 52), for example, notes that during the twelfth and thirteenth centuries, the Crusades brought Europe into close contact with the Islamic world, adding to the contact already created by the earlier Islamic occupation of Spain, which together served as 'the channel for the acculturation of medieval Christendom'. And even as late as the eighteenth century, China's system of professional examinations for recruiting government officials was admired in Europe as progressive. As fifteenth century Europe began the expansion that peaked with its global domination in the nineteenth century, this process of encounter became more lopsided in Europe's favour. The overall process was, however, highly uneven, not some smooth progression. Europe's early encounter with the Americas was highly unequal because, as noted previously, disease and technology gave the Europeans huge advantages over the indigenous peoples. But in Asia and the Middle East, formidable classical powers from the Ottoman Empire through to China imposed their own terms on the Europeans until the eighteenth and, in some cases, the nineteenth centuries. And while Europeans could exploit sub-Saharan Africa for gold and slaves, they could not occupy it until the nineteenth century. During these centuries, Europe steadily became the master of the maritime global trading system linking all of the continents together, but it was not the centre of global manufacturing until the middle of the nineteenth century, by which time it had become the dominating core region of a global-scale political economy and imperial international society. By the late nineteenth century the European vanguard was well advanced in remaking the world in its own political image, whether by repopulation, as in the Americas and Australia; colonization, as in much of Africa, South and Southeast Asia; or coercive encounter, as with China, Japan and the Ottoman Empire. This huge variety of encounters, and Europe's increasingly dominant position within them, constituted an important part of Europe's own internal development. Europe became globalized at the same time as its own internal processes of modern nation-state formation and the creation of its distinctive form of international society were unfolding.

Europe's unbroken creation is a much-told story that we do not need to repeat in detail here. The first phase of it was the move from mediaeval structures where the Roman church retained a powerful overarching position, to premodern ones in which sovereign, territorial and mostly dynastic/absolutist states became the central players (Wight, 1977; Watson, 1992; Ruggie, 1983; 1993). The second phase took off during the nineteenth century, when the multiple revolutions of modernity remade the material, institutional and ideational landscapes of both Europe and the world. Amongst other things, these revolutions replaced the dynastic state with one based on popular sovereignty and nationalism and put into place an integrated global economy driven by transnational actors and a two-tier colonial international society (Buzan and Lawson, 2015a). Europe's evolution also generated the institution of great powers: the idea that the biggest powers could claim certain rights and status privileges in return for taking on collective management responsibilities in international society. This idea emerged during the eighteenth century, as dynastic interests began to give way to national ones, and was institutionalized in the Concert of Europe after the Napoleonic Wars (Wight, 1977: 42, 136–41; Holsti, 1991: 114–37; Simpson, 2004; Clark, 2011). Although starting off as a feature of European international society, this was an important differentiation that got transferred over to GIS, initially in colonial form, but later opened to the expanding membership of GIS. Thus the great powers were initially all European, and remained Western even with the accession of the United States. But the recognition of Japan as a great power from 1902 opened the doors to this club to non-Western states that could make the grade. China was accorded great power status in 1945 by being given a permanent seat in the UN Security Council, and India and others are now knocking on the door.

Europe's evolution undoubtedly contained a strong internal dynamic, but all along the way this was in part fed by ideas and technologies from the rest of the world. And as Europe itself became globalized, this interactive dynamic got stronger, with Europe steadily exporting more ideas, goods and people than in earlier times. Europe's unbroken formation had the privilege of unfolding without foreign imposition, but it was hardly a peaceful process. Wars over religion culminated in the Thirty Years' War that produced the Treaties of Westphalia. The surfacing of nationalism produced the quarter century of French revolutionary and Napoleonic Wars. The unfolding and clashing of the ideologies of progress central to the revolutions of modernity – liberalism, socialism, nationalism and 'scientific' racism – fuelled the three world wars of the twentieth century (First, Second and Cold Wars). Indeed, writers such as Tilly (1990) and Howard (1976) argue that the intra-European dynamic of war played a pivotal role in the evolution of the modern state. Tilly's pithy phrase – the state makes war, and war makes the state – suggests a Darwinian process that selected polities according to their war-fighting efficiency. The winner in this process was the modern, rational, national state that emerged in the nineteenth century and became both the perpetrator of, and the model for, the imposition of European practices on the rest of the world. From the late eighteenth century onwards, Europe, and by this time also the United States, Canada and Australia/New Zealand, underwent a profound transformation in the nature of society.

This transformation was deep, complex and ongoing. It can be labelled global modernity, the industrial revolution, functional differentiation, capitalism, 'the great transformation', 'the empire of civil society' or 'open access orders'. However labelled, it signified a change not just in the dominant mode of production, but also in the whole political, social and economic structuring of Western societies (Rosenberg, 1994; North et al., 2009; Buzan and Lawson, 2015a). In the terms of North et al., this new type of 'open access' social order, with its distinctive separation of economics and politics, and its unleashing of civil society into both the economy and politics, was then projected outward by the West during the nineteenth century. This outward projection created an ongoing clash with more traditionally structured 'natural' states in which economics and politics remained fused, control over the means of violence dispersed, patron–client relations dominant and most access to rents restricted to elites.

In this perspective, the nineteenth century becomes a period of major world historical transformation: what Buzan and Lawson (2015a) label 'the global transformation'. The leading Western states radically remade their internal social structures, in the terms established in the previous chapter, shifting from dominantly stratificatory to dominantly functional differentiation. In so doing, they remade how they related to the rest of the world. The new forms of modern, rational, national states and the new form of colonial international society that they generated emerged in Europe and Japan during the nineteenth century. The metropolitan states at the core of these colonial empires rapidly became substantially richer and more powerful than the rest of the world, opening up the distinction between developed and developing, or developed and under-developed, countries. The social, political, military, economic, ideo-logical and knowledge revolutions of modernity that underpinned the wealth and power of the European leading edge thus opened an ongoing social and political gap between it and those peoples and polities that rapidly became the periphery to Europe's global core. As functionally differentiated open access orders took deeper root in the leading states, their relationship with the periphery shifted from the imperialism of direct territorial control typical of natural state empires, to the demand for access typical of Rosenberg's 'empire of civil society'. Open access orders make permeable the boundaries of territorial states and generate a transnational economic, social and political space in which private non-state actors can operate alongside, within and through the formal polit-ical sphere of states (Buzan and Little, 2000: 362–7). In international society terms, this constituted the shift from a Western-colonial to a Western-dominated GIS that happened after the Second World War. Since the leading colonial powers were also the most developed open access orders, their evolving, increasingly functionally differentiated, domestic structures became incompatible with old-style stratificatory imperialism, a process helped by the weakening of Britain and France by the First and Second World Wars. These two wars also undermined European pretentions to 'civilization', as Europeans applied to each other the racist attitudes, colonial practices and violent brutalities that they had previously reserved for their relations with non-Europeans. The transformation beginning in the nineteenth century to open access orders amongst the leading powers thus pushed towards the decolonization that took place after 1945.

Decolonization exposed and exacerbated the tensions between the functionally differentiated open access orders of the Western core and Japan (first world), and the mainly stratificatory natural states of the third world, many of which felt more comfortable in the company of the Soviet bloc states. By the second half of the twentieth century, open access orders dominated the core, and China's late 1970s reform and opening up, plus the end of the Cold War in 1989, marked the final victory of economic liberalism over its major totalitarian, natural state, ideological challengers. But while the core increasingly organized itself as a transnational open access order, much of the periphery remained in natural state form, unable to avoid either local conflicts or deep structural tensions with the open access order. Here we find one of the main origins of the differentiation amongst types of states, as will be discussed in more detail later in this chapter.

Repopulation

By far the most extreme form of disjuncture between contemporary states and regions, on the one hand, and the preencounter history, on the other, occurred in those places, mainly the Americas and Australia, but up to a point also in New Zealand, Israel and South Africa, where the native populations and cultures were largely displaced by European settler populations and in some places also by slaves imported from Africa and indentured labourers from Asia. In the Americas, the main work of reducing the indigenous populations to a small fraction of their preencounter size was done by Eurasian diseases. The destruction of indigenous peoples and their cultures marginalized those that remained in the social and political development of these 'new worlds', whose subsequent social and political development was dominated by transplanted Europeans (Diamond, 1998; Keal, 2003). Given the massive impact of disease, perhaps the repeopling of the Americas would have happened even in a polycentric model, and regardless of whether it was East Asians or Europeans (or both) who 'discovered' the new world. Relatively little of the historical indigenous pattern of politics or culture survived to influence the emergent states and regions, which meant that the disconnection from history was extreme. But since the people of these repopulated lands were either mostly of European stock, or if Europeans were outnumbered by slaves, they nonetheless held the political and economic whip hand, and they had a cultural compatibility with the vanguard that had created them. A key consequence of this cultural compatibility was that it made it relatively easy (which is not to say easy in any absolute sense) to create new states on the European model and to fit these new countries into European international society. The settler colonies were founded early in the process of European expansion, and they also constituted the first round of the decolonization process. The independence wars in the Americas during the late eighteenth and early nineteenth centuries, thus transformed international society from European to Western (Gong, 1984: 4–6), marking the first major step towards a GIS. Yet although there was cultural and racial affinity, many of these countries (with the notable exceptions of Canada, Australia and New Zealand) had to rebel against their European metropoles to win independence and therefore brought some revolutionist attitudes, as well as strong sovereigntism, into international society (Simpson, 2004; Jones, 2007).

In terms of how they play into the differentiation of contemporary GIS, the settler colonies split into three distinct stories: North American, Latin American and Antipodean.

The North American story is basically one of settler colonies quite quickly transforming themselves into modern states and joining the core. The European settler populations quite easily overwhelmed the remaining indigenous peoples and isolated them from the process of modern state formation. The United States pursued its own distinctive form of liberal modernity and quickly became powerful enough to dominate the region. Canada's route to modernity was via dominion status within the British Empire. After its civil war, the United States was clearly on a trajectory to becoming a great power, and after 1945, a superpower. The dominance of the United States, and the relatively peaceful relations between it and Canada after some initial turbulence, meant that North America as a region largely disappeared from view under US hegemony, being more seen as part of the West. North America is seldom thought of as a region, though its history as a post-colonial regional security complex can certainly be told in terms comparable to other postcolonial regions (Buzan and Wæver, 2003: 268–303). The United States went on to become a player at the global level, transcending its region, and during the late nineteenth century, along with Japan, becoming a non-European great power participating in international society. During the twentieth century, the United States became in its own right a principal shaper of GIS. The North American story is thus primarily about the expansion of the Western core from its Western European base to a two-continent, North Atlantic, scale. To some extent, the United States represents a differentiation of state type, but only within the modern form originating in the European core. As Americans like to point out, their state is older than most of the current states in Europe.

The Latin American story is one where a distinctive region forms after decolonization. No local power dominates this region, although it is increasingly penetrated by the United States, which, as it becomes a great power, comes to regard Latin America as being within its sphere of influence. In sharp contrast to North America, and despite their common root in being repopulated by Europeans, this region does not become seen as fully part of the West. It is quite quickly accepted into

Western international society, but interestingly becomes more differentiated from the West both in terms of state development and economic progress. Unlike the North American settler states, the Latin American ones fail to reach the leading edge of modernity either politically (a strong penchant for dictatorships) or economically (a preference for mercantilist policies). Indeed, with the major round of decolonization following the Second World War, Latin America became seen mainly as part of the third world of 'developing countries'. Both its economies and its politics remained backwards by the standards of the core, and it was subject to US hegemony and intervention in postcolonial style. The Latin American states, unlike the United States and Canada, failed to keep pace with the revolutions of modernity in the West. They drifted increasingly into postcolonial status located in the periphery of, and increasingly differentiated from, an increasingly modern Western and Northeast Asian core. One explanation for this lies in the particularity of the colonizing metropole. North America was dominated by Britain, and to a lesser extent France, which carried their own dynamics of modernity into their settler colonies early on. Latin America was colonized by Spain and Portugal, countries that not only arrived in the Americas well before modernity took hold in Europe, but also were themselves very much laggards in the nineteenth century transformation to the modern state. Latin America therefore received a very different European social and political heritage from that transmitted to North America (Jones, 2007). There is some parallel between the Latin American experience and the East Asian one. In both cases, one powerful local state, respectively the United States and Japan, modernizes quickly, becomes part of the core and proceeds to treat its neighbours as a periphery to be dominated and exploited. Whatever its causes, the evolution of Latin America has differentiated GIS both on the basis of state type and on the basis of forming a distinctive regional international society within the GIS (Merke, 2011).

The Antipodean story of Australia and New Zealand is close to that of North America, although without the impact of a local great power. Like Canada and the United States, Australia and New Zealand are mainly seen as part of the West on ethnic and cultural and developmental grounds. They went through the same dominion route to modern statehood as Canada, and they are not normally thought of as a region. These two are more often defined as not being part of East Asia, or as being some kind of periphery to it, than as being a region in their own right. Like North America, Australia and New Zealand expand the core group of modern states rather than differentiate it.

Colonization/Decolonization

A less extreme, but still sometimes large, disjuncture with the past is the story of those peoples who lost their political and economic independence to Europeans, but not their existence as peoples occupying their ancestral lands. This is the main story for most of Africa, South and Southeast Asia, the Pacific Islands, and briefly for much of the Middle East. These peoples underwent a process of colonization and decolonization by Europeans (and in a few cases Americans and Japanese) in which their political structures, and often their boundaries, were remade along Western lines and reflecting Western interests. The price of decolonization was acceptance of both the Western form of sovereign territorial state and its associated international society, and, for the most part, of the boundaries created by the colonial powers. The payoff for accepting this was not just independence, but gaining the recognized status of sovereign equality within GIS. The leaders of many colonized peoples made effective use of nationalism and sovereignty, two of the key institutions of Western international society, as well as human rights, as conceptual weapons to combat colonialism (Mayall, 1990: 38–49; 2000: 39–66).

While the outcome of the colonization/decolonization process was to create a set of states superficially compatible with Western forms, the degree of disjuncture from the local history was extremely varied. At one end of the spectrum were postcolonial states whose boundaries and people retained clear lineage to precolonial formations. This was true for most of the states in mainland Southeast Asia, for several in the Middle East (e.g., Oman, Iran, Egypt, Morocco), and for a few in sub-Saharan Africa (e.g., Swaziland, Lesotho). At the other end of the spectrum were postcolonial states that were arbitrary assemblages of peoples finding themselves corralled by boundaries drawn with little or no reference to local history, culture or geography. There were many of these in sub-Saharan Africa, and some in the Middle East and the offshore archipelagos of Southeast Asia. Many ethnic groups found themselves divided by the new borders, and most states contained anything from several, through dozens, to hundreds of such groups. For these postcolonial states, nationalism often turned into a two-edged sword. One edge was a useful weapon for mobilizing opposition to colonialism and therefore had integrating potential. But the other edge risked self-damage, tending either to fragment countries internally or lead them into conflict with neighbours, by legitimizing ethnic claims for self-government against rootless new 'national' identities such as Nigerian, Congolese or Indonesian. In the middle of the spectrum, one finds states such as most of those in the Indian subcontinent, where there was a mix of arbitrary boundaries and links to precolonial forms.

Regardless of their degree of continuity or discontinuity with earlier history, all of these postcolonial states were recast in the modernist mould of the sovereign, territorial 'nation-state', and so integrated into GIS as sovereign equals. As independent states, they were able to express once again their cultural distinctiveness from the West, and this allowed patterns of cultural identity to play into how the new regions related to, and differentiated themselves from, both each other and the Western core. These reactions fed both regional and core–periphery differentiations. These relationships were also affected by the political differentiation of most postcolonial regions from the Western core. Most postcolonial states were stratificatory natural states, often weak ones, making them very ill at ease with, and threatened by, the still rapidly evolving open access, functionally differentiated, orders of the core. All of these regions faced what was in effect a new 'standard of civilization' projected from the West in terms of demands about human rights, democracy, property rights, financial practices and such, all cast in terms of the practices prevailing in the Western core of functionally differentiated open access orders. Since the transition from natural state to open access order is fraught with difficulties, acceptance of these standards and practices had as much chance of collapsing a natural state into a failed one as of transforming it into an open access order. The formative process for these states has thus left a very mixed legacy of internal instability and an awkward combination of tension with and dependence on Western/global international society.

The extent to which postcolonial states differ from those in the Western core can be seen in Buzan and Gonzalez-Pelaez's (2009: 237–9) discussion of regional differentiation from the GIS in the Middle East:

Because the imposition of Westphalian politics onto the Middle East was in many respects flawed and dysfunctional in relation to the local societies, it created a rather unstable, coercion-heavy type of state and regional interstate politics. This flawed structure then had to endure the disruptive presence of Israel, the corrupting influence of oil, the outside interests in the Suez canal, and the region's location on the containment boundary of the Cold War, all of which brought powerful and sustained external engagements into the region.

None of this points toward a model region that is independently and consensually part of global international society while at the same time expressing elements of its own cultural distinctiveness in a regional international society. What the previous chapters have unfolded is a story which, on the face of it, points towards the conclusion that for over two centuries the Middle Eastern states-system has been so thoroughly dominated, penetrated and manipulated by the West that it would be something of a miracle to find any regional differentiation at all other than that arising from rebellions against the illegitimacy of the intrusion (Brown, 1984). The Ottoman Empire did influence aspects of the transition to the modern Middle East. But the Empire was itself a transmission belt for some Western institutions into the region, and after the First World War, European powers basically imposed the current set of states onto the carcass of the Ottoman Empire. For both the Arab world and Israel, the process of colonisation and decolonisation was a series of deals between Western powers and local elites. Decolonisation gave these elites some autonomy. But it did so not just at the price of their accepting the Westphalian rules of the game, but also with the imposition that the game had to be played on a board defined by mainly unnatural states with shallow historical roots. With a few exceptions, the new states represented a poor fit between territory and government on the one hand, and patterns of identity among their peoples on the other. One consequence of all this, whether intentional or not, was to keep the local elites dependent on outside powers for the economic and/or military resources necessary for them to stay in power. And for the reasons just given (oil, Cold War, Suez, Israel), outside powers have been willing to provide those resources. Mostly they have come from Western powers, though during the Cold War the Soviet Union did provide some choices about financial and military support, and therefore more room for manoeuvre.

In circumstances like this, it does not seem an overstatement to say that the states-system in the Middle East was not only largely created by the West, but since then has also been substantially held in place by it. Not only have local elites been sustained by outside support, but also the global norm against allowing boundary changes by force (with the notable exception of Israel) has frozen the peculiar and awkward postcolonial structure of states in place. This arrangement is hardly normal in terms of the usual assumptions of English school theory about the relationship of states both to each other and to their peoples. In the interstate domain it suggests the operation of a coercive vanguard model not just as a one-off event of colonisation/decolonisation that is now becoming old history, but as an ongoing affair in which the current US-British occupation of Iraq, and extensive US military, political and economic engagements in the region, are just the latest phase. This sustained and coercive vanguardism has created and sustained a regional system of states that has a centre–periphery structure both domestically, and in relation to external powers. Because the region lacks a dominant power within itself, what it does not have is a centre–periphery structure at the regional level. Thus especially among the Arab states, many of the regimes in the Middle East, and up to a point the states themselves, have low legitimacy with their populations. Although most of them have achieved some degree of consolidation and legitimacy their regimes are caught in a tricky balancing act between their external dependence, and the intrusiveness of external great powers on the one hand, and the anti-imperial, Islamic and Arab nationalist pressures rising from below. Holding this balance all too frequently requires the Middle Eastern states to employ coercive measures against substantial parts of their populations.

A story along these lines, but with local variations, could be told for the other regions that went through the process of colonization and decolonization.

What it points to is not just a core–periphery differentiation, but also very significant differentiations in the form and type of states in play, and some differences in regional international society.

Encounter/Reform

The least disjuncture with their own history was reserved for those states that were not colonized, but underwent a coercive encounter with the West and a process of reform towards the Western 'standard of civilization' needed to retain independence and gain diplomatic recognition as members of international society. This story is quite well told in the English School literature on China and Japan (Bull and Watson, 1984a; Gong, 1984; Zhang, 1991; 1998; Suzuki, 2009; Buzan and Zhang, 2014), and also covers the Ottoman Empire/Turkey, Iran, Siam and Ethiopia. For Northeast Asia and the Middle East (the Ottoman Empire) these encounters took place on a regional scale and involved classical era great powers that had succeeded in keeping the West largely at bay from the first contacts until the West broke down their doors in the nineteenth century. At that point, the Middle East story becomes one of colonization, whereas Northeast Asia is one of encounter/reform. China and Japan correctly saw Western-colonial international society as based on a double standard, with recognition as equals given to those deemed 'civilized' and those not so deemed treated as less than equal, as 'barbarian' or 'savage', and open to varying degrees of subordination. Japan responded to the challenge by adopting a rapid and extensive modernization programme aimed not just to enable it to match Western military strength, but also to get it accepted by the West as a 'civilized' power. It accomplished this with astonishing speed, and between the Sino–Japanese war of 1894–5 and the Russo–Japanese one of 1904–5 was accepted by the West as the first non-Western great power, although still denied racial equality in 1919 (Shimazu, 1998). China took the opposite view, seeking to adapt only inasmuch as necessary to increase its power to hold out against the West and defend its own identity and system. It failed at this, and after being unexpectedly and easily defeated by Japan in their 1894–5 war (Paine, 2003), became a failed state, spiralling into decades of fragmentation and civil war (Paine, 2012; 2017). Despite this, it achieved courtesy recognition by the West as 'civilized' and as a great power during the Second World War.

Both countries retained something close to their original boundaries and population, and in that sense a high connectivity with their own history. Yet, the depth of disjuncture caused by their remaking into modern nation-states, and the ongoing tension between modernization and Westernization, should not be underestimated. The classical social order in East Asia was overthrown both within and between states, and traditional patterns of culture, power and identity were transformed. Yet because they retain significant historical and cultural continuity, both China and Japan can differentiate themselves culturally from the West. Japan, partly through its own reforms, and partly because of its occupation by the United States after the Second World War, is a rare case of a non-Western state making the transformation to an open access order. It remains an interesting question whether Japan wants to think of itself as part of Asia or part of the West, or just as being unique. China is perhaps best understood as being in the difficult transition process from natural state to a more open access order, caught somewhere between stratificatory and functional differentiation (Pieke, 2016). While pursuing economic modernization, it retains strong opposition to both political and cultural Westernization, and quite how it wants to relate to international society is not yet clear (Zhang, 1998; Buzan, 2010b).

A conspicuous irony of these four submodels of the monocentric model is that if one looks at differentiation from the perspective of the periphery, the most extreme historical disjuncture – repopulation – underpins the least differentiation with contemporary GIS, while, arguably, the least extreme historical disjuncture – encounter/reform – triggered huge transformations and left a legacy of major tensions with Western-dominated GIS.

3   Differentiations of States and Their Distribution

These formative processes, and the particular nature of encounters with the West, have massively shaped both the member states and the substructures (regional, core–periphery, functional) of the contemporary GIS. The core–periphery theme stands out particularly strongly, and it has become something of a preoccupation of English School and some other IR writing that although the legitimacy of contemporary international society is based on the sovereign equality of states, and up to a point the equality of people and nations, it is still riddled with hegemonic/hierarchical practices and inequalities of status (Gong, 1984: 7–21; Clark, 1989; Watson, 1992: 299–309, 319–25; 1997; Kingsbury, 1999; Keene, 2002; Bain, 2003; Dunne, 2003; Simpson, 2004; Clark, 2005: 227–43, 254; Hobson and Sharman, 2005; Donnelly, 2006; Hurrell, 2007b: 13, 35–6, 63–5, 71, 111–14; Lake, 2009; Buzan, 2010a; Clark, 2011; Bukovansky et al., 2012; Clapton, 2014). An emblematic example of such hierarchy is the special responsibilities of the great powers that Bull (1977) identified as a primary institution of international society and that are formally recognized in the P5 membership of the UN Security Council.

Yet as our discussion of formative process indicates, perhaps more important for understanding the nature of contemporary GIS than the rather specific observation about the persistence of hierarchy is the broader differentiation of state types resulting from this formative process, and in some places the geographical clustering of similar types. Such clustering is of course partly true of the North Atlantic core, which is mainly composed of developed, open access orders with strong states, though Japan, Australia and New Zealand are geographic outliers. Several other regions are fairly uniform internally in the way they differentiate from both the Western core and each other. Sub-Saharan Africa is dominated by weak, underdeveloped, dependent and often authoritarian postcolonial states, in which internal conflict and the threat of state failure dominate interstate relations. Latin America is dominated by states of middle ranking in terms of weak/strong, developed/developing and democratic/authoritarian. There are elements of security community and several substantial regional powers (Merke, 2011). The Middle East, as noted previously, is dominated by weak, authoritarian, dependent postcolonial states, with again several powers of similar strength and no potential hegemon (Buzan and Gonzalez-Pelaez, 2009). East Asia is at the other end of the spectrum, arguably containing states from all four formative legacies. Australia and New Zealand were repopulated; Southeast Asia was colonized; China and Japan underwent encounter/reform; and Japan, despite its place in the encounter/reform process, might just about qualify as unbroken given the rapidity of its domestic reform and joining of GIS (Buzan and Zhang, 2014: 8–9). The general differentiation of state types incorporates and explains the core–periphery structure, and thus indirectly also the functional differentiation one.

As Martin Wight (1977: 41) observed: '. . . heterogeneity has returned. The states represented at the United Nations are more various in origin, size and structure than were the states represented at the Congress of Westphalia'. The ES has explored the evolution of states, mostly from a historical, legal and philosophical perspective (Donelan, 1978; James, 1986; Jackson, 1990; 1999; Navari, 1991; 2007; Armstrong, 1998). Yet even though the expansion story and the 'revolt against the West' set up for it, the ES has not so far discussed the systematic differences between states in any sustained way. The IR literature already contains many state typologies, and we have alluded to several of them already. Buzan (1991: 90, 96–7), for example, introduced the notions of 'weak' and 'strong' states in the early 1980s, emphasizing their level of sociopolitical cohesion – in effect, the strength of their claim to be members of the category 'state'. Migdal (1988) uses the same terms to mark the longstanding IR differentiation of states in terms of their level of power. This was followed in the

1990s and 2000s by a large literature employing terms such as 'weak state', 'failed state', 'collapsed state', 'fragile state', 'soft state', 'imaginary state' and 'absent state' (Grimm, Lemay-Hébert and Nay, 2014), again referring mainly to the degree of sociopolitical cohesion. Within and outside the ES, Robert Jackson's (1990) idea of 'quasi-states' drew attention to the problem that many formally recognized states ('juridical sovereignty') in the post-1945 era lacked the traditional positive empirical referents of statehood, at least when placed under a Western gaze. A variation on this theme is Young's (1994) distinction between the 'modern state' and the 'colonial state' in Africa (see also Herbst, 2000). Returning to the analytical horizon of the global level, Cooper (1996) established the distinction among 'premodern', 'modern' and 'postmodern' states, subsequently varied by others, for example, Sørensen (2001), who has talked about the different problems and opportunities facing 'modern', 'postmodern' and 'postcolonial' states. Economic distinctions between developed and developing countries are well embedded in the UN system, and there are all kinds of core–periphery (and semiperiphery) analyses (Wallerstein, 1974; 2004). Similarly, political distinctions between democratic and authoritarian, and many variations in between, are common in both IR and comparative politics. And moving to the margins of international society, Armstrong (1993) has explored the resistance of 'revolutionary states' to the established world order, as well as their gradual cooptation by the existing members of international society.

These are all important contributions that highlight diverse aspects of unit differentiation, and we will continue to use some of the labels they provide as shorthand classifications. But the main theme of this book is how GIS is differentiated, and before we move on to unfold the four models for that, it is worth pausing to look in more detail at just how deeply, and in multiple ways, states themselves are differentiated. In other words, to appreciate fully just how much variety there is within the category of 'state', one needs to look across the range of characteristics that define differences among them. And it is the fact of this wide-ranging and deep variety that underpins our differentiation approach to analysing GIS. The characteristics of states, which in different ways constitute the previously defined typologies, can be captured using an analogy from computing under two headings. The first is *hardware*: territory, population, government institutions and economic and military capabilities. The second is *software*: what Reus-Smit (1999) calls the moral purpose of the state, which we will look at in terms of the primary institutional package of sovereignty, territoriality and nationalism, and within that, differentiations of political ideology and culture (civilization). These two headings partly turn on the traditional material/social distinction. This, of course, should not be overdrawn. While territory, for example, is probably as material as can be, it does not obtain physical consequence outside the social and ideational state context within which it is embedded, which is why territoriality plays in the software side.

Differences in State Hardware

Territory Differences in territory are both obvious and huge, with Russia having over 16 million square kilometres, several other giants having over 5 million, all the way down to minnows such as the Vatican, which is under half a square kilometre. This distribution does not display any obvious pattern. The link between territoriality and sovereignty is foundational to the modern GIS, with territory providing the container within which sovereignty is exercised (Sassen, 2008; Elden, 2013; Buzan, 2017). Despite a long and turbulent history of territorial change, the prevailing norms in GIS now support fixed boundaries and tend to carry this static picture forward into the future: territorial change by violent means is generally considered an illegal practice post-1945. A minor exception such as Russia's annexation of Crimea does not challenge this conclusion. Indeed, the trend since the delegitimation of colonialism after 1945 has gone in the opposite direction: towards the breakup of existing units and the creation of new states (Parent, 2011: 3–4).

But while the traditional picture of states in terms of land area looks set to remain fairly stable, and highly differentiated by size, states and GIS are expanding into new spaces: sea, air, extraterrestrial space and cyberspace. Some of these, notably the seas, have been travelled by humans for millennia. Others, such as cyberspace, constitute relative virgin territory. Yet they are all increasingly subject to the sovereign claims of states. The so-called race for the Arctic (see, for example, Roughead, 2015) by the surrounding littoral states has put a spotlight on the attempt to turn the seas (and the resources below) into sovereign territory (Strandsbjerg, 2012). This is part of a longer twentieth and twenty-first century trend, a major expression of which was the monumental 1982 United Nations Convention on the Law of the Sea. In the air, transport and weapons technologies (the atmospheric test ban treaty of 1963) have been regulated by interstate agreements for some time and have been supplemented with new rights and responsibilities in relation to climate change and national carbon emissions – what Lövbrand and Stripple (2006) call the 'territorialisation of the global carbon cycle'. Extraterrestrial space is also coveted by today's leviathans. States have tried to regulate rights and responsibilities in outer space, not least in relation to claiming authority over celestial bodies (Reynolds, 2004; Strauss, 2013). Finally, a new space, cyberspace, has opened up and has equally been made the subject of sovereign attempts at control. In the early 1990s, some expressed a vision of a borderless Internet that would be regulated by citizens from below. However, states were quick to assert themselves. The Internet is presently governed by a complicated regime involving states as well as non-state actors. There are definitely artificial borders, sometimes coinciding with state borders (Goldsmith and Wu, 2006; Mueller, 2010; Nye, 2014). China is perhaps the most extreme case of attempting to territorialize the Internet.

Population Differences in population size are as huge and as obvious as those in territory and do not correlate with it. Canada has a lot of territory and not much population, while Bangladesh has a lot of people crammed into a small space. The size range is even bigger than for territory: China's 1.4 billion to the Vatican's 450 (Vatican, 2015). The population picture is more mobile than the territorial one. At current growth rates, a lot of countries in Africa and the Middle East will see their populations expand significantly, whereas in much of Europe and Northeast Asia populations will shrink. On current projections, over half of the global population growth between 2015 and 2050 will come from Africa, and by 2050 Nigeria's population will be bigger than that of the United States (United Nations Department of Economic and Social Affairs, 2015). Interestingly, a lot of people in contemporary GIS do not reside in their home states. Some are temporary or semipermanent economic migrants or people who have simply chosen to move to another country for whatever reason: 231 million in 2013, a figure that has steadily risen from the 154 million in 1990. The major trend in those twenty-five years has been a big increase in 'south–south' and 'south–north' migration (United Nations, 2013: 1–2). Other people are forcefully displaced. Currently, there are about 20 million refugees worldwide (not counting the approximately 40 million who are internally displaced within their own countries), as well as 10 million who are considered stateless. It is also notable that 86 per cent of those refugees are hosted by states that the UN categorizes as 'developing countries', with 25 per cent residing in the 'least developed countries' (UNHCR, 2015: 2). While these figures may appear trivial in comparison with a global population of roughly 7.1 billion in 2013, they nevertheless point to interesting dynamics and a partial challenge to the political system of a world of states where each individual is in principle supposed to physically belong to one state. Large migration flows are already a political issue in many places, and whether caused by war, poverty, bad government or environmental crises, such flows look set to be major issue for GIS in the coming decades.

Government Institutions States as political communities are supposed to have political institutions capable of exercising the sovereign right of self-government over their territories and populations. The extent to which they do is nevertheless subject to huge variation. Somalia, Libya, Haiti, Syria, Iraq and Afghanistan are only the latest exemplars of 'weak' or 'failing' states apparently incapable of sustaining stable self-government under modern conditions. This is an issue that goes back to the imperial era when the 'standard of civilization' was used to justify colonization, and even the League of Nations defined its 'A, B and C' mandate system in terms of degrees of readiness for self-government. That history exposes the postcolonial politics behind this issue (see Grimm et al., 2014). On the one side, the categories of weak and failed state are mostly applied to postcolonial states as measured against the standard of 'strong' Western states and Japan. On the other side, it is reasonably easy to differentiate objectively, across a spectrum, states whose governments exercise consensual control across their territories and peoples, and do so in a largely peaceful and effective manner at one end (e.g., Canada, Japan); and states that fail to do this and whose internal politics are often violent, on the other (e.g., Libya, the Democratic Republic of Congo). One measure of this is the Fragile State Index (formerly the Failed States Index), which operates with a very broad conception of 'fragility', using twelve indicators (Fund for Peace, 2016). There are perennial problems about this differentiation, especially about whether repressive authoritarian governments such as those in North Korea, Iran, China and Russia should be counted as strong (because they exercise control) or weak (because they depend on coercion). Regardless of these political and methodological quibbles, it is not controversial that this variable, unlike the previous two, shows quite marked clustering that relates strongly to the formative process of GIS. There are strong (i.e., Western-style) government institutions in much of Europe, North America and parts of East Asia and Oceania; weak ones in much of Africa, Central Asia and the Middle East; and a more mixed picture in Latin America, South and Southeast Asia and parts of the Middle East. The capacity of government institutions is fairly sticky in the sense that strong states do not usually fall apart, and weak ones do not quickly become strong. But there is mobility: Singapore has become a strong state, and seemingly strong authoritarian states such as Libya and Syria have quickly collapsed into failure.

Economic Capabilities The onset of modernity during the nineteenth century broke the traditional link between size of territory and population on the one hand, and size of GDP on the other. With industrialization, even quite small states such as Britain could achieve huge gross domestic products (GDPs) (see the authoritative account by Piketty, 2014). Modernity opened up a spectrum of levels of development that defined a core–periphery global economic structure that is still recognizable today. There are huge variations in both economic size (the United States and China around $20 trillion, and some small island states with only a few hundred million) and GDP/capita (from oil rich states such as Qatar with over $100,000 to poor African countries with just a few hundred). These underpin easily identifiable rich and poor worlds with significant regional clustering. Some countries have moved quite rapidly up the ranks within a few decades, such as Japan, South Korea, China and Singapore. There is argument about whether there will be convergence between rich and poor as the latter transform their societies and realize their inherent economic potential (Rostow, 1960; Collier, 2008; Buzan and Lawson, 2015a). Others argue that the global capitalist economy will continue to display a core–periphery structure and thus an uneven distribution of economic capabilities until an under-specified crisis point is reached (Frank, 1967; Amin, 1976; Wallerstein, 2004). There is clearly a middle group of countries, most obviously China and India, whose economic capabilities are increasing rapidly. The economic picture is thus both highly diverse, but also quite mobile, with significant shifts up and down the ranks of GDP. Overall size of GDP is quite closely associated with ranking in terms of power, but GDP per capita represents a purer picture of differentiation in terms of development, with many small states achieving high levels of wealth and development. Significant disparity in the wealth of nations looks set to remain for the foreseeable future, along with both considerable regional clustering and a core–periphery configuration, albeit one in which the core is expanding and the periphery shrinking.

Military Capabilities Military capabilities as a unit characteristic feature prominently in traditional IR debates, particularly as a signifier of great power status. Military strength is partly dependent on economic power but not totally. Wealthy states such as Japan can choose to limit their military spending, and less wealthy ones, such as Russia and North Korea, can choose to spend a higher proportion of their GDP on military capability. Differentiation in military strength is very large. The United States outspends all of the other great powers by a significant margin, while some countries are unable to secure their own borders. States living in rough neighbourhoods like Africa and the Middle East tend to spend a higher percentage of GDP on defence. So as with economic capabilities, military ones can be differentiated both in terms of absolute and relative size of military expenditure, and the degree of military effort in terms of expenditure as a percentage of GDP. Within this broad differentiation, there are several other markers that differentiate state military capacity in important ways. First is whether or not states possess nuclear weapons, a club currently thought to have nine members, but whose membership could expand quickly if nuclear-capable states such as Japan, Germany and a number of others decided they needed their own nuclear weapons. Second are those possessing blue-water navies: the ability to project naval power over and across the open oceans. This is a smaller club, and the cost and difficulty of acquiring a blue-water navy preclude rapid expansions of membership. The United States is currently in a class by itself, far in advance of all the others. Britain, France, Japan, India and Russia have limited blue-water capability, and China seems keen to expand this type of power over the coming decades. Third are those countries capable of operating militarily in space, mainly now the United States, Russia and China, but with the EU, Japan and India also in play. This, again, is a club with high entry costs. Fourth is the capability to conduct cyberwar. The membership of this club is a bit murkier, and it is probably easier to acquire the capability to join. It certainly includes the United States, Russia, China, Israel and Britain. Now as in the past, specific military capabilities go a long way to defining whether a country is seen as a great power or not.

Hardware differences are wide ranging within all of these categories. Several of them demonstrate significant clustering and status differentiation. Many are relatively sticky, though some, like choices about the percentage of GDP devoted to military expenditure, can change quickly. It would be possible to extend this list, for example by thinking about environmental vulnerability in the face of climate change. Some low-lying countries are acutely vulnerable to sea level rise, most obviously Bangladesh, the Netherlands and a variety of small island states in the Pacific and Indian oceans. Many major coastal cities are similarly vulnerable, including Shanghai, London and New York. If the world is moving into an era of climate instability, then aspects of territory such as this will become important. But we leave that for the future and turn now to differences in state software.

Differences in State Software

In a general sense, as noted previously, the software of the state is the set of ideas that defines its moral purpose by framing its identity and supporting the legitimacy of its system of government. In the contemporary GIS, there is a surprising amount of consensus about the core ideas that are constitutive of the modern state: sovereignty, territoriality and nationalism. In the ES approach, these three have standing as primary institutions, and as Buzan (2017) argues, their stories are heavily intertwined. The classical Westphalian state is constituted by sovereignty (the absolute right of self-government) and territoriality (the idea that government and people should be contained within a well-defined territorial package). The modern state that emerged during the nineteenth century added nationalism: the idea that the state should contain, protect and represent a people with a shared culture and/or ethnicity (Mayall, 1990; Buzan and Lawson, 2015a). As Ernest Gellner (1983: 1) put it, 'Nationalism is primarily a political principle, which holds that the political and the national unit should be congruent'. Sovereignty underpinned a claim to legal equality amongst states, and nationalism underpinned a parallel claim that all people(s) were also entitled to equal rights and status. Notwithstanding some difficulties about how to define a nation (ethnic or civic? historical or made?), this software package is the foundation on which GIS rests. Since it is so widely accepted, it constitutes a robust shared feature of GIS, and is the powerful basis for the idea that states are 'like-units' and GIS is fundamentally homogeneous.

Yet while this package is widely shared in a general sense, it also contains the potential for very substantial differentiation in the way that states define their moral purpose, frame their identity, and legitimate their system of government. This potential for differentiation is most obvious in relation to nationalism, which is unifying as a principle but dividing as a practice. Nationalism does either or both of taking the historical legacy of different cultures and ethnicities as a positive thing to be preserved and/or using the state to forge new nations that share a common language or languages and identity. In this sense, it is by nature differentiating and goes some way towards answering the question of how to define what constitutes a people. At its best, it can support a stable pluralism in which each nation respects the differences of the others, and the uniqueness of each is supported by a general norm of coexistence. At worst, however, nationalism is subject to the pathologies of social Darwinism and racism that reached a ghastly peak during the Second World War. It generates a practical tension with the existing territorial disposition of states and sovereignty, for there are far more nations and ethnic groups than there are states. This contradiction creates irredentism (the desire to unify nations that are spread across more than one state – think of Kurds, Koreans, Russians and Palestinians) and separatism (the breaking up of states containing more than one nation – think of Canada, Britain, Pakistan, Russia and Sudan), both of which continue still.

In addition, this package contains a large space for ideological differentiation. Without deviating from the basic principles of the package, states can and do opt for a wide variety of ideological options with which to define their moral purpose, frame their identity and legitimate their system of government. As Buzan and Lawson (2015a: 97–126) argue, nationalism was a key element in the revolutions of modernity, and one of the core ideologies of progress that transformed the ideational landscape of world politics during the nineteenth century. As it rose to the status of an institution of international society, nationalism had the effect of redefining sovereignty as popular sovereignty (Bukovansky, 2002). Popular sovereignty made the people the owners of the state, and so delegitimized the prevailing traditional political order of dynasticism, in which the monarch was the owner of the state. By pushing dynasticism to the margins, nationalism and popular sovereignty opened up a range of ideological possibilities for states to define their moral purpose. States and peoples did so with enthusiasm, building on the other ideologies of progress associated with modernity: liberalism, socialism and 'scientific' racism. This generated a very substantial ideological differentiation in the political software of states, the working out of which dominated twentieth-century world politics and is still unfolding.

During the nineteenth century, nationalism and popular sovereignty, embodied in the idea of republicanism, steadily pushed dynasticism and religion to the margins as the legitimate defining values for the moral purpose and identity of the state. The First World War and its associated revolutions destroyed most of the remaining bastions of absolutism and set in place a triangular ideological differentiation based on liberal capitalist democracy; authoritarian command-economy socialism; and authoritarian, state-capitalist fascism. Socialism had a powerful cosmopolitan streak that was opposed to nationalism, but this lost out to nationalism both in the First World War and afterwards. Both liberal democrats and authoritarians could and did play to nationalism and popular sovereignty, and despite some contradictions (mostly for liberals and socialists, hardly at all for fascists), all three ideologies coexisted with racism and empire. There was also space for a social democratic ideology that tried to marry democratic politics with a hybrid capitalist/socialist economic structure. Fascism embodied the pathologies of nationalism to such an extreme degree that it united the otherwise opposed socialist and liberal camps against it and was delegitimized and pushed into the political wilderness by the Second World War. The Third World War (the Cold War) pitched the socialist and liberal camps against each other, with social democrats awkwardly in the middle. The outcome of that was a comprehensive victory for capitalism against command economy, which was first signalled by China's move to reform and open up in the late 1970s, and then by the collapse of the Soviet Union in the early 1990s. From the 1990s, this became something of a victory against social democracy as well, as a neoliberal, globalizing form of capitalism became predominant.

By the twenty-first century, this working out of ideologies had reached a point where capitalism had won out over other forms of political economy as being clearly the most effective way to generate wealth and power quickly. But liberal democracy had not won, and authoritarianism had not been defeated. Although liberal democracy remained a powerful political ideology, unlike nationalism it did not achieve universal standing as an institution of GIS. It certainly had that standing within the Western subset, and also for some others, but globally, along with human rights, it remained hotly contested (Clark, 2009a). Authoritarians in China, Russia and elsewhere set about proving that capitalism did not require democracy. This created a world in which all were now capitalists (rather than the 'capitalist or not' rivalry of the Cold War), but capitalism came in a variety of political forms stretching across a political spectrum from democratic to authoritarian (Buzan and Lawson, 2014). This development narrowed the ideological bandwidth of GIS compared with the twentieth century, while nevertheless leaving a substantial ideological divide between democrats and authoritarians.

What this history suggests is that the core software package of GIS (sovereignty, nationalism, territoriality) remains remarkably robust, while the ideological elements can be both durable and fragile. Revolutions such as those in Russia in 1917 and 1989, China in 1949 and Iran in 1979, and wars such as that between 1939 and 1945, can quickly change ideological orientations. At the same time, democracy looks to be deeply embedded in the West, India and Japan, and the Chinese Communist Party looks set for a long run.

At the time of writing (2017), a new twist in the ideological dialectic seemed to be opening up. Both capitalism and the democratic/authoritarian divide looked pretty durable, the former because there was no alternative system on offer that could produce sufficient wealth and power, the latter because both political forms looked well entrenched in their heartlands, with neither having the momentum to overawe the other. But the votes for Brexit and Trump in 2016 suggested a powerful challenge to the globalized form of neoliberal capitalism. Authoritarians and social democrats had always been wary of globalization, and economic globalization was also a challenge to the basic sovereignty/territoriality/nationalism package. But the rejection of global capitalism in the core states of the Anglosphere that had done most to promote it, and the rise of quasifascist leaderships in the United States and some European countries, pointed strongly to the possibility of a more protectionist version of capitalism emerging as the global consensus. Part of this new twist was the impact of both terrorism and large-scale migration on Western countries. Both phenomena were related to the previously discussed international hardware differences of weak and strong, and rich and poor states. And, by putting stress on the moral purpose, identity and governmental legitimacy and competence of states, both also disturbed the core software package of GIS: sovereignty, territoriality and nationalism.

Into this mix one also needs to blend a rising tide of cultural differentiation, which partly takes a nationalist form (e.g., 'Chinese characteristics') and partly a civilizational one (e.g., Hindutva, Islamic values). In a big-picture view, it might be argued that the resurfacing of culture as Western dominance declines is replacing the ideological differentiation that marked the twentieth century. And culture, of course, is much deeper and more durable than ideology. Mostly this trend fits within the basic sovereignty/territoriality/nationalism package, although Islam has significant cosmopolitan elements that go against all three elements of the package and has played into the disruptive effects of mass migration and terrorism in the West. Elsewhere, however, cultural differentiation mainly reinforces a wariness about globalization that was heavily shaped by the fear that economic globalization had big cultural consequences – in effect, globalization equals Westernization. The era of Western domination is anyway coming to an end. After two centuries in which the West has largely shaped and led GIS, 'the rise of the rest' (Zakaria, 2009) is steadily eroding both the relative material power and the ideological and cultural legitimacy of the West. As other cultures find their own accommodation with the revolutions of modernity, the West will remain strong, but no longer dominant. This development is not just about China, though China is a big part of the rise of the rest. It is about the evening out of power and authority as the rest of the world recovers its position after the extraordinary inequality created by the rapid consolidation of modernity in a handful of mainly Western countries during the nineteenth century: what we labelled previously as 'deep' or 'embedded' pluralism.

Just as the West was both powered and changed by modernity, so other countries are following Japan in finding their own cultural fusions with modernity. The legitimacy of the Western liberal model as a universal standard of civilization will almost certainly decline. During the last two centuries, the number of democracies gradually increased, although with significant temporary reverses along the way (Huntington, 1991). By the end of the Cold War, the principle of democracy enjoyed unsurpassed international legitimacy, to the point where, as (Clark, 2009a: 569) stresses, international society (the Western bit at least) recognized it as the only really legitimate form of rule in the Charter of Paris for a New Europe in 1990. The states of Europe, organized in the Conference on Security and Cooperation in Europe (CSCE), committed themselves 'to build and strengthen democracy as the only system of government of our nations' (quoted in Clark, 2009a: 569). This hubris has now peaked, and this emergent world will display both cultural and ideological differentiation based on cultures and political forms other than Western ones. As is already visible in the case of China, culture (Confucian hierarchy) will be used to legitimize and reinforce ideology (authoritarianism). Russia and other places are finding more freedom to legitimize current authoritarianism in terms of their specific cultural heritage. For now, the state remains the dominant overall container for political communities and their ideological software. Yet one needs to keep an open mind about this. An alternative perspective is provided by Pieterse (2003; 2011: 81), who directly references Bull's (1977: 244–6) new mediaevalism in constructing his own thinking. He identifies a process of increasing hybridization of different cultural elements, a global mélange. This involves the mixing of popular culture, local culture, global culture, nation-state culture, the culture of capitalism and everything in-between in new sedentary and nonsedentary forms. This kind of work is a useful reminder that although GIS is still centred on states, that will not always be the case, and other revolutionist, world society dynamics are bubbling underneath the surface.

4   Conclusions

This chapter has laid the foundations for thinking about how GIS might be differentiated. We have exposed both very significant similarities amongst states as the members of GIS and very consequential differences amongst them and showed how both are rooted in the formative process of the modern GIS. We have shown how these differences display a considerable amount of both geographical clustering and status differentiation, and how this too is a historical product of the formative process. In principle, we could at this point construct a giant, multilayered matrix on which all states could be located, but that is not our goal. What we have established here is the historical and taxonomical basis for approaching GIS through a set of ideal-type models based on the tensions between homogeneity and differentiation.

It should now be fully clear that the monocentric formative process of GIS has left a very strong stamp on contemporary GIS, one which is still a long way from resolving the inequalities that marked its founding and remains culturally and politically insecure. Situated as we now are at the end of the era of Western dominance of GIS, it is interesting to return to the beginning of this chapter by picking up the *engagements amongst equals* submodel of the general polycentric model as a way of thinking about the future of GIS. The rise of China as a powerful new hybrid of modernity with its own traditions, when added to the relative decline of Western power and authority, opens up interesting questions about the ongoing formative dynamics of GIS. In a way, the rise of Japan, representing a similar synthesis of modernity with a non-Western culture, opened this question more than a century ago. But Japan was too much by itself, and not powerful enough, to be able to question the Western order then at the peak of its power. China is now becoming powerful enough to make such a challenge, and India may not be too far behind. Both face a relatively weaker West that is also being challenged by other rising powers and their resurgent cultural values. The less concentrated distribution of power, the opening up of cultural diversity and the substantial delegitimation of the universalist pretentions of the Western 'standard of civilization' almost certainly mean that a much more deeply pluralist GIS is about to enter into a long period of reform and renegotiation of its core intergovernmental organizations and regimes. That said, the core software package of GIS, sovereignty, territoriality, and nationalism is looking pretty robust as a framework for handling both the change in the distribution of power, and the more pluralist cultural landscape. If so, then the model for its future development will not be any of the four monocentric submodels explored in this chapter (unbroken creation, repopulation, colonization/ decolonization, encounter/reform). Those are now backward looking, representing the period of Western domination that is now ending. More likely, the dynamic that is emerging will be something like the polycentric 'engagements amongst equals' submodel hinted at in the introduction. This will take the study of GIS into new and largely unexplored territory.

With this differentiation amongst states, and its geographical, status and functional implications for clustering, we now turn to our four-model framework for analysing GIS.

Part II

Models

The five chapters in this part build on both the discussions about modes of differentiation as applied to states and international societies in Chapters 1 and 2 and the discussion of formative processes in Chapter 2. As in Chapter 2, we use Weber's tool of 'ideal-types', which Sørensen (2001: 73) helpfully describes as 'analytical constructs which seek to express "pure" forms by accentuating selected aspects of historical reality'. Our four ideal-type models draw their 'pure forms' from the principles of differentiation established in Part I. These principles make it relatively straightforward to identify the four models and relate them to the literature on GIS. The models are the following:

> *Like-units* – focusing on the similarities of units as expressed in their constitution by, adherence to, and belief in a core set of primary institutions;
>
> *Regions/subglobal* – focusing on geographical differentiations in the primary institutions of international society that express themselves in various regional and subglobal clusterings;
>
> *Hierarchy/privilege* – focusing on status differentiations within and between different types of unit, and incorporating, but also going beyond, the Wallersteinian (1974) and *dependencia* (Galtung, 1971) model of a GIS divided into a dominant, developed core, and a subordinate, less-developed periphery;
>
> *Functional differentiation* – focusing on the idea that functional differentiation within the leading-edge states has already significantly restructured the members and legitimate behaviours of GIS along globalization lines.

The first two models speak mainly to the interstate domain, while the second two open up for a wider range of units/actors from the transnational and interhuman domains. Where these models require us to look for differentiation we use the English School criteria set up by Buzan and Zhang (2014: 7):

- That there are differences in the distribution of primary institutions: some are global, but some are found only or mainly within subsets of states, and some that are widespread may not be present within one or more subsets.
- Even where the same nominal primary institutions are in place, there is considerable room for interpreting them differently and having significantly different practices associated with them. This might mean either that a given institution is associated with different practices (e.g., strong versus weak sovereignty), or that the value and priority attached to institutions within the same set is different (e.g. where sovereignty is the trump institution in one place and the market, or nationalism, or great power management, in another).

Following Weber, we do not argue that any one of these models or combinations of them, as ideal-types, represent the existing reality in its entirety. We see each of the models as representing a significant organizing principle within GIS, and thus possessing part of the necessary insight required to understand what is in front of us. To think about how each of these models plays into the question of how to assess the strength and weaknesses of any international society, we draw on the discussion of Wendt's ideas about the binding forces that hold societies together (belief, coercion, calculation) in Chapter 1. We reassemble the four models and the assessments they generate into an aggregated picture in Chapter 7.[1]

Our main purpose is to establish an overall framework for how to understand GIS and whether it is becoming stronger or weaker. Along the way, we hope to make explicit the various assumptions about GIS that are often only implicit in ES work on GIS. The key methodological difficulty in this plan is that while it is relatively easy to identify and justify the models, and to set out explicitly the assumptions and criteria that define them, it is considerably more difficult to provide exhaustive empirical evidence for assessments about degrees and types of adherence to them in the real world. Since our priority is to construct a top-down view of GIS,[2] our attempt here takes the form of a reconnaissance or

---

[1] We recognize that there may be more depth to Weber's understanding of ideal-types than presented here, including the issue of value judgement in the selection of the 'culturally significant' aspects of reality to be explored (see Keene, 2009). However, for our purposes, we will stick to the relatively simple understanding captured by Sørensen.

[2] By 'top-down', we mean that we thoroughly adopt the perspective of the detached analyst of international society, applying concepts/models constructed by us. This contrasts with a bottom-up or grounded approach in which the meaning of international society is inferred directly from the concrete, situated and variable experiences of the actors involved. See Wilson (2012) and Spandler (2015) for arguments for the latter approach.

scoping exercise, aiming to do an initial, and inevitably somewhat rough and impressionistic, survey of the landscape of GIS as seen through the lens of differentiation theory. If this works, it will provide the foundations for more detailed empirical research than we have space for in this book. An 'ideal-types' approach along these lines has paid dividends in other work (Sørensen, 2001; Buzan, 2004a: 158–60, 190–5), and we hope to make it convincing enough here to justify opening up areas for more detailed empirical and theoretical enquiry. Readers familiar with Kurosawa's classic film *Rashomon* will see echoes of his approach here: the telling of the same story several times from different perspectives.

3   The 'Like-Units' Model

The like-units model (LUM) is mainly derived from the classical historical reading of the expansion of international society. It focuses on the interstate domain and the global level of international society. It minimizes the differentiation among states (except in terms of power), and marginalizes the differentiation between states and units from the transnational and interhuman domains (except as the latter influence the formation of primary institutions among states – Clark, 2007). The LUM privileges how primary institutions held in common construct GIS, and therefore pays little attention to what, other than power, differentiates it. In this chapter, we look first at the model itself, comparing it with the neorealist one and identifying the criteria it generates for evaluating how weak or strong international societies are. We then examine its strengths and weaknesses as a representation of the GIS that actually exists.

1   The Model

The LUM is the simplest way to envisage GIS. It shares many features with Waltz's (1979) neorealism, particularly the privileging of the interstate domain, in which the assumption is of a political world composed of modern, sovereign, legally equal, territorial states that are functionally alike in terms of what tasks they perform and how they are internally structured along hierarchical and functionally differentiated lines. The only significant distinction amongst these states allowed by the model is the Waltzian one of differences in capability, which in both neorealism and the ES supports a two-tier differentiation between great powers and all the rest. An implicit assumption of the LUM is therefore that differentiation other than in terms of capabilities is minimal and not of much consequence for understanding GIS. Another shared characteristic with neorealism is a tendency to privilege the global system level: the international system for neorealists, GIS for the ES. The LUM is deeply Westcentric in its monocentric assumption that the expansion of what started as a European international society into GIS has been more or less completely triumphant, creating a world politically terraformed according to the template of the modern European/Western state.

Where the LUM departs from neorealism is in the central place it gives to shared values, norms and rules amongst the like-units that express themselves as the primary institutions of GIS. These primary institutions compose the structure of GIS and play significant roles in constituting both states themselves as legitimate members of international society and the rules defining legitimate behaviour within the society of states. Given the ES's concern about the importance of shared culture and values as a key underpinning for international society (Buzan, 2010a), a second assumption of this model is that these institutions are largely accepted on grounds of belief: states accept the rules because they see them as appropriate or right. To understand international society in the terms of this model, one needs to understand who its state members are and what primary institutions they all agree on. This can be done in static terms, like a snapshot, or in a dynamic one, like a movie, where both membership and the prevailing set of primary institutions will change over time.

Somewhat more in the margins of IR theory, in the border zone with sociology, the LUM also links to the Stanford School's culturally based concept of *world society* (Meyer et al., 1997; Navari, 2018). World culture is thought of as an explanation for the isomorphism of states through the authoritative dissemination of the standards, norms and institutions that define what states are, how they construct themselves and what is appropriate behaviour for them. In a sense, world culture is an elaboration on Waltz's idea that isomorphism occurs through socialization and competition, in which states become alike both by copying successful models and by going extinct if they don't. The difference is that world culture, much more so than the ES approach to the LUM, gives a major role to transnational NSAs in transmitting shared standards. Like the ES and neorealism, world culture is also Westcentric in seeing the main sources of isomorphism as originating in the West and flowing out from there to shape the states in the periphery.

If one looks at contemporary GIS in snapshot terms as a LUM, what does one see? The mainstream view is that there is a thin, but homogeneous, GIS based on a substantial set of more or less globally shared primary and secondary institutions. The shared primary institutions certainly include the classical ones of sovereignty, territoriality, diplomacy and international law, and also nationalism, human equality, development and the market. Great power management is still firmly embedded in a host of secondary institutions, most obviously the UN

Security Council (Cui and Buzan, 2016), but there are question marks around war and the balance of power. The standing of war has been confused by the decline of state-to-state war generally, and great power war in particular, and the rise of messy and confusing transnational 'wars' between states and non-state actors (Holsti, 2004: 283–99; Jones, 2006; Hurrell, 2007b: 163–93). The standing of the balance of power was brought into question by the near absence of the expected traditional behaviour when the United States became the sole superpower after the implosion of the Soviet Union. Human rights and democracy are contested. They have some standing as emergent primary institutions, but more in some places than in others, and whether they will reach the status of primary institutions of GIS remains an open question. Environmental stewardship has recently arrived as a thin, but more or less universally accepted, primary institution (Falkner and Buzan, 2017).

If one looks at this model in dynamic terms, what emerges is a rather Westcentric story of both the origin and the prospects of GIS.[1] This story is told in a number of classic ES works (Bull, 1977: 27–40; Wight, 1977: 110–73; Bull and Watson, 1984a; Gong, 1984; Watson, 1992; Jackson, 2000: 156–67). At some risk of oversimplification, the history behind the LUM can be rendered as three distinct phases:

- First, the emergence and consolidation of a distinctive, regional anarchical international society in Europe built around the Westphalian institutions of sovereignty/nonintervention, territoriality, balance of power, war, international law, diplomacy and great power management.
- Second, the spread of this society to the rest of the world on the back of expanding European economic and military power, mainly in colonial form but also in encounters with non-Western societies – Russia, the Ottoman Empire, China, Japan – that escaped colonization. In a sense, this generated a global-scale international society for the first time, albeit one in which the formal membership remained small, with most non-Western states and peoples folded into the colonial sovereignty of Western empires. This GIS was culturally cohesive because it was dominated by Western empires, but it was a highly coercive, and highly unequal, (colonial) form of GIS.
- Third, decolonization, the bringing in of the Third World to equal membership of GIS, and the consequent weakening of its cultural cohesion by what Bull called 'the revolt against the West' (Bull and Watson, 1984a: 217–28). This move retained the global scale but

---

[1] This account draws on Buzan and Little (2014), where the reader can find more detail.

greatly increased the number of formal members. It reduced the level of coercion and political and racial inequality. But it did so at the cost of diluting the cultural and political coherence of GIS.

The early rise of Japan to equal state status and then, by 1905, to great power status creates an awkward anomaly for this Eurocentric story. As noted previously, Japan anticipated by a century 'the rise of the rest'. In so doing, it questioned both the racial and cultural assumptions of the day and set up the problem of how to maintain the normative cohesion of a like-units GIS when the membership came from multiple civilizational roots. This cultural problem made many of the classical ES writers pessimistic about the direction of GIS because of the absence of sufficient shared culture to sustain common values and institutions. The signature hypothesis was that 'We must assume that a states-system will not come into being without a degree of cultural unity among its members' (Wight, 1977: 33). Since decolonization, this cultural divide has remained, with a still strong West trying to push liberal values such as human rights and democracy into the institutional framework of GIS, and most of the rest preferring a more Westphalian form of strong sovereignty and nonintervention.

There are arguments around the first phase about whether the initial development of the Westphalian model was a pristine event, entirely endogenous to Europe, or one that drew significantly from Eurasian inputs into European development. These do not affect the LUM, and so need not concern us here.

The second phase of this story does not bother too much with whether there were other international social structures than the European one, or if there were, what characteristics they had. It assumes that whatever was out there, it was pushed into the dustbin of history by the global overlay of the Western powers and their 'standard of civilization'. The 'standard of civilization' was the homogenizing mechanism requiring non-Western states to conform to Western criteria in order to gain entry to GIS. It could be done, as Japan did, by a process of intense reform. The nature and extent of the homogenizing test posed by the 'standard of civilization' for Japan (and others) is richly captured by Murphy (2014: 63–4):

The Meiji leaders faced three urgent and intertwined tasks. They had to build a military strong enough to act as a deterrent to Western imperialism. They had to assemble the capital and technology needed to turn their country into an industrial power sufficiently advanced to equip that military. And they had to create the institutions necessary not only to accomplish these other tasks but to convince the West that Japan had accumulated the prerequisites for membership in the club of countries that were to be taken seriously. That meant not only a credible military – preferably evidenced by victories in imperialist wars waged on weaker lands – but also such institutions as parliaments, courts, banks, monogamy, elections, and ideally, Christian churches, not to mention familiarity with Western ways and appearances in such matters as architecture, dress, sexual mores, and table manners. It was only by governing as the leaders of a convincing imitation of a modern imperialist nation that these men could persuade the West to revise the Unequal Treaties and thereby wrest back control over their country's tariff regime and security apparatus from the Europeans.

Homogenization could also be done through the process of colonization in which metropolitan powers were supposed to mentor their charges in the ways of 'civilization'. Either way, the process was a homogenizing one that would produce 'like-units' on the Western model. The 'standard of civilization' certainly reflected cultural and racial arrogance towards other cultures. But it also reflected the functional necessities of inter-action amongst equals, which required certain standards of effective government, particularly the ability to meet 'reciprocal obligations' in law (Gong, 1984: 64–93; Buzan, 2014b). Gong (1984: 24–53) shows how the European need for access (trade, proselytizing, travel) was what drove the functional aspects of the 'standard of civilization' (to protect life, liberty and property) and therefore the demand for extraterritoriality and unequal relations where the locals could not or would not provide these. He notes the clash of civilizations explicit in the expansion, and how the 'standard of civilization' created a pressure for conformity with Western values and practices, which posed a demanding cultural chal-lenge to the non-West, much of which had to go against its own cultural grain in order to gain entry.

The third phase sees the whole of the non-Western world receiving largely unconditional membership of GIS, with divided sovereignty giving way to sovereign equality. Decolonization tripled the independ-ent membership of GIS and brought into it many postcolonial states that were weak as states (in the sense of having low sociopolitical cohesion), economically underdeveloped and poor. In this sense, GIS shifted from an elite membership of empires, each of which contained societies strung across the spectrum of development, to a mass mem-bership of independent states, which were themselves ranged across the spectrum from developed to underdeveloped. The shift from an elite membership of empires to a mass one of states thus radically amplified the diversity of state types composing GIS. Decolonization weakened the cultural foundations of GIS by diluting the previously dominant Euro-pean cohesion amongst the colonial powers. Now all the world's cul-tures both great and small were inside, and this moved Wight's question about the relationship between cultural cohesion and international society to centre stage. But in order to gain independence and get recognition of their sovereignty, third world elites had to face the same test as the Japanese and accept both the Western form of the state and the basic institutions of a Western-dominated GIS. This gave some grounds for hope that the expanded GIS might be able to evolve in a coherent manner, though it also confronted GIS with both the immediate and long-term problem of how to deal with the massive economic inequalities and cultural differences that now existed within it (Bull, 1984a: 217–28; 1984b).

It is interesting that despite their significant concerns and reservations about the weaknesses of the postcolonial GIS, Bull and Watson (1984a: 433–4) took a quite upbeat view of its prospects. It is worth citing their view at length as a good example of the historical perspective underpinning the LUM:

It might be thought evidence of the underlying strength and adaptability of the international society created by the Europeans that it has been able to absorb such a vast accretion of new members, interests, values, and preoccupations, without giving rise either to any clear sign that its rules and institutions are collapsing under the strain, or that the new states have repudiated them. Indeed, the most striking feature of the global international society of today is the extent to which the states of Asia and Africa have embraced such basic elements of European international society as the sovereign state, the rules of international law, the procedures and conventions of diplomacy and international organization. In all these areas they have sought to reshape existing rules and institutions, to eliminate discrimination against themselves and to assert their own interests forcefully, but all this has been against the background of the strong interests they have perceived in accepting the rules and institutions, not only because of their need to make use of them in their relations with the erstwhile dominant powers, but also because they cannot do without them in their relations with one another . . .

In particular, Third World governments insist on the originally Western premiss that the stronger members of society have an obligation to protect the weaker, rather than licence to exploit or oppress them. In what is known as the North–South dialogue they have demanded the extension of the concept of collective security from its original Wilsonian military guarantee into a demand for collective economic security, on the very realistic ground that political independence is not enough to achieve sovereignty and that the economically powerful states also have an obligation to guarantee economic standards which a weak state cannot provide unaided. Third World governments also maintain with great firmness the European doctrine that neither collective security nor financial aid nor any other guarantee or arrangement gives the strong powers any right to interfere in the domestic relations between the new governments and their subjects. They reject any idea of a directorate or concert of great powers entitled to 'lay down the law'.

This dynamic historical view explains why the LUM can see GIS as both global and homogeneous but also thin and weak. It is global because Western power and control extended to planetary scale during the nineteenth century, incorporating all of humankind into a single international system/society. And it is homogeneous, because the non-West had to adopt Western forms and practices in return for independence, recognition and membership. But it is relatively thin and weak because it lacks cultural cohesion other than of an elite 'Davos culture' kind and is still divided by deep material inequalities. Given the ongoing 'rise of the rest' and the steady erosion of Western dominance, the problem of cultural diversity may well rise in salience, even as the issue of big material inequality between a small core and large periphery lessens. With the rise of the rest, the core is getting bigger and the periphery smaller (Buzan and Lawson, 2015a).

The LUM provides the basic framing for Buzan's (2004a: 159–60) spectrum of types of international society ranging from *power political* (based on a logic of conflict and survival – think of the warring states period in China or eighteenth century Europe), through *coexistence* (based on a logic of some desire for international order and rules of the game – think of the Concert of Europe) and *cooperation* (based on a logic of pursuit of joint gains or shared goals – think of the global economy or the pursuit of human rights), to *convergence* (based on a logic of units wanting to become more structurally alike – think of the EU's *aquis communautaire*). These four types range along a spectrum from pluralist to solidarist, and implicitly from thin/weak to thick/strong. If understood in realist/liberal terms, they also suggest a normative, progressive spectrum from primitive and undesirable to civilized and good. This rather oversimplified schema is one of the things that will come under question as we unfold our four models.

The LUM thus suggests a number of criteria for assessing whether GIS is getting stronger or weaker:

- Increasing or diminishing the number and proportion of states and peoples who have full membership of the international society. Near-universal membership makes this criterion less relevant for contemporary GIS, though it could revive if solidarist criteria such as democracy and human rights are used to create a new 'standard of civilization' that tightens the criteria for membership and makes exclusion easier (Buzan, 2014a: 159–61). But this criterion was highly relevant up until decolonization.
- Increasing or diminishing the number of primary institutions that are commonly held.

- Increasing or diminishing the elaboration and uniformity of practices within already-agreed institutions (e.g., as in sovereignty/nonintervention, the market, human rights, or diplomacy).
- Increasing or diminishing the depth or type of institutions shared. In classical ES terms, this would mean having not only institutions based on the principle of coexistence, but also ones based on the principles of cooperation or convergence, or in other words, moving from more pluralist to more solidarist institutions.
- Increasing or diminishing the degree of cultural similarity amongst the members of international society.
- A shift in the binding forces away from coercion and calculation and towards belief.

Increases in any or all of these five criteria would suggest strengthening of GIS, whereas decreases in them would suggest weakening of it. There is room for contradiction in this set. For example, movement towards solidarist institutions in some parts of GIS might cause decreases in other criteria; and increasing the membership might well decrease the cultural cohesion. We explore such contradictions in subsequent chapters.

2   Strengths and Weaknesses of the Model

This section asks three questions:

- How well does the model capture the actual nature of the units?
- How well does the model capture the actual nature of the structure in terms of the pattern of acceptance of/adherence to the primary institutions of international society?
- How well does the model capture the binding forces of GIS? To what extent is acceptance/adherence based on consent/belief (the standard assumption of the LUM), and to what extent on calculation and/or coercion; and how wide and deep is this acceptance in the sense of being accepted by the people and not just the elite?

Capturing the Units

This question is more difficult than it looks. It requires reference back to the criteria for differentiation at the unit level discussed in Chapter 1, to the more detailed looks at the formative stories behind the current member states of GIS told in Chapter 2, and to the many ways in which states differ from each other surveyed in the same chapter. In making judgements about these things, one has to keep in mind that theory

requires a significant degree of simplification from the effectively bot-
tomless complexity and endless potential for differentiation to be found
in the real world. It is not a valid criticism to say that an ideal-type fails to
capture the full reality. Indeed, it is not meant to. The issue is whether
the simplification works to expose an important essence of the full reality.
In principle, as the discussion of taxonomy in Chapter 1 suggests, the
appropriate level of abstraction and simplification will depend on the aim
of the analysis. In terms of the analogy used in Chapter 1, for some
purposes it might be appropriate to focus on what is common to the
rather general category of 'fruit'. For other purposes, one might need to
look at 'apples', or at types within apples. The suggestion in Chapter 1
was that 'states' could be thought of as analogous to 'apples' in terms of
their place in a taxonomical hierarchy stretching from very general/broad
to very specific/narrow.

On this point, it is again helpful to compare Waltzian neorealism to the
English School. We noted in Chapter 1 that the 'like-units' formulation
was common to both. But how well does it measure up against their
research aims? Neorealists are mainly interested in getting analytical
purchase on the international system in terms of power politics, but the
English School has the rather more ambitious and complicated aim of
getting to grips with international society. Regardless of what one thinks
of neorealism as IR theory, the like-units assumption works well to
underpin the level of simplification that the theory seeks. First, it confines
the definition of the international system to states, thereby excluding
NSAs. Second, by homogenizing all states in terms of function, it opens
the way for a single differentiation by capability. That move, in turn,
allows the theory to distinguish between great powers and all other states,
and to focus on the former as the important essence that gives insight into
how international relations works. Neorealism's polarity theory thus rests
on allowing a single exception – power – to the general rule of like-units.
The theory is aimed at a high level of abstraction, and is as much, or
more, about differentiation of states in terms of capabilities than it is
about 'anarchy' as structure.

But how well does the like-units assumption serve the research aim of
the English School, which is to capture the essence of GIS? Capturing the
essence of power politics is a much simpler and more mechanistic job
than finding the key to the social complexities of GIS. To start thinking
about this, it is useful to refer back to the classic definition of international society by Bull and Watson (1984a: 1):

a group of states (or, more generally, a group of independent political communities)
which not merely form a system, in the sense that the behaviour of each is a

necessary factor in the calculations of the others, but also have established by dialogue and consent common rules and institutions for the conduct of their relations, and recognise their common interest in maintaining these arrangements.

The obvious link to 'like-units' in this formulation is the idea that international society is in fact *interstate society*, in which the members are functionally alike, and the entry criterion is mutual recognitions of sovereign equality. Think again about Onuf's (2002: 228) already noted observation that for realists, 'sovereignty is the only rule that matters for the constitution of anarchy', which neatly captures the link between realism and the ES in this regard. Both privilege the interstate domain. There is significant common ground around between the ES and neorealism on the importance of both segmentary differentiation (international anarchy) and differentiation by capability (polarity theory and great power management).

But the Bull and Watson definition already begins to undermine this simple view. By raising the possibility of other 'independent political communities' being members, it opens the door to empires, tribes and even rebel entities ranging from warlords to 'Islamic State'. The inclusion of 'independent' means that this door is not opened too wide, and might still just about enable sovereignty to be applied as the criterion for membership. But while it makes room for significantly unlike units to be members of GIS, it does not allow in the wider range of NSAs from transnational corporations to INGOs that are not 'independent political communities'. The Bull and Watson definition is a pluralist understanding of international society in which it is a society of states or independent political communities, and all other entities operate by permission within that framework. More solidarist views of international society open this door wider by envisaging membership being extended to INGOs and even individual human beings on a functionally differentiated basis (Buzan, 2004a; 2014a).

Neither does the LUM deal well with the very significant differences amongst states that opened up with modernity and decolonization. As argued in Chapter 2, the formative process of GIS gave rise to huge diversity within the category of states. There are massive variations in size, development, sources and strengths of political legitimacy, stability of institutions and such. These variations are elided by the LUM's focus on the likeness of sovereignty. The LUM does allow for differences in power, and that does incorporate some of the elements just mentioned. But power is a narrow measure for a set of far-reaching differences. Nowhere is this clearer than in relation to the weak and failed states that are members of GIS. The model assumes that states have both *juridical* sovereignty (recognition by others) and *empirical* sovereignty (the capacity to exercise self-government within international society).[2] Weak and failed states may well have juridical sovereignty, but in terms of empirical sovereignty they are more like holes in the fabric of international society than part of its weave. The differences between Japan and Somalia, or Pakistan and Canada, or China and the Democratic Republic of the Congo or Haiti and Denmark are far deeper and more substantial than their differences in power or their similarity in sovereignty. Many postcolonial states are simply not the same kind of entity as their former metropoles, and the LUM is somewhat blind to this fact.

So the first issue raised by this definition for the ES is that because of its commitment to the interstate domain, the LUM potentially misses some important aspects of the actual and possible membership of GIS. The model is better for the state-centric, pluralist end of the spectrum, though even there it largely misses the diversity of state types. But because it sidelines the transnational and interhuman domains, it gets worse the further along the spectrum towards solidarism one moves. In theoretical terms, it is fairly easy to distinguish between 'states and other independent political communities' on the one hand, and NSAs on the other. But empirically it might be quite difficult to measure whether the NSAs that operate within contemporary GIS now do so more or less in their own right, thus qualifying as in some important sense 'independent', or still play their part only at the sufferance of states. This question might be put to some IGOs such as the EU, the WTO and the International Court of Justice (ICJ), some powerful transnational corporations (TNCs) such as Google, a host of INGOs from Amnesty International to FIFA and some transnational NSAs such as Islamic State.

An equally important element of this definition for evaluating the LUM is the idea of consensual agreement amongst the members of GIS about 'common rules and institutions for the conduct of their relations'. Neorealists don't have to care much about this aspect, and to the extent that they do care, they can construct international society as an epiphenomenon of great power dominance (Carr, 1946). But for the ES, this element is absolutely central and far from being wholly a manifestation of great power self-interest. Wight's hypothesis about the importance of shared culture, cited previously, leans strongly towards a like-units understanding of international society. The members must not only be states, but also share a cultural background. The pessimism

---

[2] On this distinction, see Jackson (1990).

generated within the classical ES because post-1945 decolonization unravelled the cultural coherence of Western-colonial international society is testament to the importance in ES thinking of whatever it was that provided the normative foundations for international society. For the research aims of the ES, therefore, it is vital to know how differentiations amongst the members affect the possibilities for finding and agreeing on 'common rules and institutions for the conduct of their relations'. In order to get at the essence of international society, the ES has to investigate the kinds of differences amongst its members that affect their ability to build common rules and institutions. This might include the power spectrum exception to like-units allowed by neorealists, but as the ES debate about shared culture suggests, it needs to include a lot more than that. To get at this, one needs additionally to take into account the formative stories of the membership and their differences in culture, ideology, institutions and development.

We can conclude that while the LUM does capture fairly well the key aspect of the membership of GIS centred around sovereign states, it is too narrow to do a good job of meeting the research aims of the ES. It does not allow for more solidarist views of the membership of GIS that extend into the transnational and interhuman domains, and even within the interstate domain it blocks the way to understanding how differentiations amongst the members play into the institutional structure of GIS.

Capturing the Structure

The LUM really only looks for structure in the interstate domain. It largely ignores the transnational domain, and while it does carry the interhuman domain concept of world society, the ES has barely begun to think about how this might be structured (Buzan, 2018a), only using it mainly as a normative referent against which to judge the performance of interstate society. It is strongly attached to a single-tier, global view of international society, although in principle the like-units idea could also be applied to other ways of differentiating GIS. For example, if the differentiations amongst states previously discussed tend to cluster, then a more fine-tuned idea of like-units could play into international society at the regional level: developed democratic states in Europe, underdeveloped weak states in Africa and such. In practice, however, the like-units idea with the ES has unfolded in tandem with the Eurocentric story of how GIS was made by the global expansion of the European/Western form of international society. This is essentially a homogenizing story of how the rest of the world came to take on Western political form, and that naturally leads to a single, global-level view of international society based on like units. Viewing GIS in those terms sets up a simple model for how to understand the structure of GIS. One looks to find a set of primary institutions the acceptance and practice of which are sufficiently widespread to justify thinking of them as global. Initially, this would have been about the transfer of Western practices and institutions to the rest of the world, but subsequently it become about the rise, evolution and possible decline of institutions as shaped by the GIS as a whole. The guidelines for counting a primary institution as global in this sense are similar to those applied to consensus decision-making in the UN: that opposition must be neither widespread (i.e., with a lot of states opposing) nor significant (i.e., with one or more major powers opposing). If those conditions are met, then a primary institution can reasonably be counted as global.

From this perspective, the LUM generates a plausible, and in some ways quite impressive, understanding of the structure of GIS in terms of a set of globally accepted and practiced primary institutions.[3] The classical institutions of sovereignty and territoriality are very widely accepted as the foundation of the state, and this is reflected in the way they are embedded into both diplomacy and the rules and practices of secondary institutions. Nationalism sits alongside these two as the institution that distinguishes the modern state from its dynastic predecessor. Dynasticism has not quite disappeared from international society, most notably in the Middle East, but it is now very marginal in the global picture and no longer a global institution. Diplomacy and international law both reflect sovereign equality, are widely and deeply embedded in state practice and only rarely challenged in principle. There are plenty of disagreements about what the law is or should be, but few about the legitimate existence of a framework of international law itself. The principle of great power management is firmly entrenched in the 'legalized hegemony' of the great powers and the expression of that in the common two-tier construction of IGOs, with a privileged council (such as the Security Council in the UN) and a general assembly that reflects sovereign equality (Simpson, 2004). The actual practice of great power management waxes and wanes with circumstances (Cui and Buzan, 2016), but the principle remains robust. Since the collapse of the command economy as a challenger to capitalism, first in China during the late 1970s and then in the Soviet Union a decade later, the market has also achieved global standing and is well embedded in a host of secondary institutions. There is also global agreement on the obsolescence of

---

[3] For more detailed discussion of these institutions, see Buzan (2014a: 134–63).

colonialism/imperialism and human inequality as once dominant primary institutions that have now become illegitimate. The flip side of that process is global agreement on their successor institutions, respectively, development and human equality.

The standing of the other two classical institutions, war and the balance of power, is somewhat in doubt. War presents a confusing picture. Partly it has become less relevant because the practice of great power war has become obsolete on functional grounds (i.e., nobody thinks they can win such a war in a meaningful or profitable way). Partly it has become disaggregated because some parts of the world seem to have strong practices of restraint (e.g., the EU, South America), while in others war remains a real possibility (the Middle East, much of Asia). And partly the practice of 'war' has shifted from being between states to being between states and NSAs, as in the 'global war on terrorism', with the result that war has become to a considerable extent deinstitutionalized (Holsti, 2004). Balance of power as a social institution ('associational' rather than 'adversarial' in Little's [2007] terms) has been weak or even absent since before the First World War. It might see a revival if the United States and China come to terms, or if there is some kind of new concert of capitalist powers. Within the global framing of the LUM, balance of power might be seen as a dormant institution, not obsolete, but not much practiced. War poses more difficulty because it seems to be practiced differentially across GIS.

Most difficult within the like-units global perspective on primary institutions is that set of institutions that are held to be 'emergent' (by those who support them) and either not institutions, or institutions only of some subset of GIS (by those who oppose them). The candidates here are human rights, democracy and, more recently, environmental stewardship. Human rights and democracy are clearly Western liberal values, and have long been promoted by Western powers as values that should be embraced by GIS. On that basis, and particularly with human rights, they have achieved a degree of normative influence on GIS sufficient to create tension over nonintervention, which is a key derivative institution of sovereignty (Donnelly, 1998: 20–3; Mayall, 2000: 64; Wheeler, 2000). But they are still opposed both 'widely' (by authoritarian governments) and 'significantly' (by great powers such as China and Russia). As with war, they present a very mixed and differentiated picture within GIS, being strongly accepted in some places and strongly rejected in others. Environmental stewardship has risen over the past few decades as another potentially emergent primary institution. Unlike democracy and human rights, it does not represent Western liberal values but rather has its roots in the more practical problem of the shared fate of humankind living together on a small and crowded planet from which there is no exit. Although initially contested in various ways, environmental stewardship has recently become strongly and widely enough accepted to count as an institution of GIS (Falkner and Buzan, 2017).

So while the LUM performs quite impressively in showing the general structure of GIS, it also has some significant weaknesses. It works best where institutions are deeply and widely accepted, as with sovereignty, nationalism, human equality and others. It does not work well where there is divergence of practice (e.g., war) or where emergent institutions remain contested (e.g., human rights, democracy). The problem here is that the model operates on an assumption that institutions work uniformly across GIS. It cannot easily distinguish between institutions that are emergent in a global sense, and those that are mainly confined to a subset of GIS, and which might therefore define structure on the regional/subglobal level rather than the global one. Neither does this model encourage investigation into variations of practice within what are widely/deeply accepted institutions. This was hinted at by the example of differences over nonintervention, and as we will show in subsequent chapters there is a great deal of variation of practice that tends to be occluded by this model.

Capturing the Binding Forces

Although it is not an explicit or necessary feature of the model, the LUM generally presupposes that belief in the shared values that underpin GIS is the glue that holds this sort of society together. In other words, GIS is essentially based on consensual acceptance underpinned by the internalization of shared values as the principal binding force of GIS: a logic of appropriateness rather than a logic of consequences. Implicitly, therefore, the model suggests that an institution is stronger the more widely and deeply belief in it is held. Being rooted only in the elite would make it fragile, whereas being rooted in the people as well would make it stronger. There are perhaps two explanations for the dominance of this view. First is the strong influence of liberal normative political theory in ES thinking about values. Because liberal normative theory tends to favour values posed in universal terms, such as human rights, the approach through it leans naturally towards a global-scale framing in terms of belief. Interestingly, this explanation involves a strong crossover between the interstate and interhuman domains. The second explanation is the self-serving understanding, whether true or not, that the foundational European international society was itself consensual because it arose out of a shared culture (initially Christian) and history. Recall that this was the understanding behind Wight's 'cultural unity' hypothesis, also backed up (although more arguably) by the case of classical Greece. The consensual assumption also helps to mask both the coercive colonial imposition of this European form onto much of the rest of the world and the ongoing role of coercion and calculation in the maintenance and evolution of GIS. This fits with the noted tendency of the classical ES to downplay or ignore the role of coercive colonialism in the making of the contemporary GIS.

If we take belief as the general standard set by this model, what do we see when we look out at GIS in the real world? Looking through the lens of belief certainly reveals some striking landmarks in which some primary institutions are widely and deeply accepted in this way. Perhaps the most obvious example is nationalism, which like football has become almost universally internalized as a global practice. Nationalism is everywhere understood and accepted as a key legitimizing principle for organizing political life. There are plenty of disputes about what counts as a nation (Are Kurds part of the Turkish people? Are Uighurs and Tibetans part of the Chinese nation? Etc.), but relatively few about the principle of nation-hood itself. This universalism has been achieved remarkably quickly given that this institution only rose to prominence in GIS during the nineteenth century (Mayall, 1990). By the criterion of belief, nationalism therefore counts as a very strong primary institution of GIS. Much the same argument could be made about sovereignty and development. Although there is a fringe of cosmopolitans opposing the principle of sovereignty, it has wide acceptance amongst both elites and peoples as a legitimate way of framing political life. There is not much support for world government, and state governments usually find it easy to rally their populations against supposed violations of their sovereignty. Likewise, development has become a principle with wide and deep support in most places around the world.[4] There are big arguments about responsibilities

---

[4] The colonial construction of non-Europeans as being at a lower stage of development within a single model of development carried over into trusteeship and the postcolonial discourse of development (Bain, 2003: 13–21; Holsti, 2004: 250; Bowden, 2009: locs. 1000–84, 2173–220). The colonial obligation of the metropolitan powers to bring the 'natives' up to a European 'standard of civilization' morphed into an obligation on the part of the rich world to assist in the development of the 'third world' or 'less developed countries'. Development, understood as the right to acquire modernity, became the successor primary institution to imperialism/colonialism. It appears as a goal in countless diplomatic documents and IGO constitutions and charters. It draws legitimacy from both a sense of obligation by the former colonial powers (a.k.a. 'developed states') and a sense of entitlement by the postcolonial states. It also draws legitimacy from its synergies with the welfare and basic needs end of the human rights and human security discourses, with their emphasis on rights to adequate nutrition, clean water, shelter, education and such, all of which are associated with better developed societies (Clark, 2013; Buzan, 2014a: 154–5).

and implementation, but not about the principle itself. It is probably also the case that human equality now has deep and widespread support despite lingering elements of racism and slavery. The main doubt here is over gender inequality and discrimination, which despite notable progress in some respects (e.g., franchise, employment, legal status), remain informally strong almost everywhere, and formally enacted in substantial parts of the world (most obviously under Sharia law). The point is that these deviations from the rule of human equality are now widely, though not universally, understood to be wrong, and in many places illegal, whereas before they were legitimate practices based on a widely accepted principle of human inequality.

The criterion of belief and the principle of equality also highlight democracy and human rights, but for these the picture is different. These ideas certainly register depth, and up to a point they are widespread, but they are far from being universal. On the global picture of GIS, they would show up as continents and islands, making belief a binding force for regional/subglobal structures. They face competing principles (autocracy, collective rights) and, as argued previously, it is not clear whether they are emergent institutions of GIS or institutions held by a subset of GIS. Offensive liberals such as George W. Bush, like to think that these values are in fact almost universally held by the people but opposed by self-interested elites. The outcomes in Iraq and Afghanistan, and the popularity of authoritarians such as Vladimir Putin, Xi Jinping and Hugo Chavez, suggest that even if this is true in some cases (perhaps Myanmar most obviously), it is far from being universally true.

Beyond these examples, the criterion of belief gets more problematic. A number of the classical primary institutions are about elite practices in which the general population has not much interest and, except for a few individuals (mostly academics), little knowledge. These include diplomacy, international law, the balance of power and great power management. Rather few people believe in these things with anything like the intensity and commitment that they give to nationalism, sovereignty and human equality, or democracy and human rights if they were supporters of those principles. Most people probably just accept diplomacy and international law as the way things are done. They might follow diplomatic events such as the climate change negotiations without thinking much about the underlying principles and practices of diplomacy. Occasionally, diplomacy and international law themselves might become controversial, most obviously when revolutionist states reject them (Lenin's Soviet Union) or, in the case of diplomacy, when, as after the First World War, the secretive method of diplomacy was blamed as one of the causes of that war. International law is too complicated for most people, but perhaps has a vague acceptance as a necessary way of doing business. Disputes then become about the content and observation of the law rather than about the principle of international law itself. The balance of power and great power management might likewise have some vague general support. The idea that the biggest powers have the biggest responsibilities probably resonates widely. The idea that an excessive concentration of power in world politics is dangerous and undesirable might also have some popular resonance, though much tempered by the exception that many would think it OK if it was their state that held monopoly power (viz. the 'indispensable power' rhetoric common in US presidential elections). However, the idea that might makes right does offend against the democratic sensibilities of many and is a recurring critique of decisions reached by the UN Security Council in the international public sphere. The standard of assessment in terms of belief has to be different for these institutions than for those that have more to do with mass identity. Where primary institutions are mainly about elite practices, the key criterion is whether the elite believes in them or not. It may not make much difference, as it would with nationalism, human equality and other identity-linked institutions, whether the public is supportive or just indifferent.

An institution such as the market is again problematic in terms of what holds it in place. As with democracy and human rights, a view of the market through the lens of belief would show a pattern of continents and islands, but nothing like a universal acceptance. This is a problem, because there can be little doubt that, functionally speaking, the market is now a global practice. If the pattern of belief is not universal, then other things must be holding this institution in place. There are plenty of places where belief in the market as the best organizing principle for the economy is both deep and strong. This is most obviously true throughout the West, though even there, opposition to the market principle is significant. But as noted in Chapter 1, it beggars belief that the leaders of the Chinese Communist Party (CCP) believe that the market principle is good or right in itself. When they made this decision in the late 1970s, their backs were against the wall, and Deng's turn to the market was about the failure of central planning and the immediate survival needs of the CCP. Having abandoned the core economic principle of its ideology, the CCP became hooked on increasing China's wealth and power as the key foundation for its legitimacy. Turning to the market was an instrumental decision that the market was the most effective way of pursuing these goals, not a matter of belief in the virtues of the market. The problem now for the CCP is that having successfully created a capitalist society, the people might begin to believe in the market while the CCP itself does not.

Elsewhere, the market may be accepted on mainly instrumental grounds combined with measures of coercion. The days of gunboat diplomacy to 'open' countries such as Japan and China to the market are long gone, but the capitalist powers still retain plenty of coercive tools to shape behaviour and get compliance with market norms. These range from denial of loans and credit, to denial of membership in various desirable clubs (e.g., the WTO), to denial of trade and investment, all of which can be applied to leaderships deemed unsympathetic to the market (e.g., Cuba, North Korea, Venezuela).

Environmental stewardship is another interesting case. The lens of belief would probably not show a striking picture of continents and islands in some places but not in others. Since this is a relatively new issue, many remain ignorant, and there is still a politically significant element of rejection that climate change is happening or is a problem. In comparison with the market, there is much less scope on this issue for either calculation or coercion, but it is far from clear that as yet there is a well-developed pattern of belief. There are some strong believers in most societies, but also some deniers. The picture here is perhaps one of a low landscape with scattered high points. The criterion of belief might thus capture quite well the actual condition of this emergent institution.

Although one might think that territoriality and nonintervention should belong in the first group of identity-linked institutions, along with sovereignty and nationalism, they also pose problems for the approach through belief. It would be easy to argue that territoriality and nonintervention share the same kind of quite deep and wide support as sovereignty and nationalism. Both are tightly packaged with sovereignty and nationalism as the institutions that define the modern state. Yet both are also subject to substantial differences of interpretation that make it difficult to see them clearly through the lens of belief. Put in simple terms, nonintervention is highly conditioned by beliefs about human rights, and territoriality is highly conditioned by the practices of the market. Those with liberal views about human rights and democracy will tend to see sovereignty as conditional, and therefore support interventions where those values are threatened. Those opposed to such values will take a much more unconditional line on the right of nonintervention, as the Chinese and Russian governments do. Somewhat subtler is the tension between territoriality and the market. The operation of the global market requires quite major concessions of the right of territoriality, essentially punching large and permanent holes in borders for the purposes of trade and finance. This creates a contradiction which muddies the view through the lens of belief.

3   **Conclusions**

What this review of the LUM in terms of primary institutions and binding forces shows is that the quite upbeat assessment of decolonization and the GIS in Bull and Watson, cited previously, was in significant ways not mistaken. The existing primary institutions, mainly of Western origin, have indeed been taken up, and not just by the elites of the newly decolonized states, but in several cases also by their peoples. The LUM does capture some important aspects of both the membership of GIS and its institutional structure, and it does provide a set of clear criteria by which the strengths and weaknesses of GIS can be assessed.

These criteria give a rather mixed answer to the question of whether GIS is getting stronger or weaker. The membership is already so close to universal that there is no significant scope for improvement there. Indeed, there is scope for concern about some narrowing or layering of membership if a new 'standard of civilization' based on liberal values gains purchase within GIS. From that point of view, the case that human rights and democracy are adding to the range of primary institutions can be countered by the argument that they are dividing GIS rather than unifying it by opening a rift between the offensive liberalism of the Western democracies and the defensive sovereigntism of the authoritarian states. Given the relative decline in Western power and authority with the rise of the rest, it seems more likely that human rights and democracy will define regional/subglobal structures rather than narrowing the membership of GIS with a new standard of civilization. It may also be that a broader conception of human rights focusing more on development and welfare will become a global norm (Kozyrev, 2016), with the more political view of human rights becoming a feature of the Western group. The global acceptance of the market over the last few decades is a very major gain in the extent of primary institutions that define GIS, and also a gain for solidarism. But it is something of a loss to the extent that calculation and coercion still play big roles in holding the market in place. The rise of environmental stewardship is another major addition to the solidarist primary institutions of GIS. Evidence can be found both ways for whether the practices associated with shared primary institutions are becoming more, or less, uniform and elaborate. On sovereignty and nonintervention, they are becoming less uniform. On the market and environmental stewardship, they are becoming perhaps more uniform and definitely more elaborate. We deal with this in more detail in the next three chapters.

Despite these strengths, it is also clear that this model has significant defects. It leans towards a pluralist view of GIS largely confined to the interstate domain. Its self-serving Westcentrism fails to distinguish between an ongoing and successful monocentric, coercive expansion and a genuinely consensual GIS. Such Westcentrism looks increasingly out of place as the West gets weaker, and the rise of China and the rest facilitates authoritarian resistance to Western values. The model does not allow for membership of GIS other than states and therefore excludes much of the solidarist spectrum. Its homogeneous view of states occludes both the quite serious problem of weak and failed states and the question of how the differences amongst states discussed in Chapter 2 affect the institutional structure of GIS. Bull and Watson's (1984a: 432) prescient insight is relevant here:

... the Western-educated leaders of the Asian and African countries have come to be challenged by the representatives of indigenous cultures. It has become evident that Western culture has not in fact had any easy triumph over non-Western traditions of behaviour, which have reasserted themselves vigorously in many parts of the world, the resurgence of Islamic consciousness being only the most striking example.

This nativist dynamic is still unfolding. As the West declines in relative (not absolute) terms in relation to 'the rest', GIS is becoming more intensely differentiated culturally in ways that affect both what primary institutions are acceptable or not, and what kind of practices are used to implement those institutions that are shared. Sovereignty and nonintervention are the obvious examples here. Yet at the same time, there are also significant degrees of cultural convergence, partly from the embedded legacy of GIS in such things as sovereignty, territoriality, nationalism and human equality; partly from the logic of necessity pointed out by Bull and Watson previously quoted; and partly by the rise of new shared-fate institutions such as the market and environmental stewardship.

The like-unit model's privileging of belief as the main binding force of GIS does capture quite a lot of the reality, but also raises awkward questions. It does not allow for an easy assessment of elite institutions that don't have much impact on mass identity issues. It has difficulty dealing with 'emergent' institutions that might in fact more accurately be seen as belonging to subsets of GIS. And it misrepresents important cases such as that of the market, where there are clearly binding forces other than belief in play.

To what extent can our other three models, with their more differentiated view of GIS, compensate for the deficiencies of the like-unit one, and what can they tell us about the strength or weakness of GIS?

4   The Regions/Subglobal Model

The regions/subglobal model (RSM) grows out of a relatively new debate within the ES that started in the late 1990s and early 2000s (Ayoob, 1999; Diez and Whitman, 2002; Stivachtis, 2003; Buzan, 2004a) and which is forcefully represented in contemporary ES research (Buzan and Gonzalez-Pelaez, 2009; Merke, 2011; 2015; Schouenborg, 2013; Buzan and Zhang, 2014; Stivachtis, 2015). Like the LUM, the RSM is largely located in the interstate domain, with some spillover on matters of identity into the interhuman one. In contrast to the LUM, its starting premise is that GIS is a fundamentally differentiated social structure, and that the formative process of GIS outlined in Chapter 2 has a lot to do with this. That is why the expansion story (Bull and Watson, 1984a) and Wight's (1977) and Watson's (1992) comparative studies of the evolution of the modern states-system are usually taken as precursors to this contemporary debate. The RSM picks up on the idea floated in earlier chapters that both cultural differentiations and differentiations of state type arising from the formative process play into a geographical differentiation of GIS.

1   The Model

The central principle of differentiation in this model is geography. The assumption is that social structure, in domestic society as well as international society, varies with both location (the impact of physical geography) and agents' local histories of being implicated in larger social assemblages (e.g., whether peoples have been part of extensive empires and/or religious and economic circuits that link them with entities other than their local one). This is a fairly uncontroversial assumption in sociology, and is more or less the raison d'etre of disciplines such as anthropology and history. It is also compatible with Rosenberg's (2013; 2016) theory of uneven and combined development (UCD) (see also Buzan and Lawson, 2016). Rosenberg argues that UCD is a powerful way to theorize how the political and economic dynamics of its operation

96

necessarily generate 'the international' in the sense of multiple units linked together in ways that reproduce the differentiations amongst them. Whereas Waltz (1979) sees anarchy as driving a tendency towards homogenization and 'like-units', Rosenberg sees it driving dynamics of differentiation.

The ES appears to have approached the issue of geographical differentiation of social structure mainly through the notion of regions, and one region in particular: Europe (Ayoob, 1999; Diez and Whitman, 2002; Stivachtis, 2003; Buzan, 2004a). This makes a lot of sense. To the extent that IR scholars in general have engaged with geographical containers other than individual states or the global system as such, this has mostly been in the form of regions. Moreover, it is quite common for IR scholars to possess a particular regional expertise, although the intermingling with area studies has traditionally been low (Hurrell, 2007a: 135–6). To simplify, regions have generally been understood within IR as involving a bounded geographical area, sometimes with signs of a common transnational identity and corresponding regional secondary institutions and actor qualities. Furthermore, scholars have pointed to the increasing relevance of regions, in addition to the global level, for understanding security dynamics and international politics following the end of the Cold War (Buzan and Wæver, 2003; Katzenstein, 2005: 22–4).

The ES focus on Europe (and the wider West) is also not surprising considering the biographies of the first generation (Bull, Watson and Wight) and many contemporary contributors, including ourselves. As we have previously discussed at length, they were, as Westerners, concerned about what the expansion of European international society to the rest of globe would do to the social cohesion of that society and to the pursuit of international order. The expansion story can be read as the trials and tribulations of one regional international society trying to cope with having transcended, or lost, its geographical and cultural roots in becoming global. This view from the core, with its driving concern about order at the global level, easily lost sight of the perspective of those in the periphery whose local arrangements had been overridden, and on whom the European model had been imposed (Suzuki, 2009; Zarakol, 2011; Suzuki, Zhang and Quirk, 2014). The expansion also led to a chronic confusion in ES thinking between European/Western international society on the one hand and GIS on the other. Buzan's rather tortured construction of 'Western-global international society' captures this confusion about levels perfectly (Buzan and Zhang, 2014: 208). This was not just about how Europe, and the EU in particular, had been taken as an explicit or implicit model for how GIS might develop in the future: generally towards a more solidarist or 'thicker' international society (see, for example, Diez and Whitman, 2002; Buzan, 2004a: 147–8; Diez, Manners and Whitman, 2011). It was more deeply about how the expansion produced a GIS that was both Western (because the West and Western values were the driving core) but also global in geographical reach. This history produced a form of core–periphery structure that sat uncomfortably with the like-units model of GIS, and one of our aims in this book is to find clearer formulations for talking about this.

But is it really the most logical solution to look to regions when exploring geographical differentiation in GIS? It may be that social forms tend to cluster geographically (consider, for example, both ghettos and gentrification in urban societies), but it does not appear to be a logical necessity. It is perfectly feasible to imagine, as well as possible to observe, similar social forms (for example democracy, dynasticism and human rights) in several noncontiguous geographical locations around the world (Schouenborg, 2013: 9–10). This thus sets us up for looking at two distinct types of geographical differentiation in GIS: the regional and the subglobal. The first type implies regional clustering, as in 'Europe'. The second type refers to a geographical scatter pattern, but a geographical pattern nonetheless, as in 'Western'. Furthermore, these options may be logically combined: global scattering of regional clusters. Earlier ES work has gravitated towards the regional, but at the cost of overlooking or ignoring the subglobal, which may or may not prove a significant dimension of the past, present and future GIS. This justifies its inclusion as a central part of the model of geographical differentiation. Furthermore, as we shall argue in subsequent chapters, the subglobal easily plugs into other forms of differentiation, notably functional differentiation (see Chapter 6).

What about the social content of geographical differentiation? The main approach within the ES is to look at the distribution of primary institutions (Diez, Manners and Whitman, 2011; Schouenborg, 2013; Buzan and Zhang, 2014). The core question is how Bull's five traditional primary institutions, as well as other candidates, are interpreted regionally and subglobally. A logical concern, most recently articulated by Costa-Buranelli (2015), is whether the global diffusion of these originally European institutions will inevitably be followed by a fragmentation in meaning as these are adapted to a plethora of local contexts and practices. It is a valid concern. Yet it seems to involve the same general problem of classification that we have already discussed several times (recall the fruit and apple example). In a sense, all social practices can be considered unique for some analytical purposes. However, we also insist that for other analytical purposes they can have common characteristics. A marriage is still a marriage regardless of whether wedding rings are worn on the left or right hand. The balance of power as a primary institution may have a general identifiable form across several geographical regions, albeit with specific local variations. It is the same principle that underpins all other commonly accepted classification systems, be that for stars, animals, fruit, languages, religions or music genres. Moreover, scale need not always be correlated with increasing fragmentation. In fact, standardization has often been the outcome of geographical amalgamation, as shown by Scott (1999) and Tilly (1990), and as indicated in Chapter 6.

Hence, instead of adopting the default conclusion of fragmentation, as Costa-Buranelli does, it appears more appropriate to talk about the open-ended nature of institutional differentiation. Fragmentation (the erosion of core meaning) is still an option, and probably a clue to conceptualizing a weakening GIS (more on this later in the chapter), but not the only one. This understanding of the geographical differentiation of primary institutions resonates with Lasmar, Zahreddine and Lage's (2015: 476–7) claim that all primary institutions can be considered to have an identifiable core, around which lies a flexible 'protective belt' of associated ideas that can be adapted to local contexts and practices. Lasmar et al.'s case study is international law and human rights conventions, and they are able to document, through a concrete mapping of states' adoption practices, significant regional and subglobal variation. However, the core can be breached, for example, if we observe a return to the acceptance of human inequality rather than human equality, or if sovereignty is widely rejected as a guiding political principle. Then those primary institutions are compromised and subject to fundamental fragmentation. This appears to be a logically sound and analytically profitable approach to modelling geographical differentiation.

In addition to this, Buzan and Gonzalez-Pelaez (2009) and Buzan and Zhang (2014: 7) have outlined three options for thinking about the differentiation of primary institutions at the regional level. The first scenario is that a regional international society contains primary institutions not present at the global level. The second is that some primary institutions present at the global level are missing at the regional level. The third scenario is regionally specific interpretations of global institutions (more or less the same position as that of Lasmar et al.). It is an appealing schema, and the train of thought behind it is readily intelligible to most ES (and IR) scholars: we start with a global international society and observe hints of variation within it. Therefore, being used to levels thinking (the domestic and the international most prominently) and regions, we naturally gravitate towards the position that this may apply in this instance as well and conceptualize difference as that between a global and a regional level.

But where, exactly, is the global level? Where do we locate the global set of primary institutions and the authoritative, as far as core meaning goes, interpretation of them? This is an obvious problem. Think in particular of Buzan and Zhang's second scenario: how can something, in this case a primary institution, be globally present at the same time as being absent from one or more regions? If we accept that the word 'global' does in fact refer to the whole world geographically, then that is logically unsustainable (see also Schouenborg, 2013: 9). This dilemma is the source of Buzan and Zhang's (2014: 208) solution of adding the prefix *Western*-global international society. This is in one sense a neat solution in that it both fits the historical circumstances and makes it possible to locate the global set of primary institutions, as well as their authoritative interpretation, somewhere. However, it does not solve the problem of keeping levels distinct. It is also Eurocentric in privileging the Western set of primary institutions. If GIS really is global, why should the West have a monopoly over the authoritative interpretation just because it was the origin of GIS, and how does that square with the dominant 'like-units' model? To use an analogy, today we do not look to contemporary Greece for the authoritative interpretation of what it means to be a democracy just because it was the first country to practice it. What Buzan and Zhang's solution does is basically to privilege the West, as it sets up a core–periphery structure. That is a very interesting principle of differentiation, but it does not follow logically from the principle of geographical differentiation. The principles are distinct, and one of the contributions of this and the following chapter is to untangle these two dimensions of GIS that are often conflated. The present chapter is about geography as a principle of differentiation; the following one is about the principle of privilege and hierarchy, of which core–periphery is one form. True, there is often a geographical dimension to core–periphery relations: think of, for example, the physical distance between the centre of a city and its suburbs or that between an imperial centre and its provincial backwaters. But core and periphery necessarily imply privilege: the core is above the periphery. That is the principle's distinct meaning, and it opens up to thinking about GIS well beyond the interstate domain.

There is a final dimension to this geographical differentiation of social structure that the ES has paid a lot of attention to: the relative 'thinness' or 'thickness' of international society. This concern grows out of the debate between pluralists and solidarists within the ES and is generally about the extent to which global and regional international relations have become more cooperative and less conflictual over time and/or the extent to which individuals have gained greater standing in international affairs, supposedly indicating a shift towards a world society. As noted previously, Buzan, trying to increase the analytical specificity of this debate, has developed a taxonomy for thinking about the degree of cooperation and conflict in an international society: it ranges from 'asocial' and 'power political', through 'coexistence' and 'cooperative', to 'convergence' and 'confederative'. Moreover, he has suggested that the vague notion of world society in the ES should be used specifically to refer to a social structure where states, individuals and non-state actors are in play together and none of the three dominate over the other two (Buzan, 2004a: xviii, 159–60). These concepts have been used to investigate the character and relative thickness of regional international society in the Middle East and East Asia respectively (Buzan and Gonzalez-Pelaez, 2009; Buzan and Zhang, 2014). In regards to Europe, Stivachtis (2014: 324) has also made use of the thin/ thick distinction and Diez and Whitman (2002: 48–9) have discussed the world society dimension in their early work. The attractiveness of these ES schemas is that they provide a novel take on major concerns of the general IR community as well as the policy world, and offer a language for talking about some of the signposts that many consider central for building a sustainable world order.

This is, however, also a pointer to the schemas' normative baggage, i.e., that they reflect the enduring ethical priorities of the West. This becomes problematic in a historical perspective: what are the grounds for associating 'thick' social relations with cooperation? We have quite a few examples of non-European international societies in the more distant past where war was a dominant and accepted social norm as opposed to institutionalized cooperation (Schouenborg, 2017). From a neutral analytical perspective, how can we consider these any less social? Europe's history equally offers plenty of examples, including the more recent one of the fascist international society composed of Nazi Germany and fascist Italy (and Japan) (Schouenborg, 2012: 138–41). While almost universally considered morally abhorrent regimes, is there any reason to judge them less social from a neutral analytical perspective? If 'social' means what humans have done at all times and in all places, then the answer is logically no. We have to emphasize that with this conclusion we do not want to bar anyone from ethically assessing present or past social arrangements. We gladly deposit this task with the normative wing of the ES. Yet we do want to develop a model, an ideal-type, that comes close to analytical neutrality and can be used for cross-cultural and transhistorical comparisons. In this perspective, warrior international societies are as valid as liberal ones and equally subject to analysis about thickness and thinness, weakness and strength.

Our aim is to capture all of the norms and values that have been, or might be, used to form international social orders. That, however, also requires us to say something about what 'thick' might mean from this neutral analytical perspective. Intuitively, and partly in line with early integration literature (Deutsch et al., 1957), the best candidate for measuring thickness would seem to be the volume, scale and range of social interactions. Taking a cue from the following chapters, for example the range of social functions shared or the number of recognized privileged positions. To use a biological analogy, it would be the difference between simple and complex organisms. According to this standard, the war-prone and complex Maya culture should be considered thick, whereas a small and undifferentiated, but peaceful and cooperative, island society in Polynesia should be judged thin. However, that would only be part of the answer. The issue of institutional fragmentation would have to be factored in as well. Density of interactions is not all (indeed, it is not possible to imagine human interaction without social content). If there are no recognizable social institutions in these interactions, or more likely, significant fragmentation of these institutions, then that would seem to count as a weak or thin social structure. To provide an example that might mirror a future scenario for GIS, it could be a condition of strong globalization (multiple and diverse interaction flows) and the parallel retreat of the classical primary institutions of GIS. One can imagine the possibility that this would be driven by institutional expansion in the transnational and interhuman domains and would thus manifest as a weakening of interstate society only. With these final reflections, the astute reader will notice that we have in fact opened the door to a merging of strength and thickness (and weakness and thinness). To us, initially, they appear to be tied together. Keeping them separate would, in a sense, smuggle in the system/society distinction through the back door. We have to stress, though, that this is a preliminary hunch, not our final statement on this issue. In the chapters that follow, we will further probe the appropriateness of this conceptual move. However, to reflect this hunch or working hypothesis, the terms will henceforth appear together as strength/thickness and weakness/thinness. And thus our overall working definition of strength/thickness is the volume, scale and range of social interactions and functions shared, as well as the relative absence of PI fragmentation (including regionally and subglobally). Assessment of which direction GIS is moving is based on the more specific criteria formulated with reference to each model in this and the other chapters.

Let us briefly recapitulate the RSM of GIS and its basic elements:

- The core principle of differentiation is geography.
- Geographic differentiation comes in two main forms: regional and subglobal. Regional entails a geographic clustering of social content

and the possibility of some boundedness (close to the traditional understanding of regions in IR). Subglobal entails similar social content in two or more noncontiguous geographical locations, manifesting in a global scatter pattern.

- The approach to conceptualizing social content is through primary institutions. If such institutions are globally present (meaning the whole globe), they are understood to have a core meaning, a kind of lowest common denominator, around which are changing sets of interpretations and practices that vary according to local contexts.
- There is no normative judgement of social content in the model. A regional international society, for example, is not considered 'thicker' because it displays relatively more cooperation or respect for human rights. Thickness/strength, rather, depends on the volume, scale and range of social interactions and functions shared, as well as the relative absence of PI fragmentation (including regionally and subglobally).

Application of the RSM

What does a snapshot picture based on this model reveal about contemporary GIS? As we have noted in previous chapters, it is remarkable that a range of primary institutions are broadly adhered to globally both in the interstate domain and sometimes significantly also into the transnational and interhuman domains. These include sovereignty, territoriality, diplomacy, international law, great power management, the balance of power, nationalism, human equality, development and the market. For each institution, it appears possible to identify a core meaning – in the case of the market, a consensus on the international exchange of goods, capital and services (because people have been excluded since the banning of slavery, and also because free movement of people threatens the institutions of nationalism and territoriality) – while at the same time finding particular local interpretations and practices. For example, a global primary institution such as nationalism may be said to display subglobal patterns if we consider its different forms and practices: ethnic versus civic or what Reus-Smit (2011: 223) terms 'aggregative' and 'communal' nationalisms.

There is a spirited debate within the ES about whether some institutions are more foundational to GIS than others and whether some of the latter are derived from the former, which need not detain us here (see Buzan, 2004a: 161–204; Schouenborg, 2011; Wilson, 2012). Suffice it to say that most academics, as well as most practitioners of international affairs, will probably be able to agree on the global presence of the previously indicated institutions when presented with a rough outline of the core meaning of each. The interesting question, for our purposes, is obviously whether some of the associated ideas and practices around an institution's core tend to cluster regionally and/or scatter subglobally. Take sovereignty, which several ES scholars have identified as the bedrock institution of GIS (see the table in Buzan, 2004a: 174). It retains a core meaning globally: the right to exclusive and supreme authority within a circumscribed territorial space. Yet in some regions, particularly East Asia, it is interpreted in a very restrictive way, even to the extent that it is frowned upon to publicly comment on the domestic actions of another government (Costa-Buranelli, 2015: 506). In other regional contexts, for example the EU, sovereignty underpins efforts to pool authority amongst governments, and in yet others it allows for coercive external intervention into the internal affairs of states (Libya, Mali, etc.). Similar stories can be told about the regional and subglobal interpretations of the remaining global primary institutions.

What about regionally or subglobally specific primary institutions? This is Buzan and Zhang's (2014: 7) first scenario mentioned previously: primary institutions not present at the global level. So far, the ES literature suggests that this type of differentiation is relatively rare, and to the extent that it can be found is more obvious in the Western core than in the rest of the world. While non-Western regions show a lot of variation in practice within primary institutions, there is as yet nothing comparable to the distinctiveness of, say, the Sinocentric tribute system as a key primary institution of classical East Asia. That said, Buzan (2018b) makes the case that within the Confucian cultural zone in East Asia, 'face' and hierarchy deserve consideration as local primary institutions. The EU is a more distinctive case of regional institutions for having already internalized human rights and democracy, primary institutions that remain contested in many other parts of international society. In the Middle East, dynasticism still retains considerable legitimacy, having once been global, but since the nineteenth century having mainly been displaced in the West and elsewhere by nationalism (Bukovansky, 2002; Gonzalez-Pelaez, 2009: 108–10; Buzan, 2014: 108–11, 157–8).

Another potential candidate for distinctive regional primary institutions might be long-running wars or conflicts such as the Arab–Israeli conflict in the Middle East, explored by Buzan and Gonzalez-Pelaez (2009: 232–3). The ES is used to thinking about war as a primary institution (Bull, 1977; Holsti, 2004; Jones, 2006; Pejcinovic, 2013), but has traditionally not considered specific wars as belonging in this category. However, as Buzan and Gonzalez-Pelaez argue, some long-running wars seem to take on this meaning when they become stabilized into a semi-permanent social structure and start to impact on local interpretations of other primary institutions. The same argument can be made with regard to other regionally specific wars, such as the simmering war (official armistice since 1953) between North and South Korea and their respective allies. Along these lines, one can even consider the Cold War as a global primary institution, again with local and specific interpretations. A similar argument can be made about the so-called global war on terrorism (see, for example, Buzan, 2006). Perhaps it is sufficiently institutionalized at this stage to count as such a global institution. From a conceptual perspective, one might also argue that such specific wars are derivative institutions from the master institution of war.

Other potential candidates for regionally or subglobally specific primary institutions are local interpretations of what it means to be a state. This partly echoes the discussion of state typologies in Chapter 2. Schouenborg (2013), for example, has argued that the Scandinavian welfare state, with its unique ideology of social rights as universal citizen's rights, amounts to a primary institution that sets Scandinavia apart from the rest of the European regional international society, as well as GIS. There are obvious similarities between the Scandinavian welfare state and other welfare states in Europe and overseas, but the former does display significant and unique characteristics. In the same way, Buzan and Zhang (2014: 209) contend that the developmental state may be considered a distinctive East Asian primary institution. It can be argued, though, that with these examples we are still operating with local interpretations of the global primary institutions that define the state. To that extent, they do not fulfil the criteria for inclusion in Buzan and Zhang's first scenario of being absent from the global level.

As already suggested, the best candidate for distinctive regional institutions is the EU. In the context of arguing that Bull's traditional five institutions have undergone radical transformation, have become obsolete or substituted, Diez, Manners and Whitman (2011: 133) claim that the EU has moreover succeeded in producing one entirely novel primary institution, what they term multiperspectivity: 'Rather than competition and a concert of great powers, the regional order of the EU is one where a multiplicity of perspectives from different locales come together.' However, after having made this assertion, they immediately backpedal and say that this is obviously also true of other regional international societies. The EU's claim to fame, so to speak, is in how far it has taken this principle of governance (Diez, Manners and Whitman, 2011: 133–4). What this then seems to boil down to is again a variation in the interpretation of global primary institutions backed up by an unprecedented level of secondary regional institutions, not some fully unique regional primary institution. The EU case raises some difficult questions about the issue raised earlier of whether institutions such as human rights and democracy are mainly regional phenomena or should better be seen as emerging primary institutions at the global level. Solidarists will mainly want to see them as emergent at the global level, but pluralists might see them as institutions characteristic of regional (mainly European) or sub-global (Western culture, Islam) substructures of GIS.

What about subglobally unique primary institutions? Here the RSM does yield a richer tapestry. All of the contested primary institutions that we have discussed (e.g., democracy and human rights) manifest in a global scatter pattern and/or the global scattering of regional clusters. This is the basis for viewing them as globally emergent. The Freedom House (2015) survey of worldwide democracy suggests a general division between a 'free' West and 'not free' East, but also a series of subglobal overlaps and mixed zones. Adopting a military metaphor, there are presently a couple of clear frontlines and several distinct pockets of resistance in this global contest of ideas.

There may also be other candidates for subglobal primary institutions that perhaps do not fully qualify as such, but which may help us develop our collective thinking on this topic. Consider, for example, the global religions Christianity and Islam. These are intimately intertwined with the society of states, yet, as Buzan and Gonzalez-Pelaez (2009: 26–9, 229–36) argue, are as much located in the interhuman and transnational domains as in the interstate one. Religion and ethnonationalism may well count as key institutional forms in the interhuman domain, an issue not yet much addressed by the ES (see Buzan, 2018a). Sometimes religions provide an identity foundation for state legitimacy: Iran is an official Islamic state; Denmark is an official Christian state (note that we do not claim that religion is the only source of state legitimacy in these two cases nor the most important one!). Furthermore, one Christian sect, Catholicism, has managed to gain state recognition in the form of the Vatican (permanent observer status in the UN). Similarly, an Islamic sect is still, at the time of writing, trying to set up an Islamic State/caliphate in the Middle East. The latter example is the more interesting for our purposes because it does not seem to vie for recognition by the rest of international society, but rather presents itself as a revolutionary challenge to that society on the basis of establishing empirical sovereignty. Islamic State may eventually be either defeated or socialized into international society, just as other revolutionary states have been in the past (Armstrong, 1993). Yet the challenge it poses signifies a wider challenge to the society of *states* that we also touched upon in the previous chapter: new or old non-state polities may seek to gain access to this society or, in a more radical scenario, set up competing societies alongside it or in direct competition with it. The two religions covered here, Islam and Christianity, are global, but also reveal themselves in regional and subglobal formations, as do other religions and other ideological communities. Huntington (1996), for example, sees Orthodox Christianity as separate from the other forms of Christianity, though he does not do the same for Sunni and Shi'ia Islam. Whether and how religions will crystallize as political formations in the future seems to be of profound importance for GIS and its primary institutions.

Another issue that is worth considering in the context of this discussion regarding the subglobal presence of unique primary institutions is the issue of new spaces introduced in Chapter 2: sea, air, extraterrestrial space and cyberspace. While some of these can be made to follow a territorial logic (think about the notions of 'territorial airspace' and 'territorial sea'), they also open up for a three-dimensional extension of the principle of geographical differentiation. Cyberspace takes us one step further: the physical infrastructure underpinning it is certainly tangibly located in territory, but the Internet's inherent logic of immateriality appears to defy our standard notions of space. The argument can be made that GIS has so far managed to 'colonize' these different spaces with adaptations of its existing set of primary institutions, and hence it is not presently possible to observe any unique subglobal institutions. China in particular has been pretty successful in territorializing the Internet, and the corporate world pursues 'closed garden' strategies to considerable effect. However, it is possible to imagine that separate primary institutions and separate societies might grow out of these spaces (it is another question whether this is likely or desirable). To capture the spatial distribution of these social structures, we may have to develop a taxonomy with new spatial categories – in addition to regional and subglobal. We may also have to rethink domains, though at the moment it seems that all of these new geographical spaces, just like the traditional ones, have been occupied by actors from all three domains: states; TNAs, both corporate and social, and civil and uncivil; and individuals.

That was the snapshot picture of geographical differentiation in GIS. Does a dynamic picture bring out additional facets? It certainly does if we think about the roster of primary institutions and its changes over the history of international society. Some primary institutions go back a long time, and some are more recent. Sovereignty, notwithstanding the extensive debate about its contents and precise emergence, has been practiced in European international relations for more than three hundred years. Nationalism and democracy, as principles of state legitimacy, are respectively of nineteenth- and twentieth-century vintage. Environmental stewardship is perhaps the most recent candidate for a global primary institution (Falkner and Buzan, 2017). And this is obviously a history with a large geographical component to it, as we have discussed in previous chapters. Most primary institutions emerged in Europe and were carried to the rest of the world on the back of European imperialism. Some institutions of the colonial era even implied a partly geographical division of the world: divided sovereignty, racism and the standard of civilization were all about separating the European core from the extra-European periphery, though this line of argument begins to trespass onto the conceptual territory of the next chapter. One can debate the precise ideological origins of the anticolonial struggle in the twentieth century (was it mainly rooted in European Enlightenment ideas, or more a traditional revolt against weakening imperial rule?), but it manifested as a geographical challenge to colonial GIS at the time in that political communities around the world demanded recognition and equal access to that society and changes to some of its defining primary institutions. Furthermore, today we have global secondary institutions that explicitly express regionalism. The multilateralism of the UN is partly based on regionalism. It is mentioned as a specific principle in the UN charter (articles 33, 52 and 53), and regional groups elect their representation on the Security Council. Similarly, until the Paris agreements of 2015, the UN climate change regime operated with a strong notion of 'common but differentiated responsibilities', which practically speaking meant a geographically differentiated allocation of responsibility for cutting CO_2 emissions between a developed North and a developing South.

It is hard not to detect a geographical homogenization trend in this dynamic story. Following Philpott's (2001) so-called second revolution in sovereignty, the UN declaration on the end of colonialism in 1960, a more or less standard roster of primary institutions has taken hold globally. There are, of course, exceptions. Contested primary institutions such as democracy and human rights are not accepted globally, but it is hard to identify states that completely ignore either of these. Even one of the worst global violators of human rights, North Korea, has signed and ratified a number of UN human rights conventions, and the state's official name invokes 'democracy'. Up to a point, the world is now made up of like-units that display formal core homogeneity, while at the same time adopting specific regional and subglobal interpretations of individual primary institutions. The spreading out over the globe of European social content seems to have been the dominant mode of transformation.

At first sight, this appears to be a hugely controversial assertion of Eurocentrism. Yet that becomes less controversial when one takes into account the well-established arguments within the ES about the extensive non-European inputs into the formation of 'European' international society itself (Buzan, 2014: 70–2; Suzuki, Zhang and Quirk, 2014). Because European international society evolved as it expanded, many of its institutions developed as a result of its encounters with other international societies. The development of what became GIS was thus from the very beginning a two-way street. Yet that said, it remains true that there does not seem to have been two-way traffic to the extent that institutions from one of the 'historical regional international systems' (their term) discussed by Bull and Watson (1984b) in the opening chapter of *The Expansion of International Society* got incorporated into GIS. To give but one example, the tribute institution of the East Asian system could have been integrated into GIS and/or fused with Western institutions of trade and diplomacy. This simply did not happen. To state the argument bluntly, it is hard to identity a distinct, substantial and unique non-European primary institution that made it into the contemporary GIS. There is some indication that this might happen in the future. For example, China presents itself simultaneously as both a strong defender of sovereignty/nonintervention and a power that is increasingly thinking in Confucian terms about hierarchy/harmonious relations, *Tianxia* (all under heaven) and such (see also our discussion of privilege–equality nexuses in the following chapter). This is a scenario that, however, has not fully crystallized yet. Perhaps the concept of the Islamic Umma, and its institutionalization in the Organisation of Islamic Cooperation, merits more attention in this regard than it has so far received.

Talking about the future, one might also go further back in the evolution of international society to tease out some potential trajectories based on past experience. As Watson (1992), Buzan and Little (2000) and Suzuki, Zhang and Quirk (2014) have argued, before the expansion of European international society, the world was made up of several distinct premodern international societies/systems that sometimes thought of themselves as universal but were geographically regional. Often these societies were centred around great empires, and they could almost take on actor qualities vis-à-vis other regions. Applying these observations to the present GIS, one can imagine the further strengthening of the regional dimension in international relations, such as an increasing role for regional IGOs and their representation at the UN. Moreover, one can also imagine an additional differentiation of the primary institutions of GIS in regional patterns to an extent where we again end up with fully distinct regional international societies. Some primary institutions would probably still be shared globally to secure the foundation for at least a minimum of social interaction, but the bulk of institutions would be located in distinct geographical regions. Scenarios such as Kupchan's

(2012) 'no one's world', Womack's (2014) 'multinodal world order', Acharya's (2014) 'multiplex world order' and Buzan and Lawson's (2015a) 'decentred globalism' all point in this direction. Such a scenario also could work in combination with the one suggested by Huntington, where people would more and more identify with regional civilizations (Huntington, 1993; 1996).

Another scenario would take us back and beyond Bull's (1977: 244–6) 'new mediaevalism'. It would be based on some of the complex and variegated constellations of legitimacy, governance, authority, territory and distributions of power that Schouenborg (2017) has explored in the historical regions of Central Asia, the Central African rainforest and Polynesia. The idea would be that future regions would not just display an increasing differentiation of primary institutions, they would also fundamentally rewrite the rules for the kinds of units and social inter-actions that would be contained within them. Segmentary differentiation, if we can call it that, would in a sense come to an end, and the regions would become fundamentally unalike.

What does this discussion suggest about how we can evaluate the weakening and strengthening of international society? Unlike for the LUM explored in Chapter 3, the question of strengthening or weakening for the RSM in this chapter is more complicated, involving a two-level problem. Since this model rests on a geographical principle of differ-entiation, it involves both GIS and whatever regional and subglobal international societies are in play within it. We have to consider not just what strengthens or weakens GIS, but in addition what strengthens or weakens regional and subglobal international societies within themselves. We also have to consider the relationship between the two. Is there a zero-sum game between the two levels in which stronger formations at the regional and subglobal level necessarily mean that GIS is weaker, and vice versa? Or is it possible that there could be synergies between the two levels, suggesting a positive-sum game in which stronger formations at the regional and subglobal levels could contribute to strengthening GIS? From the existing evidence, it seems that both relationships are possible. There is not much doubt, for example, that both the fascist international society during the interwar period and the communist one during the Cold War were in a zero-sum relationship with the rest of GIS. That fact underpinned the Second World War and the Cold War. On the other hand, there can be equally little doubt that the regional international societies in Europe and Latin America represent less defiant regional differentiation within GIS. These regions are not challenging the rest. Rather, they go further than the rest of GIS in some areas, but do not threaten the basic institutional structure of GIS. The big question about

China is whether, if it attained regional primacy in Asia, it would construct there a regional international society that was mainly challenging, or mainly complementary, to the rest of GIS?

The preceding discussion leaves us with a number of principles additional to those outlined in the previous chapter for thinking about the criteria by which one might evaluate the strengthening or weakening of international societies:

1. Fragmentation of a primary institution's *core* meaning regionally and sub-globally (in Lasmar et al.'s terms, penetration of an institution's protective belt of associated ideas)
2. Fragmentation of a primary institution's *associated* ideas regionally and subglobally
3. Fragmentation of *foundational*, as opposed to derivative, primary institutions regionally and subglobally
4. The emergence of regionally and/or subglobally specific primary institutions
5. Weakening or strengthening as international society expands into new spaces (air, sea, extraterrestrial space and cyberspace).
6. The extent to which any of the preceding developments are driven relatively more by coercion, calculation or belief

The first four principles obviously revolve around the issue of primary institutions. Principles 1, 2 and 4 seem fairly self-explanatory and follow logically from the preceding discussion. Here fragmentation points to a zero-sum relationship between the levels, with differentiation along these lines meaning a weakening of GIS in the sense of lower uniformity and/or number of institutions and practices, and correspondingly stronger regional and subglobal formations with distinctive packages of institutions and practices. Any such evaluation, however, has to be carefully assessed against principle 6. It is conceivable that strengthening at the regional/subglobal level by a package of institutions and practices better tailored to the cultural patterns at that level might produce an all-round strengthening of GIS by increasing the role of belief as a binding force at both levels. A GIS with a relatively high level of coercion, as some might see present GIS to be, could become institutionally thinner, but more legitimate, and therefore stronger, in a world in which regional and subglobal international societies were also more legitimate. If those societies were complementary rather than challenging to GIS, the result might be higher levels of belief, and thus legitimacy, at both levels. Only if the regional and subglobal formations were challenging to the rest of GIS would the global level become weaker.

Principle 3 received less attention, but highlights the point made by many ES scholars that some primary institutions, notably sovereignty, are more foundational or more crucial to setting up the 'game' of international society. To switch metaphors, if you change the basic syntax, then the whole language may be subject to change. This would imply a weakening of GIS at a deeper level. Following up on the afore-mentioned scenario regarding regions as agents of change, they could in this context be thought of as agents of fragmentation and hence weakening as well. It is quite easy to point to historical examples of this: revolutionary America and revolutionary France in the eighteenth and nineteenth centuries, and the fascist international society and the com-munist bloc in the twentieth century (Schouenborg, 2012; see also Armstrong, 1993). However, all of these revolutionary challenges were eventually absorbed by GIS. Islamic State (IS) as a form of regional revolutionary challenge (at the time of writing, it still has footholds in several Middle Eastern states, as well as in parts of Africa and Asia) is perhaps likely to suffer the same fate. Challenging core institutions, as IS seems to do with sovereignty and territoriality, and other revolutionary regimes have done before it (e.g., the Soviet Union before Stalin adopted 'socialism in one country'), is a formula for a zero-sum relationship between the two levels.

Principle 5 is essentially about extending our model based on (terri-torial) geography into new spaces. Whether this will lead to weakening or strengthening of GIS will depend on the degree to which the societal logics of the different spaces can be made to coalesce. As we stressed previously, increasing scale is not necessarily associated with increasing fragmentation of GIS, and the same argument can be made about GIS's 'colonization' of new spaces.

Principle 6 is concerned with the question of to what extent any of the developments captured by the previous five principles are propelled by different mixes of coercion, calculation and belief. If we assume that a belief-based social structure is necessarily stronger than one based on coercion, then that, as noted, potentially matters a lot for an overall assessment of the relative strength or weakness of GIS. A basic reading of the geographical evolution of GIS will arguably yield an impression of a double movement of coercively imposed change. The first move-ment is the predominantly coercive expansion of the Western set of primary institutions, reaching its zenith in the late nineteenth century. The second movement is the equally predominantly coercive 'revolt against the West' (Bull, 1984a) that removed (albeit imperfectly!) most of the political vestiges of colonial GIS, much less so the economic ones.[1] Today the global picture appears to be mainly one of mixed belief- and calculation-based acceptance. Most states, most of the time, do not need to be coerced into accepting Bull's core five, as well as a range of other primary institutions. There are obviously exceptions such as human rights, democracy and the market that are sometimes coercively and conspicuously imposed on certain states. The former two are not global primary institutions but rather contested subglobal ones, as was the market before the end of the Cold War. Moreover, the mix of binding forces seems to manifest in regionally and subglobally specific configurations. For example, in Europe, most primary institutions, global as well as contested subglobal institutions are sustained predominantly by belief. By contrast, the market as a global institution is held in place by quite different mixes in different geographical locations. It seems relatively safe to say that China does not believe in the market to the same extent as do traditional trading nations such as the Netherlands or Singapore. China is driven by a calculated acceptance of the market and some of its associated capitalist practices. Working out the potentially quite complex patterns of legitimacy in terms of the balance amongst coercion, calculation and belief is the key to evaluating the strengthening/weakening effects of the RSM on GIS.

A highly interesting question is the composition of binding forces in the new spaces referred to under principle 5. On the one hand, some of these are partly empty spaces (there are no permanent human inhabitants of extraterrestrial space and most sea and air space). This, in a sense, leaves GIS with no one to coerce. On the other hand, states and private actors do operate in these spaces, and in some of them the great powers enjoy an augmented presence due to superior material and technological capabilities. This makes the latter, the great powers, key to understanding the binding forces operating in these spaces, which leads us to another interesting question about how the great powers view their own roles, separately and collectively, in these spaces.

2   Strengths and Weaknesses of the Model

We now turn to the strengths and weaknesses not of GIS, but of the RSM, and again ask the following three questions:

---

[1] Note that Bull discussed five separate revolts. Here we are mainly referring to the second revolt, the anticolonial struggle.

- How well does it capture the actual nature of the units?
- How well does it capture the actual nature of the structure?
- How well does it capture the binding forces?

Capturing the Units

The model in the previous chapter essentially represented sameness and was thus in important respects aligned with the parsimonious theoretical objectives of neorealism. Where it parted ways with neorealism was in stressing the constitutive role of values, and more specifically the primary institutions of sovereignty, territoriality and nationalism and their effects in terms of creating the structure of international anarchy in the first place. Nevertheless, the model's starting premise was still the predominant homogeneity or sameness of GIS. The models in this and the remaining chapters are closer to the traditional theoretical aims of the English School (see Butterfield and Wight, 1966). These models all emphasize differentiation in GIS and thus naturally its historical and sociological complexity. Yet, they are, as models, obviously simplifications of reality that necessarily leave things out at the same time as bringing other things into sharper focus. How well are the units of GIS captured when viewed through the RSM lens?

Since the RSM, like the LUM, is mainly located in the interstate domain, what we mainly see is a host of very different states. These are differentiated not so much in terms of what we called hardware in Chapter 2 – the regional international society literature has been less preoccupied with the material properties of states – but in terms of software, the principles of legitimacy underpinning individual state constructions. We have noted the presence of what can be described as regionally unique state forms or primary institutions: the Scandinavian welfare state, the East Asian developmental state, the weak postcolonial states in much of Africa and the Middle East. It is also possible to observe fine-grained regional and subglobal variations in the interpretations and practices associated with the whole ensemble of institutions we traditionally associate with the state in international society: sovereignty, nationalism, territoriality, etc. Going further, one can moreover see more 'extreme' forms of state challenges to the dominant state norm in GIS. These are, for example, the revolutionary states explored by Schouenborg (2012) and Armstrong (1993), notably Nazi Germany, revolutionary France and the Soviet Union. In this category, one can also include the whole list of 'black' and other 'coloured' states that drove the anticolonial struggle forward, all the way back to the pioneers in San Domingo (on the latter, see James, 2001) or even Islamic State today.

Lastly, we have the quasi- or weak states discussed by Jackson (1990) and others. The model thus provides us with a more nuanced picture of the state units of GIS, one that is sensitive to the local histories that lead to substantially different state trajectories. To the extent that differentiations amongst states tend to cluster geographically, the RSM lens provides a clearer view of this factor than does the LUM one.

As conceived in this chapter, there is nothing in the RSM that demands a focus on states. There is a tendency to focus on states in the regional international society literature, but at the same time there is an awareness of other types of actor. This is notable in the edited volumes by Buzan and his collaborators on the Middle East and East Asia (Buzan and Gonzalez-Pelaez, 2009; Buzan and Zhang, 2014). It is also evident in other work on East Asia (Quayle, 2013), as well as analyses of the EU (Diez and Whitman, 2002; Diez, Manners and Whitman, 2011). In some of these regions, NSAs are becoming increasingly involved in policy making at different levels and are gaining standing and recognition in the process. If we adopt Buzan's (2004a: xviii) understanding of 'world society' as a condition in which states, non-state actors and individuals are in play together and none of them dominate over the other two, then we at least have one rough tool for assessing the extent to which non-state actors and individuals have been incorporated into the traditional society of *states*. According to this exacting standard, no regional or subglobal international society is close to making the transition to a world society. Individuals, say, have now been recognized as subjects of international law in several regions and at the UN, but their formal and active political standing in GIS is still close to nonexistent. One small exception is the EU's Citizens' Initiative, which allows for direct participation of individuals in EU policy making. With one million signatures, EU citizens can direct the European Commission to develop a legislative proposal. A concrete example of this was the successful 'One of Us' initiative, which called for a ban on financing activities presupposing the destruction of human embryos. However, this specific initiative was later vetoed by the European Commission (2016). Buzan's standard for world society, premised on equality between actors, is perhaps too exacting. Maybe an analytically more rewarding approach would be to develop a taxonomy similar to that developed by Donnelly to assess what he terms the different forms of 'hierarchy in anarchy' (Donnelly, 2006), with the difference being that this taxonomy would not be restricted to states. Now, however, we are again trespassing on the subject of the following chapter.

One issue arising from allowing multiple types of actor is the relative standing of individuals and NSAs vis-à-vis states, another is the principles of legitimacy underpinning their political claims on international society. Here the RSM opens up for looking at primary institutions that are specifically tied to these types of actor. Nevertheless, so far little has been done to pursue this research path in the regional international society literature. There are references to how nationalism (especially pannationalism), democracy and religion can be used to claim political standing for individuals and NSAs, just as they can be sources of legitimacy for the state. But we do not get a lot on primary institutions (with the obvious exception of human rights in relation to individuals and some types of NSA, and the market in relation to economic NSAs such as firms) that are specifically tied to either type of actor, regionally and/or subglobally. This is because too little has yet been done to think about primary institutions in the transnational and interhuman domains. Much of the thinking about human rights has focused on states, and the ES has still devoted little effort to exploring the market as an institution that ranges across domains.

Lastly, the RSM also opens up for viewing geographical regions as units. These may take on actor qualities and adhere to or challenge the prevailing conception of GIS. The EU is a highly interesting example of this, widely recognized by other states as an independent actor that is within itself reinterpreting or abandoning a number of central primary institutions of GIS: the balance of power, war, diplomacy, etc. In line with the way we have set up the RSM in this chapter, this would provocatively suggest that, for example, the balance of power is no longer a global institution seeing that it has been abandoned in one region (it is still practiced, though, in the EU's external relations with other regions and states). That would put it in the company of other contested primary institutions such as democracy and human rights.

Capturing the Structure

Probably the greatest strength of the RSM is how it captures variation in primary institutions, both those that define the units (e.g., sovereignty, the developmental state) and those that shape the units' interactions (e.g., diplomacy, the balance of power). The weaknesses of the LUM discussed in the corresponding section in the previous chapter hence turn into an obvious strength for the RSM. Largely, this is a story of variation in interpretations of global institutions. As we have stressed several times in this chapter, most of what we observe regionally and subglobally are distinctive associated ideas of primary institutions such as sovereignty, the market and the great powers. The core meaning of these primary institutions remains intact. Those primary institutions that can be considered regionally unique seem limited to those that define the units: the East Asian developmental state, the Scandinavian welfare state, the Middle Eastern patrimonial state. These all have a clear regional anchoring. However, if we instead focus on democracy and dynasticism, then they appear in complex subglobal patterns. The same applies to religion, albeit in an even more complex configuration: it can be the sole source of legitimacy for some states (e.g., the Vatican); and it can sanction democratic leaders (e.g., the United States), dynastic heads of state (e.g., Jordan, Morocco) or a mix of democracy and dynasticism (e.g., Denmark, Britain). Again, there is nothing in the RSM that demands a focus on states. However, as we pointed out previously, relatively little research has been undertaken to explore those primary institutions that are focused on other types of actor. This is a shortcoming not of the model but rather the still state-centric orientation of most ES scholars.

A recurrent theme in the ES literature has been that some regional international societies are 'thicker' than others, as well as thicker than GIS as a whole. Buzan (2004a: 208), in particular, has made use of a fried egg metaphor, with regional international societies represented as the thick yolk surrounded by the thin white of GIS. As we have argued, this conceptualization no doubt appeals to policy makers and to solidarist scholars in the ES. However, it equally seems to constitute a normative colonization of the RSM model: there are no ipso facto analytical grounds for considering cooperation or respect for human rights intrinsically more social than, say, conflict. Contemplating a reconfigured version of the distinction between thick and thin confers distinct advantages, one of which is the ability to capture potentially thick/strong social forms (understood as the volume, scale and range of social interactions and functions shared, as well as the relative absence of PI fragmentation, including regionally and subglobally) that nevertheless display an open commitment to violent conflict. The so-called fascist international society of the 1920s, 1930s and 1940s could arguably be considered thick/strong according to this standard (Schouenborg, 2012).

A clear weakness of the RSM is that it obviously grows out of a territorial logic (geography), and this at least superficially aligns it with the state, which shares a similar logic. That puts the model at a disadvantage when it comes to some of the nonterritorial spaces explored in this book. As noted, air and sea spaces can to some extent be territorialized. Near-earth orbital space is much more problematic (Deudney, forthcoming), as is cyberspace, although the Chinese experiment in territorializing the latter is worth watching. If these spaces grow in importance for GIS, as they seem likely to do, the model might throw up an increasingly distorted image of global political relations.

Capturing the Binding Forces

In the corresponding section in the previous chapter, we made extensive use of geographical metaphors to discuss states' (and elites' and peoples') adherence to primary institutions: islands and continents, a low landscape with scattered high points. The present chapter and model are obviously about geography, but we would like to start somewhere else, with the notion of the good life. In a justly famous essay, Wight (1960: 48) stated the following: 'Political theory and law ... are the theory of the good life. International theory is the theory of survival.' What he meant more specifically with reference to the latter was the following:

The principle that every individual requires the protection of a State which represents him in the international community, is a juristic expression of the belief in the sovereign State as the end of political experience and activity which has marked Western political thought since the Reformation. That belief has absorbed almost all the intellectual energy devoted to political study. It has been natural to think of international politics as the untidy fringe of domestic politics (Wight, 1960: 38).

Adopting Wight's perspective, there is little in international society that can muster the wholehearted belief of people. The sovereign state and the other institutions of international society are at most necessary and unattractive means to the pursuit of the real end in the form of the good life in domestic society. Wight had a tendency to put things in bleak terms, but his observation does push one to consider whether many of the institutions we observe in GIS are devoid of belief-based adherence and instead founded on grudging or disinterested calculated acceptance. Nevertheless, such a view seems to disregard belief in those institutions that help define the very content of domestic life, such as nationalism and territoriality. Moreover, it similarly appears to ignore those institutions that promote the good life, not just in domestic society but also internationally, and of which Wight arguably should have taken note. These are institutions such as human equality, human rights, environmental stewardship, development and, perhaps more arguably, the market. Development and human equality in particular appear to be accepted globally, by the UN and by all regional international organizations. And the notions of development deployed in those contexts are seldom exclusively about domestic development, but also joint regional and planetary development. Of course, there are many different notions of what constitutes development, from the cold economic logic of GDP growth to the eclectic approach of the UN Human Development Index. Here we arrive at a central contribution of the RSM: the different state forms captured by it express different conceptions of development.

The Scandinavian welfare state represents a particular take on development domestically *and* internationally – a particular notion of the good life (Schouenborg, 2013). The same applies to many of the other state forms discussed in this chapter (see also Kupchan, 2014 on how hegemonic states project their domestic normative orders onto international society).

A related point is that these beliefs in the good life arguably reach deeper into states. Similar to nationalism, they are in many cases political projects embraced by elite and people alike. There is an international development project with a large measure of popular support in China, just as there is in the United States. A second related point is that some of these projects can influence adherence to other primary institutions regionally and subglobally. To take the familiar example of the EU, this political project has in important respects removed even calculated acceptance of the balance of power and war in intra-EU relations. Indeed, this political project has partly been about eradicating or overcoming these institutions (Diez, Manners and Whitman, 2011; Schouenborg, 2012: 145–7). In other regions, the Middle East and East Asia (Buzan and Gonzalez-Pelaez, 2009; Buzan and Zhang, 2014), such institutions remain inconvenient necessities for the promotion of the good life domestically.

Another advantage of the RSM is that it allows us to gauge the distribution of binding forces geographically. Schouenborg (2013: 68) has attempted this with reference to four regional and subglobal international societies. He, for example, finds that the EC/EU, from 1952 to 2010, was sustained by a low level of belief, a high level of calculation and a low level of coercion. By contrast, the fascist international society was sustained by a low level of belief and high levels of calculation and coercion. If we combine this with the idea of regions or subglobal formations as agents of change in GIS, we may have one approach to determining the potential success of these. Arguably, coercion is a costly and fleeting means to achieve backing for a new social order, belief is more sustainable in the long term and calculation sits in between the two. We would hence expect that a belief-based challenge should have greater odds of success (of course, remembering that the coercive European imperial expansion was quite successful). However, it is perfectly possible to imagine that the mix of binding forces in an international society might change in the course of expanding. The fascist international society, for example, appeared to rely on a large degree of belief in its core states (Germany, Italy and Japan). Yet it coercively imposed its social order on other states through war (though Spain and several Eastern European and Latin American states were ideologically sympathetic and did not have to be convinced by the sword). The story of the communist bloc and its rapid demise is an interesting mix of belief and coercion, with calculation in the middle. The Sino–Soviet part of the story shows what happens when the core of belief breaks down. The Central and Eastern European and Central Asian parts of the story show what happens when the coercion part of the binding force suddenly disappears. This contrasts with the Western bloc, which has had, at least until 2016, much less division over its ideological core, much less coercion as a binding force and perhaps similar amounts of belief and calculation.

3   Conclusions

While the challenge posed by the RSM to the LUM is in principle potentially rather strong, in terms of current practice, it is not that fundamental. If we put the two models in a head-to-head contest, the like-units model seems to prevail: there is generally more sameness to GIS at the deeper levels of core meaning than there is regional or subglobal differentiation, which is more in the sphere of associated interpretations and practices. Largely, this is because the 'game' of international politics is still one predominantly constituted by states. This locks in some core defining institutions (because what defines states has some basic components) while leaving scope for differentiations in practice arising from both differences in state type and differences in culture. Other actor types have not gained equal standing in any regions (not even the EU), and the primary institutions sustaining these (for example, human rights) have been coopted or 'colonized' by the society of states. Neither have regions themselves made much headway in establishing autonomous actor quality as units within GIS. The most promising such development, the EU, is now in a considerable crisis of legitimacy, facing difficult choices between its scale and the degree and type of integration that it represents.

However, the RSM is invaluable for capturing some of the complexities of contemporary GIS, as well as past, present and future salient dynamics. It helps us get a handle on the numerous variations of the state form in GIS, with their variegated implications for adherence to different primary institutions and conceptions of world order. The model is thus a natural heir to some of the traditional research priorities of the ES. As conceived in this chapter, with the regional–subglobal distinction and with its more nuanced take on the debate about thinness and thickness, the RSM furthermore allows us to go beyond the orthodox mental frameworks of IR scholars and policy makers (geographical regions and the privileging of cooperation) and explore the emergence of new principles of legitimacy that sometimes violently challenge the present state order and the territorial understanding of space with which it is bound up. However, as the RSM is itself tied to a geographical notion of space, it faces certain limitations when GIS moves into, say, the sea or into cyberspace. Moreover, as conceived here, it excludes considerations of hierarchy and core–periphery relations, the subject of the following chapter.

What does the RSM tell us about the strength/thickness or weakness/thinness of GIS? First, it provides us with a provisional working definition and six principles for thinking about this issue. The initial three principles have to do with different kinds of fragmentation in meaning (understood as weakening GIS). There appears to be little evidence to suggest much fragmentation in most primary institutions' core meaning. Sovereignty, territoriality, diplomacy, international law, great power management, the balance of power, nationalism, human equality, development and the market all seem to have a recognizable common form across the globe (although some of these appear to be challenged in the EU). Where there is fragmentation, it mainly manifests as differences in associated ideas (principle 2). The market, for example, is a hugely complex global institution, with a host of variegated local practices and beliefs. Consider only the recurrent debates over free trade versus protectionism and the corresponding policy packages. According to principle 2, we are therefore presently witnesses to substantial fragmentation, as several institutions, not just the market, are getting ever more complex. Interestingly, and contrary to the traditional thin or thick understanding in the ES literature, the EU could then represent a weakening of GIS. To the extent that the EU challenges dominant interpretations of primary institutions and seeks to formulate alternatives, it contributes to the fragmentation of GIS. Arguably, the same applies to contested subglobal primary institutions such as democracy, human rights and, to a decreasing extent, dynasticism. They can also be viewed as promoters of fragmentation. By contrast, if the overall trajectory of GIS tends towards an engagement amongst equals, differentiation at the regional level need not be a problem and may in fact strengthen the coherence of GIS. The crucial issue is whether regional differentiation is approached predominantly as a positive-sum or zero-sum game by the actors in GIS, and whether upload (from region to global) or download (from global to region), for example environmental stewardship, is considered dangerous. To assess this, we need to carefully observe states (and other actors) and see whether they deem certain ideas and practices compatible or incompatible with their conception of international society. The weakening or strengthening potential of a particular idea, a particular primary institution, cannot be neutrally judged by the analyst in advance. This only becomes evident in actual (state) practice.

The key implication that emerges from a consideration of principles 4 through 6 is that the deep-felt belief in different, sometimes conflicting, notions of the good life domestically and internationally can lead to a similar fragmentation of GIS. This, however, depends on the degree to which these versions of the good life pose challenges to the content of the primary institutions of GIS: core meaning and associated ideas. Because these notions of the good life tend to have not just elite but also popular backing, they appear to pose more potent challenges both to GIS and to an understanding of GIS filtered primarily through the interstate domain. Yet considering the present wavering popular and elite support for the EU, this need not be a foregone conclusion. The movement of GIS into new spaces equally represents potential fragmentation as new principles of legitimacy may emerge and the old primary institutions of territorial international relations are perhaps deemed inappropriate for handling the societal problems encountered in these environments.

5   The Hierarchy/Privilege Model

Although much of IR and ES theory is built around the ideas of sovereign equality and international anarchy, there has always been a significant place for hierarchy and privilege, even within the interstate domain. Empire and colonialism are the most blatant forms of the hierarchy/privilege model (HPM). They were neglected in traditional ES research, a problem that has been raised and partly rectified by scholars such as Keene (2002), Keal (2003) and Holsti (2004: 239–74). By contrast, the 'standard of civilization' (SoC) received some early attention (Gong, 1984), but then largely lay dormant as a concept until recent years (see, e.g., Donnelly, 1998; Stivachtis, 2006; Bowden, 2009; 2014; Suzuki, 2009; Towns, 2009; Phillips, 2012; Aalberts, 2014; Buzan, 2014b; Keene, 2014; Schulz, 2014; Zhang, 2014). Furthermore, the evident hierarchy between states in international society has been addressed intermittently by various authors over the past forty years, including by Bull and Watson (see, e.g., Bull, 1977; Holbraad, 1984; Clark, 1989; 2011; Watson, 1992; 1997; Bain, 2003; Dunne, 2003; Simpson, 2004; Clapton, 2014). The current everyday language of 'great powers' and 'superpowers' and the more recent postcolonial language of 'core–periphery' (Galtung, 1971; Wallerstein, 2004) all suggest the central role of hierarchy/privilege in thinking about interstate IR. The ES for a long time preferred thinking about the flatter, anarchical, like-units model of GIS, largely setting aside Wight's and Watson's early interest in hegemony and suzerainty as important forms of GIS (Buzan, 2014a: 51). Yet the ES also embedded the privilege model in one of its five classical primary institutions: great power management (Cui and Buzan, 2016). All of this scholarship points to a salient dimension of the structure of international society (and probably all societies): the existence of privileged positions. In this chapter, we will attempt to make sense of this dimension and explore its implications for thinking about the strength and weakness of GIS, not only in the interstate domain, but also in the transnational and interhuman ones, and in the relationship among the domains.

1   The Model

Whereas the central principle of differentiation in the previous chapter was geographical location, in this chapter it is *positional* in a social sense, implying subordinate–superordinate relationships (see also Ayoob, 2010: 129–30). These status relationships can express themselves vertically, in which case we refer to them as hierarchy (think a pyramid), and horizontally, in which case we refer to them as core–periphery relations (think concentric circles). Vertical status relationships are often formal, as in empire, dominion, suzerainty and the privileged position of great powers in some IGOs (e.g., the P5 in the United Nations Security Council). Horizontal status relationships are often informal, as in hegemonic and core–periphery structures, or 'informal empires'. We are interested in capturing both in this chapter and have thus given our model the general label hierarchy/privilege model. However, focusing in on vertical and horizontal privileges between and amongst states only takes us so far. A great many issues are raised in the ES literature referenced previously, and hence we find it useful to further subdivide privilege into the following three elements, which we discuss in turn. While these elements can be separated analytically, they are in practice often intertwined.

• Within the interstate domain, the privileged political position of some states vis-à-vis other states based on the identity they carry within GIS
• Between the interstate domain and the other two, the privileged position of states vis-à-vis both NSAs, whether political, social or economic, and individuals
• Within the interhuman domain, the privileged position of broader, general status roles and classifications based on race, gender, class and civilization within GIS

The Privileged Political Position of Some States vis-à-vis Other States Based on the Identity They Carry within GIS

Perhaps the most obvious position of privilege to casual observers of world politics is that of being a great power or superpower. References to this status are commonplace in news coverage of international affairs, and most informed people know that the great powers enjoy special rights on the UN Security Council. As noted, the institution of the great powers was central to Bull's (1977) account of order in GIS. At a very basic level, the institution implies a hierarchy between states. It is first and foremost a *recognized* status that confers certain formal entitlements and obligations upon states. That recognition comes mainly from the other great powers, but to be properly institutionalized, great power status has also to be accepted by lesser states. Great power status generally requires appropriate material capabilities, though it is difficult to say exactly how substantial these have to be. There have been a few instances of honourary great power status being awarded to states that once had such capabilities but did not possess them at the time: Sweden in the late eighteenth century, China and France in 1945. Furthermore, like all the other privileged status roles we will discuss in this chapter, it is a social phenomenon with a particular historical origin. In its modern form, it can be traced back to the Congress of Vienna in 1815 and the institutionalization in the so-called Concert of Europe of the idea that a small set of states should have an extraordinary responsibility for managing international affairs. Above all, the great powers should prevent a hegemonic challenger from gaining dominance, both through the careful manipulation of the balance of power and through the remaining order-maintaining institutions that Bull discussed in his landmark contribution (see also Simpson, 2004; Bukovansky et al., 2012, 26–7).

That is perhaps the IR baseline understanding of what this part of the HPM is about. However, this understanding leaves space for quite a bit of variation. For example, it says nothing about the number of great powers that can exist in GIS at any given time. In practice, the number has remained low, both in absolute and in relative terms. The recognized great powers at the Congress of Vienna were Austria, France, Britain, Prussia and Russia. Today there are also five permanent members of the UN Security Council, but a number of other states have been considered great powers for much of the twentieth century (Germany and Japan) and some are aspiring to this status in the twenty-first century (Brazil and India). Another forum, the G7, also has some claim to fulfilling great power management functions in the economic sphere, as does the relatively new G20. While some members of the G20 are certainly not presently considered great powers by the other states in GIS, the G20 does pose the question of how much the great power club can logically grow. Can it, for example, expand to fifty states or even a majority of states (ninety-seven based on the current member roster of the UN)? At some point, this would seem to push against the conventional understanding that this is an exclusive club with special entitlements and obligations. Yet it is hard to say exactly where such lines should be drawn. In this way, the problem is similar to the one concerning the indeterminate requirement of superior material capabilities; what does it take to be 'great'? Alternatively, a case can be made that in the vastly more complicated contemporary GIS, it is not so much that great powers are becoming more numerous but that the management functions previously seen as great power responsibilities have proliferated wildly, and perforce are now dealt with in more specialized ways by a wider range of states and NSAs (Bukovansky et al., 2012). In this perspective, great power management is fusing with global governance (Cui and Buzan, 2016), pushing what was a privilege model towards the functional differentiation one discussed in the next chapter.

This discussion naturally leads to a consideration of other gradations of hierarchy and privilege between states in GIS. During the Cold War, for obvious reasons, the status of 'superpower' entered the global diplomatic vocabulary. It became clear to everyone that the capabilities of the United States and the Soviet Union were of a different order of magnitude compared with the rest of the members of the putative great power club, both materially and as representatives of competing ideologies. Retrospectively, some have applied superpower status to Britain during the nineteenth century (Ferguson, 2004: 222), and prospectively it is increasingly common to refer to China either as a superpower or a country that will soon reach that status. Superpower status is not just a recognition of material facts. The recognition translated into what Simpson (2004) termed 'legalized hegemony': the general acceptance of special rights and responsibilities for this class of states. Even here, however, the ambiguity about capabilities persisted. Other than in the military sphere, the Soviet Union never came close to matching US material capabilities. During the 1980s, the Soviet Union retained recognition as a superpower, even though its economy had been surpassed by Japan's and its ideological leadership challenged by China. Because of its military self-restraint, Japan was not even universally acknowledged as a great power after 1945. Following the end of the Cold War, the membership of the superpower class was reduced to just one, the United States, and the management function of privilege had in a sense, paradoxically, morphed into what it was originally designed to prevent: the near hegemony of one state (see Clark, 2009b; 2011 for an extensive discussion of the United States and the limits of its hegemony in GIS). Some argue that we will soon be in a world without superpowers, albeit one in which great powers and regional powers remain prominent in the hierarchy of states (Kupchan, 2012; Acharya, 2014; Buzan and Lawson, 2015a).

It is also appropriate to discuss the purposes this formal standing can serve. We have already noted the manipulation of the balance of power and countering hegemony as a core traditional purpose. However, this is just one functional purpose, albeit perhaps a foundational one.

Kingsbury (1999: 78) points to three instances of formal great power privilege: the UN Charter (including the Security Council), the nuclear nonproliferation treaty and the IMF. The former two can arguably be categorized as having to do with security, and by extension with the balance of power and the counterhegemony project. The latter is more concerned with an economic management purpose, which also finds expression in the G7. In addition to these purposes, there is environmental stewardship, in relation to which the great powers (the great CO_2 emitters) are increasingly viewed as having special responsibilities too. Moreover, as argued in previous chapters, they also seem to enjoy a special standing in extraterrestrial space. Lastly, but importantly, great powers govern the very possibility of entry into GIS as the UN Security Council grants or withholds recommendations concerning admission of new members to the UN. Cui and Buzan (2016) argue that great power functions have largely been defined in terms of the security agenda. As that agenda has widened and deepened away from traditional military-political issues towards economic, identity and environmental security, great power functions have expanded into, and increasingly overlapped with, the broader processes of global governance. This underpins the previously noted argument of Bukovansky et al. (2012) about the diffusion of special responsibilities in GIS and begins to anticipate the discussion in the next chapter.

Going in the other direction, towards inferior gradations of power, GIS has also historically dabbled with the concept of 'middle powers'. A lot of intellectual energy has been put into elucidating what this status entails (see Holbraad, 1984, for a thorough investigation). It has been taken to signify everything from the capability to mount a nuclear weapons programme to a special role in international mediation. Canada has functioned as the main 'spokesperson' for, and exemplar of, this status role, with Sweden and Australia as other significant examples. However, as Holbraad (1984: 75) argues, unlike the great powers, and 'Despite their efforts in the early years of both the League of Nations and the United Nations to secure some recognition of their own, the middle powers have no such formal standing in international society'. Their influence comes not from formal status, but from their individual willingness to put disproportionate resources into diplomacy, and their skill at building up positions of trust within IGOs specifically and GIS generally.

Less acknowledged in most of IR, but in practice more important, is the category of regional power (Buzan and Wæver, 2003). Regional powers have not achieved the level of formal status recognition accorded to great powers, but informally, within their regions, they can have a lot of status. For example, Brazil and Argentina are expected, and expect themselves, to provide leadership within South America. The same can be said of France and Germany within the EU, of Nigeria within West Africa, of South Africa within southern Africa and of Indonesia within Southeast Asia. In various other regions, there is little or no consensus about which of the regional powers should legitimately be considered as having regional leadership responsibilities. This is true in South Asia, the Middle East and Northeast Asia. The effectiveness or not of regional power leadership is a key variable in the strength or weakness of the regional international societies discussed in the previous chapter.

Moving further down the gradations of powers, we find small powers, or what is usually referred to as small states and microstates. These are probably the ones most at risk of being subjected to different sovereignty-diminishing statuses. Donnelly (2006:149–50) has done a very good job of explicating these different formal hierarchies that he terms practices of 'semi-sovereignty'. The first kind is treaties of *guarantee and protection*. They grant special rights of intervention to an outside state, or set of states, to uphold certain specified internal conditions in the target country. As contemporary examples, one can point to the international trusteeships in Bosnia and Herzegovina, East Timor and Kosovo in the 1990s and 2000s (see also Bain, 2003). A related category is *financial controls*. These are different claims over states' financial resources that were popular in the nineteenth and early twentieth centuries. Today this kind of formal hierarchy is forcefully expressed in the international creditor agreements with Greece, which grant the creditors extensive influence over the conduct of Greek fiscal policy and administration. A third category is *servitudes*. These secure use rights or access rights to other states. For example, waterway regimes, military basing rights and leasing of territory, but also demilitarized zones and permanently neutralized states, belong in this category according to Donnelly. There are moreover certain *general rights of intervention* that are not created with particular target states in mind. The UN Security Council has the right to act on threats to international peace and security, and in the 2000s this right was supplemented with a more specific obligation to uphold the Responsibility to Protect (R2P). A final category is *imperfect unions*, where an ambiguous international legal personality is created. Donnelly's contemporary example is the EU, which has achieved an international legal personality for some purposes, while its constituent units continue their legal lives as sovereign states.

Even further down the list of gradations of power exist Jackson's (1990) so-called quasi-states, which appear to invite near permanent external intervention by GIS, because although enjoying juridical sovereignty (recognition by other states within GIS), they remain deficient in empirical sovereignty (the capability to govern a population and territory up to the expectations of the 'standard of civilization' of the day). Quasi-states blend into failed states, where practically all of the sovereignty is juridical and very little empirical (e.g., Somalia, Libya). Such states effectively become either holes in the fabric of GIS or wards of GIS, even though the post-1945 illegitimacy of empire and colonialism does not allow frank use of language to say this. During colonial times, when sovereignty was divided, the language was much starker, and often more racist: 'civilized', 'barbarian' and 'savage' correlated with the League of Nations mandate statuses of capable of modern self-government, likely to be so capable after tutelage and unlikely ever to achieve modern self-government.

Quasi-states as a phenomenon provide a neat transition from the issue of gradations of powers to other dimensions of privilege based on the kind of state you are, your state identity. This is where some of the insights of the SoC literature become relevant. As discussed in previous chapters, GIS had its origin in Europe and was characterized by some degree of cultural homogeneity. It was a Christian commonwealth made up of Christian states. Yet at the same time it was shot through with differentiation based on hierarchy. The very problem that we have discussed, how to differentiate between different types of powers (referring to entities and their rulers), was a much debated topic in European international relations both before and after the Peace of Westphalia, and it manifested in a range of different rankings of sovereigns (Reus-Smit, 1999, ch. 5; Keene, 2013). For example, Rousset de Missy, in his mid-eighteenth-century work on diplomatic ceremonial, detailed a sovereign order of precedence based on emperors, kings, princes, dukes, marquises, counts, barons, etc. (Keene, 2013: 275–6). Most of the pre-modern international societies that we know about had similar cultural/civilizational status differentiations, whether it be the Sinocentric tribute system in East Asia, the classical Greek City states or the Amarna society in the ancient Middle East (Cohen and Westbrook, 2002). Over the centuries following 1648, many of these sovereign statuses in Europe gradually lost their currency, so that states were either mostly led by emperors or kings (with a few duchies and republics as notable exceptions). The key point, though, is that European international society exhibited hierarchical, privileged tendencies well before its expansion to the rest of the world. However, in the course of the expansion and afterwards, new dimensions of 'being' were added to these status debates in response to interaction with the foreign other.

While we agree with Keene (2014) that it is problematic to overdraw the distinction between the pre- and postexpansion phases,[1] the expansion did result in a number of state categories coming into common usage: for example, non-Christian states, black states or even black Christian states (Ethiopia). These statuses and their incorporation into a Europe-centred hierarchy of states start to blend into the preceding discussion about general status roles and classifications. They provoked the requirements associated with the SoC and documented by Gong (1984: 14–15). These were requirements concerning what you, as a state member of GIS, were supposed to be and do: (1) to guarantee the basic rights of foreign nationals; (2) to carry out basic governmental functions; (3) to adhere to international law and have an appropriate domestic system of law; (4) to engage in diplomatic interchange; and (5) to conform to the customs and norms of the civilized (European) international society. The whole idea of the SoC was strongly linked to the hierarchy of development that opened up during the nineteenth century between early modernizers and those who lagged behind (Buzan and Lawson, 2015a). The development hierarchy remains strong despite the rise of the rest. It is even formalized in the UN status of 'developing country', which, as in various environmental agreements, allows different terms than for developed states. Other elements of the SoC have endured up to the present, for example in the idea of democracy as a favoured form of government or outright SoC (Hobson, 2008; Clark, 2009a), as well as in the special obligation of GIS, as a collective actor via delegation to the great powers, to deal with so-called outlaw states (Simpson, 2004).

Lastly, there is the layer of privilege standing above those representing the relative standing of individual states and addressing structures of hierarchy and privilege covering GIS as a whole. In its older, more vertical and formal instantiation, this is about empire, or suzerainty or dominion, and captures the relationship between metropolitan cores and colonial peripheries. In its more recent, horizontal and informal instantiation, this is about collective hegemony and captures the relationship between a more developed economic core and a less developed economic periphery. In its formal, imperial form, this status has mainly been viewed as the negation of international society in ES work. Empire and hegemony were exactly what primary institutions of anarchical international society such as sovereignty, territoriality, diplomacy, war, great power management and the balance of power were supposed to prevent or contain. In addition, since the delegitimation of the institution of

---

[1] Keene is right in stressing that interaction and stratification between Europe and the outside world predated the traditional 'entry' in the nineteenth century.

imperialism/colonialism after 1945, this form is widely seen as no longer relevant to GIS. It is hence not surprising that the most detailed ES account of empire is substantively dedicated to exploring it historically, before the creation of the European international society (Watson, 1992). And it is equally not surprising that the imperial relations expressed in colonialism have featured as blind spots in traditional ES scholarship.

In a *longue durée* perspective, it makes sense to follow Watson (1992: 16) in his understanding of empire as 'the direct administration of different communities from an imperial centre'. It is thus a more formal and possibly more extensive dominance relationship than hegemony, though one should not underestimate how extensive and dominant an informal hegemonic relationship can be. It is entirely legitimate to see core–periphery hegemony after decolonization as the postimperial form of core–periphery relations, and thus in some important ways, especially economic, functionally similar to empire in its effects, even though less formal and less vertical in its forms and practices. And although core–periphery relationships are less formal than imperial ones, they have achieved significant levels of institutionalization within GIS. The developed-states core, for example, is institutionalized in the OECD and the G7 and G20, and the less-developed periphery is institutionalized in the G77, the UN Conference on Trade and Development (UNCTAD) and the Nonaligned Movement (NAM). While the institution of imperialism/colonialism and its associated institution of human inequality have been delegitimized, both the language and the idea of empire remain active in the discourse of IR and world politics. Accusations of 'imperialism' and 'neocolonialism' still mark the Marxian and postcolonial discourses about core–periphery relations. The United States has often been accused of imperialism, and up to 1989 that charge was also thrown at the Soviet Union. More recently, both China (in the South China Sea and Central Asia) and Russia (in Ukraine, the Caucasus and Central Asia) seem to be increasingly thinking and behaving like empires.

Empire, hegemony and core–periphery have become hotly debated ideas in IR, influenced in large part by increasing economic globalization (perceived by some as a form of empire, by others as hegemonic) and by the actions of the former US Bush administration abroad (see Kettell and Sutton, 2013, for a detailed review). The empire debate did not really get going until the United States achieved 'unipolar', sole superpower states after the end of the Cold War. Conceptual ambiguity abounds. The United States is labelled as an empire mainly by those who want to exploit the illegitimate political connotations of the term to criticize

Washington's policies, though it was also embraced by a few in the United States who liked the idea of Washington as the new Rome. Hegemony is more like informal empire, where the United States sets the rules and standards and generally runs the system to its own advantage while also providing significant collective goods. Empire suggests a more coercive relationship, but one should not forget that the dynasticism/empire combination could also carry a lot of legitimacy from both calculation (the trade and security benefits of a large-scale political order) and belief (the legitimacy of dynasticism expressed in phrases such as 'For king and country'). Hegemony suggests a more consensual relationship, where calculation, and even belief, play alongside a smaller degree of coercion. Either way, and regardless of whether the core is understood to be the United States, the West or a group of developed states, the outcome is an unequal structure of interstate relations in which the core states have more control and more status and the periphery states less of both. This can be constructed both as exploitation of the periphery by the core (*dependencia* theory) and as an extension of the imperial responsibility to bring colonial peoples up to the SoC via the new post-1945 primary institution of development (Buzan, 2014a: 153–7).

In sum, then, we can see that amongst states the HPM reveals a wide range of unequal relations both formal and informal. Despite the delegitimation of empire, the idea that there should be privileged actors in GIS has been remarkably durable and is deeply institutionalized. There is still considerable strength behind the formal privileges of great powers, though this may be changing to add in giving special responsibilities to actors possessing the relevant functional skills. There nevertheless seems to have been a shift from formal to informal modes of hierarchy and privilege as the core–periphery structure has replaced the imperial one.

The Privileged Position of States vis-à-vis Both Non-State Actors and Individuals

The ES narrative about GIS has naturally been pulled towards states, as these are the defining actors of this social order. The institution of sovereignty claims to give states automatic precedence over all other types of entity. However, over the past fifteen years or so, scholars have started to give more attention to world society (Buzan, 2004b; 2018a; Clark, 2007; Ralph, 2007; Pella Jr, 2013; 2015b; Cantir, 2016) and to entities placed outside or submerged within GIS in the course of colonization (Keene, 2002; Keal, 2003; Pearcey, 2015). Inevitably, this has put a spotlight on the cross-domain subordinate–superordinate relations between states and non-state entities as well as individuals. These relations of hierarchy and privilege come in different forms.

The first form awkwardly straddles between the hierarchies amongst states discussed in the previous subsection, and hierarchies between states and other kinds of entity. It is about the relationship between states and what might be thought of as prestate entities, and thus overlaps with both colonial and weak/failed state hierarchies. It is mainly expressed in the process of righting this basic inequality by erasing the distinction between state and 'non-state'. Here we are referring to the various attempts (some successful, some not) by different actors to gain entry into GIS by being recognized as a state by other states. A major benchmark date for colonial entities was 1960 (Philpott, 2001). As discussed previously, this may be considered the point at which a truly global international society of independent states, as opposed to a global imperial one, came into existence. Other entities have been less successful. Pearcey (2015), for example, has documented the failed attempt of Chief Levi General to get the Six Nations (formally part of Canada) recognized at the League of Nations in the early 1920s. In this category, we also place the different 'contested states' (Kosovo, Palestine, South Ossetia, etc.) that have so far only received limited recognition by GIS (Geldenhuys, 2009). What this boils down to is a class of NSAs that aspire to become states and whose main purpose is to gain membership into GIS. They can do this by establishing a claim for recognition on the basis of one or more criteria: national identity, historic right and/or ability to exercise empirical sovereignty. There is a fuzzy frontier between this category and what might be called genuine NSAs: those which have no desire to become states. Should entities such as Taiwan and Islamic State, or in earlier times those 'states' and peoples classified as 'barbaric' or 'savage', be thought of as states or NSAs? How should one classify the peoples identified by Keal (2003) as being submerged within postcolonial states? Prestate actors are, in a sense, supplicants to the prevailing interstate order.

The second form is about the relationship between states and 'genuine NSAs'. Genuine NSAs come in a huge variety of forms. If the basic criterion for 'genuine' is that they have no aspiration to become states, then this range would include most TNCs, most INGOs and most IGOs. It is not beyond imagination that a few TNCs and INGOs might aspire to statehood. The Vatican might be seen as an example of the latter. Even IGOs might do so, as some have suspected of the EU's mission towards 'ever closer union'. In relation to both INGOs and TNCs, there is also a distinction to be drawn between what might be called global civil society (GCS) and global uncivil society (GUS), with the latter comprising transnational criminal and terrorist entities and networks (Buzan, 2004b). In general, the sovereignty-based construction of GIS places genuine NSAs in a position of legal subordination to states, and on the GCS side this hierarchy is broadly accepted. On the uncivil side, however, this relationship is more complicated. Transnational criminals and even terrorists (if they see themselves as prestate entities) might in some sense accept the legal hierarchy even while attacking and subverting existing states. Even on the civil side, there is a well-established line of thinking that TNCs are powerful enough to overwhelm smaller and weaker states and even to subvert the politics of more powerful ones. This thinking ranges from specific cases of 'banana republics' to the wider critique of neoliberalism and globalization as making the world safe for big capital and the super-rich.

Given that most genuine NSAs, especially those on the civil side, accept their legal subordination to states, this highlights the distinction between the formal status of NSAs within GIS on the one hand, and their actual power and influence on the other. Clark (2007) has certainly shown that GCS can influence the formation of primary institutions at the interstate level. Since 2001, transnational terrorists have succeeded in getting the sole superpower to declare war on them, thereby giving them a status (as parties in the formal activity of war) in GIS previously reserved for states and the potential to become parties to diplomatic negotiations. If big capital has in fact pushed states to accept neoliberal globalization, then that would have demonstrated a very considerable ability to influence the agenda of interstate society. If big capital was indeed the power behind the throne, then the formal hierarchy of state dominance would have been effectively hollowed out. Pella (2015b) has demonstrated how actors associated with world society were crucial to the European colonial expansion into Africa, not just as go-between subordinates, but as active agents pushing states into this partly resisted political project. In a similar fashion, he has shown how world society actors were instrumental in setting up the institution of slavery in the fifteenth century and in pulling it down again in the nineteenth (Pella, 2013: 69–74). To use his phrasing, it may be that world society exists as a 'parasite' on international society as it is dependent on its institutional framework. But as in nature, when it comes to actual influence the parasite can sometimes steer the larger organism. This suggests that the distinction between formal recognized privilege and the privilege of actual conduct stands as a common aspect of the different elements of the hierarchy/privilege model.

The third form is about the relationship between states and individuals. Within the GIS, this relationship occurs at three levels: individuals;

large-scale human collectivities based on identity, such as nations, religions and civilizations; and humankind as a whole. In the ES tradition, this relationship has never been one of a clear formal hierarchy of states over individuals. Indeed, it has defined the central tension in the ES between pluralists (who tend to privilege the state and sovereignty) and solidarists (who emphasize the independence of human rights against sovereignty and/or the conditionality of sovereignty on the provision of human rights) (see Cochran, 2009; Bain, 2014; Buzan, 2014a: 83–167). Even a firm pluralist such as Bull (1977: 318–20; 1990: 83) argued that the society of states could only be justified by how well it served the needs of the great society of humankind as a whole. There is thus an important sense in which individuals are both legally subordinate to the state as individual citizens but collectively as humankind stand in a position of moral primacy to it. This already complicated picture is made even more so by adding in the middle level of human identity collectivities, particularly nations. While nationalism is a primary institution of interstate society, it also gives collectivities of individuals defined in this way a considerable moral leverage if they assert a claim to statehood. If a middle-level collectivity can establish credentials as a nation or a people, it can create real leverage against the existing disposition of sovereignty and territoriality, a dynamic forcefully illustrated by the tortured history of Israel/Palestine.

In terms of formal standing, individuals have to some extent managed to be incorporated as subjects and not just objects of the interstate order. This is the familiar story about the Nuremberg and Tokyo trials and similar tribunals in the post–Cold War period that held individuals accountable for crimes against humanity and, most recently, the creation of the International Criminal Court. It is, however, also the story about individuals suing sovereign governments in, for example, the European Court of Human Rights (Armstrong, 1999; Holsti, 2004: ch. 5; Ralph, 2007). These developments give rise to complicated constellations of legal and political hierarchies that sometimes in effect appear to put the interests of individuals above the interests of states, again playing to the tensions within the ES between solidarists and pluralists. It is not necessary to rehearse this debate here, except to say that the binary or dichotomous framings of it can tend to obscure what is at stake (Buzan, 2014a: 85).

The Privileged Position of Broader, General Status Roles and Classifications within GIS

Although hardly the most researched topic in the ES literature, this is a crucial element of the HPM. In some ways, general ideas about race, gender, class and religion generate their own status hierarchies, while in other ways these ideas can operate through the structures of states and NSAs, reinforcing notions about what it means to be a state or which kinds of non-state actors should have a voice in GIS. The privilege of broader, general status roles has garnered some attention in thinking about GIS but needs much more development. Race and gender, and up to a point class and religion, relate closely to the primary institution of human equality/inequality. For pretty much all of human history up to 1945, the prevailing norm was human inequality, and this norm underpinned dynasticism, empire and slavery. Particularly in the larger and more powerful polities, the position of women in society was inferior to that of men, and it was normal practice in such societies to arrange themselves in hierarchies of masculine gender privilege. Within societies there were masters and slaves, and aristocrats and commoners. Between them there was almost always a 'standard of civilization' where some saw themselves as civilized and looked upon others as barbarian. So-called 'universal' religions worked in a similar way, creating privileged insiders and inferior, discriminated-against outsiders: think of Islamic taxes against nonbelievers and Christian restrictions on the social position of Jews. In one of the more remarkable, yet little noticed, transformations in the primary institutions of international society, the norm of human inequality was replaced by the norm of human equality after the Second World War. Declaring all humans to be equal quite effectively delegitimized dynasticism, empire, racism and slavery, but has so far been much slower and more limited in countering gender discrimination. The shift to human equality reduced or marginalized many, though by no means all, of the discriminatory behaviours, and cut down, though not eliminating, the influence of this type of privilege.

Perhaps the most remarkable turnaround was achieved in relation to race. As Bell (2013: 1) notes: 'for the opening few decades of the [twentieth] century, race was widely and explicitly considered a fundamental ontological unit of politics, perhaps the most fundamental unit of all'. This dark past has largely been forgotten about in the IR and ES literature, but for more than a century, 'scientific racism' legitimized racial hierarchies and empire, with 'white' being closely associated with civilization and modernity (Buzan and Lawson, 2015a: 118–25). After decolonization, racist views were still certainly held privately, but they were largely eliminated from public discourse and diplomacy, and eventually even from the two most stalwart apartheid states, South Africa and the United States. In the ES story, one notable case is the inability of Japan to get racial equality recognized as a principle at the Paris Peace Conference following the First World War (Vincent, 1984: 245;

Shimazu, 1998; Kingsbury, 1999: 74; Zhang, 2014: 681). Not long after this event, Japan made a 180 degree turn and began to pursue an international order largely based on racially defined regional blocs in the 1930s and 1940s. This was in cooperation with the fascist states Germany and Italy (Schouenborg, 2012: 138–41). The influence of racism on GIS reached its ghastly apex during the Second World War, providing much of the impetus to institutionalize a norm of human equality. The racism of the colonial era remains a huge source of resentment in much of the nonwhite world, but as a source of formal, and to a lesser extent informal, privilege has now lost most of its influence.

Gender has by and large been overlooked in the ES literature (True, 2005; Blanchard, 2011). Although in some ways very similar to racism, being based on discrimination on the grounds of biological markers, its impact on GIS has been much less obvious (or much less noticed) and certainly much less politicized than racism. So far, there have been no big gender stories active in the discourse about GIS that parallel or match the racism ones told about Japan and about postcolonial resentment. This might be about to change if the argument put forward by feminists such as Sjoberg (2012), that gender hierarchy is a structural feature of world politics, and a better explanation for war than Waltz's anarchic structure, gains purchase. From that perspective, there is a very powerful story to be told about the impact of gender hierarchy on the whole structure and operation of GIS, including the definition of power, and the ways in which states locate themselves and others in international status hierarchies.

But if we shift our gaze from the high-level abstraction of masculinity/femininity to the more personal level of how gender hierarchy has affected women, then an interesting difference with racism opens up. Although there were differences in the forms and degrees of gender hierarchy that discriminated against women, such discrimination was a common feature in the male-dominated logics of dynastic hierarchy and preference. This hierarchy was widespread across many types of societies, and especially so in the larger and more powerful types of polity. As Sjoberg (2012: 7) observes, masculine and feminine behavioural traits, and the hierarchies associated with them, show 'surprising similarities across recorded history'. Because gender privilege was so widely practiced amongst the major powers in the international system, it did not so obviously create the status differentiations *between* states and societies that gave racism its big impact on GIS. By contrast, race differences, especially before the mass migrations of modern times, were generally much stronger between societies than within them.

Gender hierarchy, and the privileged status for men and masculinity that it supports, remains influential, despite being delegitimized by the principle of human equality, and can reinforce other privileges. Towns, for example, discusses how the status of women worked as a SoC in the nineteenth century GIS. In particular, she argues that the nineteenth-century version of the standard suggested the 'full-scale exclusion of women from politics' and the linkage of female roles in politics to 'savagery', and female exclusion from politics with 'civilization' (Towns, 2009: 683; see also 2010; 2012). A shared language developed in GIS whereby inferior states and peoples were feminized and superior ones masculinized: feminine traits were ascribed to colonized peoples and 'savage' areas as a way to mark their inferiority (Nandy, 1983). Such practices continue today, albeit usually without the crude language and analogies with 'savagery' (Sjoberg, 2012). As with racism, under the broad pressure of the human equality norm, some things have obviously changed a lot since then. Women have become enfranchised in many countries, and international society has moved the status of women up the political agenda. In 2000, the UN Security Council adopted the pioneering Resolution 1325, which aimed to strengthen the participation of women in national and international politics and to protect them from harm. It has since been followed by seven subsequent resolutions, spelling out initiatives and goals in different issue areas (Kirby and Shepherd, 2016). As with racism, and to a greater degree, gender discrimination remains an active force even though it no longer has the legitimacy necessary to sustain formal and explicit hierarchies of privilege.

Class as a status role has hardly been touched by ES writers, which might be a consequence of the general reluctance on the part of the school to engage with international political economy noted by Buzan (2005). Moreover, it might be possible to see the whole ES/international society body of classical theory as the attempt of an old 'aristocratic class' of white men to understand and justify their own position in the world in the 1950s and 1960s (Callahan, 2004). However, from the perspective of social structural theory adopted in this book, there seems to be no way of avoiding the issue of class in GIS. As with race, class was once an enormously powerful basis of privilege and hierarchy in GIS. It shared with racial hierarchies the biological idea of the importance of breeding, and 'good stock'. Before it was displaced by the rise of nationalism and liberalism during the nineteenth century, dynasticism embodied a system of formalized class privilege. Like discrimination against women, the dynastic political principle of aristocratic superiority was very widely spread across cultures, albeit differing in practices from place to place. This form of status hierarchy was giving way even before the First World

War, and was largely gone after that war, clinging on only in a few places, most notably in the Islamic world. In this sense, class, like race and gender, has lost much of its formal, and even a lot of its informal, influence as a status hierarchy.

That said, there are other ways in which class plays into GIS. There have been attempts by some communist states, and by Marxist intellectuals more generally, to elevate the status of both the proletariat and, for Maoists, the peasantry in GIS in the twentieth century. One of the bizarre features of Mao's Cultural Revolution was the way in which class status classified in terms of birth generated a major split in the Red Guards between those from good class backgrounds (e.g., the children of Party cadres) and those from bad, incorrect class backgrounds (the children of landlords or the bourgeoisie). The former tended to defend the Party, the latter to attack it (Gray, 2002: 334–44). Armstrong (1993: ch. 4) has explored class in relation to the Bolshevik revolution in Russia, and Schouenborg (2012: 141–5) has focused on the whole communist bloc in Eastern Europe as a regional international society during the Cold War. The latter two authors document the ultimately failed attempt to liberate the transnational proletariat from its subordinate status role in GIS. Of immediate interest in this connection today is that communist China appears to have given up on this mission too and is now promoting some form of capitalism domestically and internationally, as well as embracing the more traditional role of being a great power.

Perhaps the main element of class hierarchy still in play is to be found in the economic management of the great powers, and by extension the G20, which makes it abundantly clear that a club or class of capital-rich states are on top. The class distinction implied here is perhaps not as clear-cut as the traditional Marxist one between the proletariat of workers and the capital-owning bourgeoisie, or that between the periphery producers and core consumers of primary resources in world-systems theory. But differentiated economic capability certainly turned into a recognized privileged status in terms of positions within the IGOs and regimes that manage the global economy. This hierarchy is perhaps most clearly expressed in world-systems theory (Wallerstein, 1974; 2004) and other approaches focusing on core–periphery economic relations (Galtung, 1971). These mainly informal, but sometimes formal, privileges are inextricably linked to the material capabilities that help define gradations of state power (element 1 of the HPM) and the capacity of NSAs such as transnational firms to have a say in state affairs (element 2 of the HPM). Since class analysis has largely faded out of the study of IR, whether this phenomenon is best thought of as a general status role or simply a combined manifestation of capabilities in the other two elements is an interesting analytical question.

Religion as a source of status hierarchy works differently from race, gender or class. If we understand religion to be based on belief in a specific set of stories and rituals, then it automatically creates insiders (those who share a belief) and outsiders (those who don't). There is a strong tendency for the insider/outsider structure to morph into a status hierarchy where insiders see themselves as being superior to outsiders. This is most obvious where the members of a religion see themselves as a chosen people of some sort. In premodern times, there were strong links between civilization and religion, with each religious core seeing itself as central and superior, whether Christendom, the Islamic Umma, the Hindu world or the Confucian world. For a time, Christianity had the status advantage of being associated with dominant Western power. But while religion can and does create status hierarchies, this no longer works on a global scale in relation to GIS. The post-1945 shift against empire and human inequality has also affected religion and to some extent has enforced a norm of tolerance and mutual respect in place of competition for central status. There are, of course, some local exceptions to this, as well as a worrying imperial tendency in some of the extremist fringes of Islam. But in general, religion, like race, gender and class, has largely lost its formal capacity to sustain formal hierarchies of privilege.

To sum up, we have thus elaborated the three elements of the HPM and discussed how they intersect. The next step is to explore the static and dynamic stories about GIS that they engender and to expand on the horizontal/informal and vertical/formal dimensions of privilege as well. In doing this, we will pay attention to how the different elements of the model can coalesce (and reinforce one another), move in opposite directions and gradually increase or diminish in force. Furthermore, we will be on the lookout for principles that can help us determine whether GIS is getting weaker or stronger.

Application of the HPM

The snapshot picture today is one where privilege endures in multiple ways, both formal and informal and both within and between the three domains. Perhaps the most surprising aspect of this is that empire seems to be back as a practice, albeit without the legitimacy within GIS that it once enjoyed. Amongst the great powers, the most obvious examples are Russia and China, which, as noted previously, seem to be thinking – and where they can get away with it, acting – like empires. Russia's annexation of Crimea in 2014 and China's ongoing land grabs and reclamations in the South China Sea are the lead examples, and the competition between the two in Central Asia has much of the feel of rival suzerainties competing for spheres of influence. The US's temporary occupation and direct control of Iraq and Afghanistan in the early 2000s also had an imperial feel about it, albeit without a true empire's intent to occupy permanently. A few smaller states also display imperial mindsets and practices. The most obvious example here is Israel, whose practice of expanding settlements aims at permanent occupation of contested land. Saddam Hussein's attempts to seize Kuwait and parts of Iran also had the appearance of an imperial project, and the same might be said of the attempt of so-called Islamic State to create a new caliphate. All of these mindsets develop and practices take place against the grain of GIS's institutions of sovereign equality, nonintervention and the sanctity of existing borders, and struggle against the illegitimacy of claiming ownership of territory seized by force (Fazal, 2007). They are both demonstrations that imperial thinking still has legitimacy within some societies and are exercises in what can still be achieved by the ruthless use of force.

It can also be argued (e.g., Keal, 2003) that the domestic practices of some states look like those of empires colonizing peoples who happen to be caught inside their national boundaries. Pakistan (in Baluchistan), China (in Xinjiang and Tibet) and Indonesia (in various of its islands) all adopt the practice of moving majority populations (respectively Punjabis, Han and Javanese) as settlers into minority areas in order to change the ethnic composition of the population. Israel might also be understood in this way. Although redolent of long-ago imperial mindsets and practices, these countries can and do argue that their behaviour falls within their domestic rights as sovereign states and are nothing to do with empire in an international sense, and therefore no business of GIS.

Much less surprising is the continuity in the formal privileges of great powers. The main secondary institution in GIS, the UN, is still built around great power privilege in security management and, through the Security Council's ever-expanding definition of threats, management of everything from the environment to human and gender rights. Moreover, the Non-Proliferation Treaty (NPT) guarantees the P5 a monopoly on the legitimate possession of nuclear weapons, at least in law (Walker, 2012: 5–6). There is also the privilege of some states, including the great powers, in economic management, both formally in their positions in the IMF and the World Bank, and less formally in IGOs such as the G20. However, there are at the same time mounting challenges to these privileges from subordinate actors across the three elements of the HPM. The ongoing debate about reform of the UN Security Council is a case in point. Some interventions in this debate aim at justifying the expansion of the great power club so that it more accurately reflects the actual distribution of material power in the GIS of the twenty-first century. These are voices arguing for permanent or semipermanent seats to be offered to, for example, Brazil, Germany, India and Japan. But there are also interventions that envisage a greater role for the democratic principle of majority rule by limiting the potential use of the veto. And then there are those who champion another democratic principle, that of appropriate representation. This principle is used to construct arguments for a more balanced regional representation or for seats specially reserved for some of the many small states in GIS (Pouliot, 2014). These democratizing arguments seemingly chip away at the idea of great power privilege.

Extending this discussion of the UN to global governance more broadly, Cui and Buzan (2016: 208) argue that the academic literature on global governance (GG) has generally viewed great power management (GPM) more as a problem than a solution. The literature has celebrated the presumed 'power shift' (Mathews, 1997) to non-state actors (NGOs, IGOs, TNCs, etc.) and these actors' influence on world politics, whether benign or malign. Although it is exceedingly difficult to assess these claims regarding the relative power standing of NSAs vis-à-vis states (and it is not for lack of trying in the literature), it seems indisputable that NSAs have become increasingly involved not just in international decision-making (as lobbies and as providers of information, interpretation and resources) but also in the implementation of policy. This greater engagement combines with the strong growth in the number of NGOs in the post–Cold War era. However, under international law, article 71 of the UN charter functions as 'the de facto charter for NGO activities', and ascribes them a less-than-privileged consultative role (Charnovitz, 2006: 357). They have not been granted independent political standing as such. Other (regional) international organizations such as the African Union and the Organization of American States follow this interpretation of the status of NGOs (Charnovitz, 2006: 359). Similarly, while IGOs can have independent actor qualities (Barnett and Finnemore, 1999), they still serve at the behest of states under international law. TNCs might wield considerable power, especially over weaker states, but they are still formally subordinate to the states-system.

The increasing involvement of NSAs in international decision-making is no doubt an important development with further potential for change, but at the moment it does not seem to have fundamentally upset the formal state-based order and the privileged position of the great powers in law and in practice. Two partial exceptions to this, as already previously noted, are the International Criminal Court and the European Court of Human Rights. However, the standing of the former is contested by the United States (see Ralph, 2007), and it is indeed hard (but not impossible) to imagine that the court would pursue prosecution of nationals of those great powers who have ratified the Rome Statute. The court's activities do appear to be targeted predominantly at weak states in Africa, which has led to en masse withdrawal being openly debated in the African Union. Thus, while NSAs might well have informal privileges at various points, they have little in the way of formal hierarchical standing and mainly have to operate as subordinates with the.

Focusing on element 3 of our model (race, gender, class and religion), the hierarchy inherent in great power management has also come under critique from this angle. For example, a putative 'new' member of the great power club, India, has accused the 'old' great powers of perpetuating a 'nuclear apartheid' system through the NPT (Ayoob, 2010: 137). Pakistan, North Korea and Iran appear to share similar misgivings, notwithstanding the latter's recent acceptance, under conditions of considerable coercion, of an international agreement concerning its nuclear programme. In this form, as well as in postcolonial and core–periphery politics generally, racial contestation of more general political, economic and cultural hierarchy is far from absent from contemporary GIS. But whereas race differentiation might once have been the main issue, since decolonization and the shift to a principle of human equality, race is now more just an associated feature correlated with dissatisfactions over the unequal distribution of wealth and power. The shift to a norm of human equality has been extremely important to this change, and it is worth emphasizing that human equality, like inequality before it, is now both formal and largely sustained by belief.

Gender and sexual rights are perhaps now more important than race as a source of tension in GIS. The issue is redolent with SoC politics and appears to have reinforced existing core–periphery hierarchies to some extent. Much of Africa, the Middle East and Russia remains highly resistant to the opening up of gender rights and recognitions. A prominent recent example was the sanctioning of Uganda following its decision to enact severe penalties for homosexuality in 2014 (the law was later ruled invalid by the constitutional court). This led to widespread international critique of the country, and a pause in, and review of, different aid programmes by certain Western states. In this way, the law brought up the issue of what it means to be 'good citizen' in GIS and what counts as civilized behaviour, the old 'standard of civilization' question (see also

Onapajo and Isike, 2016, on normative contestation over this issue). However, LGBT rights also feature prominently within the domestic politics of core states (the United States) and in divisions between Eastern and Western Europe in the EU.

Like racial hierarchies and practices, gender ones certainly still exist in many, perhaps most, countries, generally informally, but in some places formally, most notably in the Islamic world. But they are no longer legitimated by GIS in any 'standard of civilization', and female heads of state and government are becoming common. Religion has local hierarchical effects, and some states (e.g., Iran and Saudi Arabia), political parties (the BJP in India, AK in Turkey, Komeito in Japan) and NSAs (e.g., Islamic State, Al Qaeda and their many offshoots) accord it a kind of political primacy. The individual and collective right to religion is generally supported in human rights. But there is no global sense in which religion creates a position of privilege, either formal or informal.

The picture is rather different when we turn our attention to class. It appears to be mainly a nonissue in GIS. Despite the disastrous human consequences of the 2008 financial crisis, most states, even communist China, still embrace the market internationally, and domestically maintain different versions of capitalist economic regimes with all that that structure implies for class and class relations (Buzan and Lawson, 2014b). There is presently no class-based alternative with significant political backing from the global have-nots to the economic management performed by the G20. At most, resistance takes the form of the limited concessions that the developing countries have sought to wrest from the developed countries in the stalled Doha trade negotiations that were initiated back in 2001. This, of course, means that economic inequality is perpetuated, domestically and internationally. In that sense, real horizontal and vertical privileges endure. These privileges are contested by the antiglobalization movement, sometimes hotly, but this contestation is not primarily about class in the way it would have been when Marxism was a strong political force. What is mainly at issue now is not so much class as jobs and a fairer sharing of the spoils of capitalism. That said, economic capabilities, using the crude measure of GDP, have shifted relatively from the Western core to the non-Western periphery in the post–Cold War era, and this shift is sustaining different states' claims to being emerging powers. To that extent, some international 'class', or core–periphery, privileges are being eroded, while inequality within states has tended to increase. Whether emerging powers can maintain their growth trajectories is an open question (consider, for example, the economic slowdowns in Brazil and South

Africa and the wild stock market fluctuations in China).[2] But given slow growth in the old core, the gap is still closing.

The overall picture from this snapshot is that contemporary GIS displays relatively little formal privilege, but quite a lot of informal hierarchical and privileged practice. The main exceptions to this rule are the specific, ongoing formal privileges of great powers, and the general privileging of states over NSAs, both of which remain deeply institutionalized within GIS. General status classifications of race, gender, class and religion do not in themselves generate legitimate privilege in GIS (though they may locally) but are still effectively deployed to challenge the privileges of core states, elites and great powers.

What happens if we switch to the dynamic perspective? Have the hierarchical and core–periphery characteristics of GIS become more or less pronounced over time? One way to get a quick sense of the dynamics of privilege in GIS is to compare the preceding snapshot with the situation during the nineteenth century, and to do so in terms of the three general forms of hierarchy within GIS.

In terms of the first form of the HPM, hierarchies amongst states, the main impression over the last three centuries is of a rather dramatic shrinkage of formal hierarchy, with a messier picture on the informal side. The extraordinary rise of European material and ideational power in the nineteenth century (Buzan and Lawson, 2015a) was characterized by the establishment of formal hierarchies of divided sovereignty under empire, and core–periphery economic relations, with colonialism playing a key role in both. This structure lasted until after the Second World War, supported more or less formally by 'scientific' racism, and up to a point by the semiformal primacy of Christianity, though colonialism was also opposed on religious and class grounds. The period since 1945 has been characterized by the breakup of the institution of colonialism and the formal privileges associated with it. This quintessentially hierarchical institution of international society came under increasing attack, culminating with the UN General Assembly resolution on the granting of independence to colonial countries and peoples in 1960, and the institution can today be judged as obsolete (Holsti, 2004: ch. 8). There are still several existing formal hierarchies in anarchy, to use Donnelly's (2006) phrase, but with the ending of colonialism, the arguably most significant one was removed, giving way to a universalization of sovereign equality (Buzan, 2017). Despite a very considerable degree of political and legal equalization, the core–periphery economic structure stayed

---

[2] We are referring to developments in the first half of 2016.

substantially in place, though with much less formal standing than under colonialism. Even this began to erode with the economic rise of China, India and 'the rest' from the 1990s. Moreover, informal privileges have mostly replaced formal privileges in the interactions between weak and strong states (that is, if we exclude the formal privileges of great powers in different IGOs).

The ending of colonialism seemed to spell the end of racism's prominent role in GIS. Our argument is not that racism disappeared – we have on the contrary stressed its enduring presence in GIS in the preceding paragraphs – but that it became largely unimportant in itself as a principle of hierarchical legitimacy, both in terms of defining what it meant to be a state and in terms of state conduct in GIS. One of the legacies of these developments, however, is the substantial informal hierarchies that are expressed in GIS's involvement in postcolonial weak states (Jackson, 1990) and its attempt to help those individuals categorized as 'vulnerable' (Clark, 2013). Here we are referring to the whole spectrum of activities associated with the development agenda, which replaced the colonial obligation to bring colonized peoples up to the 'standard of civilization'. The development agenda covers the spectrum of what are still essentially core–periphery relationships from relief aid and the funding of basic services to the promotion of good governance and the imposing of economic conditionalities in return for loans or debt forgiveness. Up to a point, these can be deemed instances of neocolonialism and are perhaps some of the most important contemporary core–periphery relations in GIS. Yet as we have noted, such policies are now also being pursued in intra-European relations, between supposedly developed states. Broadly speaking, based on this dynamic story, we will argue that the formal inequality of colonialism has declined overall, but that different forms of informal hierarchy endure in core–periphery relations and the postcolonial institution of development.

An interesting question in this respect is the degree of GIS consensus on these informal practices. Initially, one might be tempted to conclude that consensus is largely absent. Thinking about humanitarian intervention in support of human rights and democracy, or the perhaps less invasive practices of economic and 'good governance' conditionalities, the impression one gets is that these informal hierarchies are fundamentally contested, pitting Western states against notably Russia and China.[3] However, picking up a metaphor from Buzan and Lawson (2014b), it at the same time seems as if the 'ideological bandwidth' in GIS has

---

[3] We recognize that these are to an extent also formal hierarchies in that they partly express the legalized hegemony of the great powers in the UN.

narrowed considerably compared with the Cold War and earlier eras. There may be significant differences of opinion between authoritarian and democratic states in contemporary GIS, but they are not of the same order of magnitude as that between communist and capitalist states before 1989 or between dynastic and republican states in the nineteenth century. It is probably going too far to term the present disagreements in GIS the narcissism of small differences, but the salient point is that there seems to be more basic consensus today about the rules of the game of GIS amongst states than there was in the past. Even China and Russia, for example, support R2P in principle and have voted for its application in a series of resolutions in the UN Security Council. Moreover, they do not challenge the basic right of democracies to be democracies: democracies are not portrayed as inherently evil (although some recent rhetoric comes close, and former US president George W. Bush certainly did not shy away from using such language with reference to some authoritarian states).

Within the state-to-state story, the one big element of formal privilege that has remained is the 'legalized hegemony' of the great powers, though even this has been subject to subtle change. Great power management has endured, but the membership of this club has slowly but surely moved beyond the West. First Japan and much later China gained entry into the great power club, and now India is increasingly counted as a member too, making the club ever less white and Western. This is in line with Buzan and Lawson's (2015a) idea of a shift from (West-)centred to decentred globalism (see also Kupchan, 2012; Acharya, 2014; Womack, 2014).

In terms of the second form of the HPM, the hierarchy between states and non-state actors, the dynamics move in the opposite direction, with states consolidating their formal privilege over NSAs. During the eighteenth and nineteenth centuries, European states had to deal with a host of very different non-European polities, sometimes on equal terms. Furthermore, European states existed in a symbiosis with some very powerful European non-state political actors such as the Dutch and British East India companies (see Stern, 2011; Phillips and Sharman, 2015) or King Leopold's Congo Free State. However, during the nineteenth century, the emergence of much more powerful and effective modern states, and the shift from natural to positive law, strengthened the relative position of states. By the early twentieth century, states were clearly the dominant power brokers in GIS and were recognized as such both in practice and in international law. The recent inroads made by various types of NSA are, as previously noted, still mainly informal, and despite the great growth in all types of NSAs, from TNCs to INGOs, they still remain formally subordinate to states. On this basis, and recognizing that Spruyt's (1994) well-known argument was mainly aimed at a previous era of history, one can nevertheless still say that the sovereign state is presently, at least in formal terms, a good distance ahead of its closest competitors.

Yet while powerful corporations have not challenged states' formal sovereign rights, they can both manipulate states, and evade or subvert state regulation and taxation. This underpins the suspicion of some anti-globalizationists that big global capital is, in effect, running a hollowed-out state system in its own interest, and they can point to a long list of corporate tax avoidance and unrepentant bailed-out bankers. While such a proposition is arguable, it is plausible enough not only to be politically effective but also to raise interesting questions about the relative importance of formal and informal privilege. The antiglobalization view paints a picture not unlike that of late nineteenth-century Qing China. The formal sovereignty of the Chinese government was hollowed out by foreign powers who (except for Japan and Russia) wanted to keep a Chinese government in place to save themselves the trouble and expense of having to rule China. On this basis, it is possible to imagine scenarios in which informal hierarchy becomes more powerful and important than the formal arrangements. Such arrangements are quite normal in East Asian politics, where a de facto leader such as Deng Xiaoping ruled without holding the formal offices of power.

The story between states and individuals goes somewhat in the opposite direction. Until the nineteenth century, individuals were mainly subjects, with dynastic polities having relatively few rights against their rulers. As nationalism and popular sovereignty pushed dynasticism aside during the nineteenth century, absolutist states increasingly gave way to nation-states, and people moved from being subjects to being citizens. Where nation-states became democracies, citizens accumulated formal rights, although this was much less the case where modernity generated fascist or communist totalitarianisms. The delegitimation of racism and empire and the shift to a norm of human equality after 1945 underpinned the growth of human rights. Some views of human rights put individuals in a position of moral, and up to a point legal, superiority over states, but in practice human rights are largely mediated, interpreted and controlled by states. Thus, although states still retain a privileged position over individuals, it is much less extreme than before, with perhaps a slow and highly unevenly distributed tendency for the status of individuals to be increasing against the state.

In terms of the third form of the HPM, race, gender, class and religion mainly appear to have become less globally important as formal status markers. As already argued, the ending of colonialism and the shift to a formal, belief-based norm of human equality removed any formal legitimacy for racial privilege, though not of course a certain amount of racist practice. The formal exclusion of women from the politics of 'civilized' countries has ended, though again there is still significant informal discrimination in practice, and sexual identities and rights remain hotly contested in many countries. Compared even to the nineteenth century, when dynastic rule and aristocratic privilege were still common, class today confers no formal privilege in GIS and has largely been superseded by concerns about inequality. Whatever primacy Christianity might once have had largely disappeared with decolonization. While formal elements of all of these types of privilege can still be found locally, they no longer operate globally in international society.

Principles for Thinking about Strengthening or Weakening of GIS

That takes us to the discussion of the principles that can be used to think about whether GIS is getting stronger or weaker. Because of the multiple forms that privilege and hierarchy can take within the HPM, this model is unusually complicated. It covers not only privileges and hierarchies amongst states, but also between states and NSAs, and status roles and conditions embedded more broadly in society. In all three forms, there is the issue of whether the privilege is formal or informal. There is also the issue of overlap in the three forms. While they are easily distinguishable in principle, in practice they often combine. As noted in the preceding discussion, for example, empire was strongly entwined with racism and class. Core–periphery structures likewise informally empowered a variety of NSAs against weak states in the periphery. This complexity in the HPM makes it inherently tricky to assess strengthening and weakening because both might be going on at the same time.

We need first to clear the decks by addressing a normative issue that potentially affects the HPM as a whole. The very principle of privilege, in public and academic discourses about politics and IR, is often treated as a fundamental problem that necessarily undermines societal cohesion. We are used to normatively privileging the principle of equality for both people and states. Yet this seemingly obvious conclusion appears to be contradicted by both historical and contemporary experience. Arguably, the history of human society on this planet is one of persistent and stable privilege where some significant degree of hierarchy is the norm (Watson, 1992). Many, if not most, societies before the eighteenth century, especially dynastic ones, celebrated privilege in its different forms and were far from exposed to revolutionary upheaval each and every year. Indeed, where privilege established legitimacy in the minds of those subject to it, as with innumerable cases of dynastic rule and religious hierarchy down the millennia of human history, this may have been the very reason why such societies remained stable. (With this, we are suggesting that longevity is evidence of societal strength but not a direct criterion for measuring it. If the latter were the case, we would only be able to judge strength or weakness retrospectively.) It is no accident that dynasticism and empire worked so well together for so long until their legitimacy was torn down by nationalism. Anyone doubting this need only to visit the Vasa Museum in Stockholm to see how a seventeenth-century Swedish king thought it appropriate to adorn the bowsprit of his new flagship with statues of Roman emperors. This was a thousand years after the fall of Rome and in a part of Europe that was never under Roman rule. The British similarly celebrate such Roman ruins as remain in their country as evidence that they were part of the civilized world from an early time.

Modern Western societies, which are supposed to be standard-bearers of equality, still incorporate formal privilege in seemingly unproblematic combinations with equality, what we will term privilege–equality nexuses. For example, representative democracy is based on the idea of one person, one vote. This is equality. However, once the votes have been counted, the electorate finds it completely normal and acceptable to convert those votes into different hierarchical systems of government, with a prime minister or president at the top. One can extend this example to any number of contemporary organizations in modern societies, from joint stock companies to professional associations. Citizens generally consider this mixing of equality with privilege unproblematic, and there does not seem to be much to suggest that it is ipso facto a sign of a weakening society. A good case can be made that in the Confucian societies of Northeast Asia, hierarchy is the dominant way of thinking about both domestic social and political order and international relations (Buzan, 2018b). If we apply these conclusions to the global arena, then privilege is in the same way not a sure sign of a weakening GIS. Weakening only occurs under two conditions: first, when principles of equality are actively mobilized to mount a revolutionary challenge to principles of privilege, implying fragmentation of GIS, or the other way around; and second, when there is a contest for legitimacy between different forms of, or claimants to, privilege, again implying fragmentation. It could be argued, for example, that from the 1890s to 1945, the rivalry and war between Japan and China were not about the basic ordering principle in East Asia. Both believed in a hierarchical tribute system but disagreed as to which one of them should be at the core of that system. States can accept sovereign equality for some purposes while at the same time accepting great power privileges for others. And this can make for a strong and stable GIS. Whether privilege, and its specific combinations with equality, is contested thus appears to be one approach to thinking about the potential weakening of GIS. It is not privilege/hierarchy itself that is necessarily problematic, only whether its legitimacy is strongly contested, whether in principle or by an alternative provider, leading to fragmentation.

Contestation over principle points us in the direction of an auxiliary principle for thinking about weakening and strengthening: does contestation take the form of a fundamental challenge, or does it merely refer to certain minor elements of a given privilege–equality nexus? This principle is similar in logic to the one in the previous chapter concerning whether challenges are to a primary institution's core meaning or merely to its associated ideas. We are in other words dealing with degrees or levels of contestation. For example, when the newly independent United States argued that it would seek a divorce from European international society's institutions of great power management and the balance of power (Schouenborg, 2012: 136), it was engaged in fundamental revolutionary contestation, although one that did not last. By contrast, China and Russia are not fundamentally challenging R2P but rather contesting some of the (admittedly important) details of the doctrine's practical application. Whether the imperial practices of China and Russia are challenging the principles of sovereign equality and nonintervention is as yet unclear. Both countries talk a strong line supporting sovereign equality and nonintervention while violating it in practice.

A third principle follows closely on the heels of this and also points back to the previous chapter. The principle is based on the idea that fragmentation in meaning can lead to fragmentation in the consensus surrounding privilege–equality nexuses. Within the HPM, this points to whether the mode of privilege is formal or informal. Our hypothesis here is that informality breeds ambiguity and in turn conflicts over interpretation. If we see increasing informality, we are likely to experience increasing contestation. And precisely the rise of informal privileges both in state-to-state and NSA–state relations was one of the things we emphasized in the preceding dynamic story (though there were also signs of formalization in some areas such as human equality). Take, for example, the informal privilege expressed in a developed state advising a weak postcolonial state on good governance. This may result in growing conflicts over privilege–equality nexuses. To be sure, informality need not always be a problem. The UK political system, for example, thrives on informality, as it is not based on a unified written constitution. However, it appears to be a system that is characterized by strong and semifixed informal rules. That is, there is a fairly solid consensus about how the system is supposed to work. There is also the possibility that formalization may be used as a strategy to compensate for the perceived weakness of a given social structure. One can easily point to a host of examples where coup-makers or revolutionaries have tried to put a legal stamp of approval on their actions *post facto*. In these cases, formalization is indeed a sign of weakness. However, we will still maintain that the overall hypothesis that informality, other things being equal, breeds ambiguity and hence leads to fragmentation, is valid.

Lastly, there is the principle revolving around binding forces: is privilege held in place predominantly by belief, calculation or coercion? As in previous chapters, we assume that a belief-based social structure is the stronger one. In the context of privilege, that would mean that great power management or, to take the extreme case, a racial apartheid GIS accepted based on belief should be deemed strong. Assessing the strength or weakness of an international society is not the same as assessing its moral worth. The former is a structural theory issue, while the latter is a normative one that will vary according to the beliefs of the assessor. Thus, from our (structural theory) point of view, if the subordinate actor believes in the legitimacy of his or her own subordination, then it does not matter whether this is caused by 'false consciousness' or one of the other reasons pointed to by emancipatory political theorists. If slaves accept that the master–slave principle is a legitimate social order, then that order is strong. By contrast, a social order characterized by calculation and a large measure of coercion would imply a missing consensus on privilege and thus a social order ripe for revolutionary challenge. As the previously discussed example of the formal, belief-based norm of human equality suggests, the normative and the structural are not always in opposition.

From this discussion, we can extract four points from the HPM about whether GIS is getting stronger or weaker:

- Fundamental contestation of privilege–equality nexuses will weaken GIS strongly.
- Contestation about either the associated ideas of privilege–equality nexuses or rivalries about who exercises an accepted privilege will weaken GIS but less strongly.
- Both of these types of weakening will be more likely when privileges and hierarchies are more informal than formal.
- Both of these types of weakening will be more likely when privilege–equality nexuses are sustained by coercion and calculation more than by belief.

2 Strengths and Weaknesses of the Model

Our next task is to again assess the strengths and weaknesses of the HPM through the usual three questions:

- How well does it capture the actual nature of the units?
- How well does it capture the actual nature of the structure?
- How well does it capture the binding forces?

Capturing the Units

As with the model in the previous chapter, the HPM directs our attention to some of the complexities of GIS as they manifest with respect to units. To that extent, the model easily aligns with traditional English School epistemic goals. Interestingly, however, the model also takes us quite close to neorealism's parsimonious focus on great powers. From the perspective of the HPM, the great powers and great power management stand out as one of the important privileged positions in contemporary GIS. It is, nevertheless, a quite different understanding of great powers that comes out of the HPM as compared with neorealism. Neorealism looks exclusively to material capabilities to determine inclusion within this category, whereas the HPM emphasizes the social recognition underpinning privilege. This does not mean that material capabilities are irrelevant, but that they are always filtered through a process of social negotiation before they transform into positions of privilege. This can, for example, result in actors that are nominally weak (based on material capabilities) gaining recognition as moral or normative great powers or even superpowers. It has to be stressed, though, that social recognition is more than an intervening variable between capabilities and positions of privilege. Social recognition fundamentally shapes what meaning we give to the material aspects of social life and has real consequence for world politics.

This thus yields an understanding of GIS that highlights multiple, graded and overlapping privileges. Some are closely tied to the social status role of being a state. Amongst the latter, we can include all the different status roles that are premised on interpretations of power: weak power, small power, middle power, great power, superpower, etc. We can moreover include all those status roles that emphasize a state's progressive or regressive standing as viewed from the prevailing SoC. Arguably, today, examples from the liberal progressive end of the spectrum are democratic states, developmental states, welfare states, gender-conscious states and so on. And each of the latter can arguably be combined with the former, so that we may end up with a gender super-power such as Norway. This is a clear example of an overlap between elements 1 and 3 of the HPM: privilege based on what you are combined with gender as a general status role. Turning from positive to negative evaluations of status, you can have gender-rogue states such as Uganda, or at the other end of the (social) power spectrum Bull's (1980) 'great irresponsibles'.

Where the HPM really shines, however, is with respect to non-state actors and individuals. One can argue that the very act of speaking about an international society in the first place is premised on accepting the historically contingent privileging of states in global social relations. Make no mistake, the privileged position of states today is real in that it is generally accepted (sometimes tacitly and unknowingly) by the great majority of individuals on this planet. But it is at the same time a historically contingent social order, and the HPM allows us to address how it emerged and how it is maybe in the process of being challenged. The model captures all those political units that were excluded from, and thus hierarchically subordinated to, GIS as it expanded across the globe. Here we are thinking about the 'tribes' and 'kingdoms' of Africa, the Aboriginals in Australia, the indigenous 'nations' in North America and a whole range of other polities. The model moreover does well at captur-ing the different units aspiring to formal state status (for example, Soma-liland, Kurdistan, Western Sahara and Kosovo). These units are, of course, subordinated to international society as such, but they are often also implicated in more direct hierarchical relationships with specific sponsor states (for example, Transnistria and Russia, and Northern Cyprus and Turkey).

The exclusion of unwelcome polities and the inclusion of aspiring states are forms of privileging basically aligned with the state-based order and does not seem to pose a direct challenge to it. That, by contrast, is the potential consequence of the increasing involvement of non-state actors such as NGOs, IGOs and TNCs. As we have repeat-edly stressed, these actors are still formally subordinate to states today, but given their increasingly strong informal strengths, that may change in the future, not least as their growing informal power destabilizes the prevailing privilege–equality nexus. Through almost any IR theoretical lens, their formal inclusion in GIS as actors with equal legal standing vis-à-vis states would be a momentous political change, significantly extending the pluralism of GIS. It would at the same time, though, most likely be accompanied by novel patterns of privilege between the different actors, regardless of their equal legal standing – that is, if history is any guide. To that extent, it is indeed difficult to imagine

Buzan's (2004a: xviii, 159–60) world society scenario: a situation where states, individuals and non-state actors are in play together and none of the three dominate the other two. Dominance will probably always endure, but it will be channelled through different privilege–equality nexuses. An interesting perspective on this is that a potential lessening of today's sharp contrast between state and non-state may in turn push the whole question of units into the background of GIS, and forefront general status roles such as race, gender, religion and class. This scenario would be based on a fairly straightforward domestic analogy: in domestic societies, during normal times, we do not tend to discuss the status of different corporate entities but are instead preoccupied with the general status roles captured by element 3 of the HPM. For example, we do not debate the legal standing of corporate entities such as parliament or unions, but rather class- and gender-relevant issues such as austerity and gay marriage. To use another analogy, during normal times we are less concerned with how the game is constituted and more concerned with how it is played and the specific outcomes for different groups and individuals.

Capturing the Structure

On a macro scale, what the HPM reveals clearly is the core–periphery structure of privilege and hierarchy that is largely occluded by both the LUM and the RSM. This structure has been durable for at least two centuries. During that time, it has shifted from being highly formalized during the colonial era to being mainly informal, but nonetheless highly effective, after decolonization. As we write, the rise of the rest and the relative decline of the West seem to be eroding the core–periphery structure. The core is expanding, and the periphery shrinking, meaning that international relations are increasingly driven by dynamics typical of the core, and less so by the dynamics of a core–periphery structure (Buzan and Lawson, 2015a: 269–81). At the same time, as we have argued, hierarchy is becoming less formal and more informal, and perhaps less belief based and more resting on calculation. What the HPM exposes here is a long crisis of legitimacy for the core–periphery structure of privilege. This crisis, now looking to be in its terminal phase, has massive implications for how we think about the strength or weakness of GIS. This is discussed in more detail in Chapter 7.

More specifically, privilege appears to be a feature of all known primary institutions. This is obvious when we are talking about institutions such as great power management and colonialism that are based on fundamental inequality between actors. Yet it also, somewhat counterintuitively, applies to an institution such as human rights. The signs of this are the heated debates about what it means to be human, what rights follow from this and the extent to which either of the former can be said to be universal (Donnelly, 2007). This has historically led to privileged and unprivileged actors pushing different understandings of human rights, such as the right to private property versus the right to housing (Hoover, 2015). Moreover, different human rights standards have been used to impose a privileged interpretation of what it means to be civilized, and indeed to justify colonial practices in the past and in the present (Donnelly, 1998). The HPM helps us get a handle on this and allows us to connect these dimensions of primary institutions to the units of GIS and the broader debates about general status roles in GIS and in domestic societies.

Going further, one might even consider the relationship between individual primary institutions as one of privilege. Buzan (2004a: 182–6), for example, has argued for a 'nested hierarchy' understanding, with 'master' and 'derivative' institutions. To provide an illustration, in this scheme nonintervention is a derivative institution of the master institution of sovereignty, and alliances a derivative institution of the master institution of the balance of power. Partly this seems to be a genealogy scheme of the sequence of emergence of the different primary institutions, but it can also be read as an assessment of the relative standing of individual primary institutions in GIS. There is, for instance, an ipso facto argument to made for considering sovereignty as more important for the overall functioning of GIS than, say, the market or nationalism. Lastly, there is the opportunity to connect this to primary institutions and associated practices that are tied to different non-state actors. An example here could be the emerging rights of corporations to sue sovereign states for infringements of investment treaties through international tribunals, putting government regulation under strain and subjecting states to multibillion dollar claims (Poulsen and Aisbett, 2013). A development along these lines would be a significant marker of a change in the formal balance between states and NSAs in GIS.

Pursuing the HPM perspective on the structure of GIS no doubt results in a quite complicated and unwieldy social assemblage. In this sense, it parallels the argument in Albert, Buzan and Zürn (2013: 228–45) that the contemporary international system is not dominated by any single type of differentiation but is a complex mix of segmentary, stratificatory and functional differentiation. Yet it importantly brings into focus the many facets that are missed when viewing GIS as a state-based, like-unit, sovereign equality order, as well as pointing us to past and current strains and future development trajectories.

Capturing the Binding Forces

As we have pointed out, Westerners, or perhaps more broadly those who favour liberal democracy over other political forms, are used to thinking about privilege as something to be naturally resisted. From this perspective, political, economic and social disparities are an affront, and a good amount of political theory is dedicated to the project of emancipating us from them. The equality ethos is strong in many modern societies. Buzan (2004a: 187) even designates 'equality of people' as a master institution of contemporary GIS. Yet, paradoxically, privilege and hierarchy are also accepted, indeed legitimate, features of many modern societies. Often this comes in the form of some of the aforementioned privilege–equality nexuses. But at the same time, we should not discount the purer instances of privilege. As previously noted, if the slave believes in his or her own subordination and considers it legitimate, then it is a belief-based social structure. This has certain implications for how we tell the traditional expansion story and for how we view the binding forces holding privilege in place in contemporary GIS.

The revisionist accounts of the expansion story (e.g., Keene, 2002; Keal, 2003; Suzuki, 2009; Pella, 2015a) have rightly stressed the large measure of coercion involved. Indeed, a prominent scholar, although not associated with the English School, has recently described the European overseas expansion from 1415 to 1914 as 'The Five Hundred Years' War' (Morris, 2014: loc. 3073). Yet that should not blind us to the fact that much of the European expansion over this long period was negotiated with local actors and only partly rested on elements of coercion (Suzuki, Zhang and Quirk, 2014). And even when we get to the late nineteenth century, the height of European power primacy, the expansion of GIS does not appear to have been an exclusively coerced affair. The technological and scientific advances on which Europe's power was based made Western civilization look superior in the eyes of many of the peoples subjected to its influence (Howard, 1984: 33; Watson, 1984: 31–2). No clearer example of this can be found than in the many detailed analyses of the nineteenth-century encounter between the West on the one hand, and China and Japan on the other. Both of these Asian societies were deeply torn between traditionalists, obsessed with preserving their own cultures against the revolutionary upheavals of modernity, and reformers, desperate to modernize their countries so as to give them the power to stave off Western imperialism (e.g., Jansen, 2000; Schell and Delury, 2013). Neither side doubted that the West had found a path that gave it profoundly superior access to wealth and power, especially the military power and its machinery that was so prominently on display. Yet neither side (barring a few extreme reformers) wanted their cultures to become mere copies of the West. Backed by the Europeans' spectacular machines and medicinal abilities, Western privilege therefore took on an air of legitimacy. Interestingly, as a result of their missions to study the West, the Japanese quickly learned that Western modernization was a recent development, and the gap therefore not as big or insurmountable as it might at first appear to be (Jansen, 2000: locs. 5364–5438).

The history of European colonization is littered with examples of the awe displayed by locals in different encounters with the 'white masters' and their knowledge and technology. It was the historic contribution of Japan to be the first to break the myth of white invincibility by beating Russia not just in a battle, but in a whole war fought in the modern way, with modern armies and navies. To be absolutely clear, this is not an apology for European colonial domination. It is only an observation about its partly belief-based underpinnings, and therefore about how this may, for a time, have produced a relatively stable social structure. As Philpott (2001) has noted, that structure did eventually succumb to revolutionary challenge. As the shock of Western superiority wore off, and the revolutions of modernity diffused, empowering a wider circle of states and peoples, so the legitimacy of Western privilege declined, leaving GIS in the troubled transition phase that it now occupies.

Moving forward in time, there are some similarities between the technological superiority that so impressed non-Europeans in the past and the esteem accruing to developed states today. It is hard not to notice that the different measures captured by the UN Human Development Index are the ones on which developed (and mainly Western) states do remarkably well: life expectancy, education and gross national income. This seems to confer upon these states a degree of at least informal privileged standing. Up to a point, many elites in developing countries appear to admire these states' achievements and want to emulate them. At a popular level, affluence makes these states look attractive and is a pull factor for immigration. Furthermore, economic acumen is at the end of the day what supports states' claims to being great powers. Yes, you need a big population, and you need to show potential for military greatness. But you will not get there before you have demonstrated economic greatness. This is the hurdle aspiring powers such as Brazil and India are currently facing. Behind all this, there seems to be a widely shared consensus across GIS that economic performance is a legitimate path to privilege. This argument comes with qualifications. The anticolonial struggle was partly about ending coercive economic privilege in the form of outright exploitation, and the legacy of the 1970s proposals for a New International Economic Order is still with us. However, the privileges born of economic performance do appear to be sustained by more than grudging and calculated acceptance. The ruling party in China has certainly noticed this and plays on it relentlessly to improve its standing within GIS. It is not so much that the principle that once underpinned Western privilege has changed, but more that the West now faces challengers to be the holder of that privilege.

Thus, there is more than coerced or calculated acceptance in play when we consider a range of primary institutions that define privilege in contemporary GIS. Sovereignty is widely accepted as a legitimate privileged position, putting states above NSAs and individuals. The same goes for nationalism. It very concretely puts the nation above minorities and foreigners. Even territory can be said to occupy a superordinate position in relation to air space, sea space, cyberspace and extraterrestrial space. Most people (elites and commoners), most of the time, appear to believe in the rightness of this. Viewed from this perspective, privilege is not a challenge for GIS. It is rather what largely holds this social structure together. Whether that is right or wrong in an ethical sense is a different question, and one that should be of primary concern to pluralists and solidarists.

3   Conclusions

The model in this chapter puts a spotlight on what can arguably be termed a collective taboo of sorts in GIS: privilege. The principle goes directly against the lauded ideals of sovereign equality (like-units), as well as the equality of peoples and individuals, and reminds us of our shared colonial past. Yet, like other taboos, this one only shrouds what we are already painstakingly aware of: the privileges of the great powers; the subordination of non-state polities and NSAs; and the enduring, if now mainly informal, role of various forms of human inequality. Furthermore, the model draws our attention to what for many must be an even more unsettling proposition, namely that privilege and hierarchy are constant fixtures of society, global and domestic. That seems to suggest that when it is held as legitimate, privilege is not a problem for society, nor a disintegrative element, but that it may, as proponents of hegemonic stability theory argue (Gilpin, 1981; 1987; Keohane, 1984), actually help hold the structure together.

Over the past two hundred years, there appears to have existed a relatively stable division of labour between an oligarchy of great powers, a wider society of sovereign 'patron' states and a range of subordinated 'client' NSAs and individuals. This social order has been subject to different upheavals. Bull (1984a: 220–3) captured the most significant ones with what he termed the five phases of the revolt against the West: the struggle for equal sovereignty, the anticolonial struggle, the struggle for racial equality, the struggle for economic justice and lastly the struggle for cultural autonomy. To these we may add the struggle against the racial supremacy projects of the Axis powers during the Second World War and the struggle between capitalists and communists during the Cold War. Both of the latter upheavals had the potential for fundamentally upsetting the prevailing order of privilege in GIS and instituting something fully new. However, like the Roman social order from which we borrow the concept of patronage, the order of privilege in GIS has proved rather resilient over time. Some of this resilience is probably due to tacit acceptance, simple inertia or path dependence. But as we have argued in this chapter, it may also be due to a significant amount of belief in the institutions sustaining this order and in the specific privilege–equality nexuses that are part of it.

Is this order of privilege presently weakening or strengthening? There seems to be a *prima facie* case to be made for weakening based on the principles elaborated in this chapter. Most pertinent is the waning of the core–periphery structure. More subtle is the growing informality and complexity of privileges that may lead to fragmentation and hence weakening. This could combine with some of the regional fragmentation observed in the previous chapter to produce ever more potent undercurrents of change. Another source of fragmentation may be the rise of non-Western states such as China to the position of great powers. As Kupchan (2014) has argued, this could result in them projecting alternative visions of hierarchical order onto the international scene based on their own domestic cultural, ideological and socioeconomic histories. Obviously, China has been a member of the great power club for some time now, without any fundamental challenges to the present order of privilege. However, the world is becoming more decentred with the redistribution of economic and military power, and the Western authors of the present order are in relative decline. Nevertheless, the formal principle of great power privilege still seems robust, surviving the shift from being a white/Western club to being a multicultural one. But the normative content of great power management may well change as the non-Western members grow relatively stronger. As Bukovansky et al. (2012) note, the merger of great power management and global governance will certainly change the style of great power privilege by diffusing 'special responsibilities' more widely through GIS. That diffusion may also, ironically, be the key to maintaining the legitimacy of great power management.

The HPM thus presents a rather complicated perspective on whether GIS is getting stronger or weaker. Privilege in itself looks to be a durable and often stabilizing feature of GIS. The form and content of that privilege are, however, changing significantly, and doing so in ways that may simultaneously both weaken and strengthen GIS.

6   The Functional Differentiation Model

Of our four models of international society, the functional differentiation model (FDM) is without doubt the one furthest removed from mainstream discussion in the ES. The like-units model (LUM) has been dominant since the beginning of the ES. The regional/subglobal model (RSM) and hierarchy-privilege model (HPM) were late developers but could be seen as implicit in some of the thinking of the classical ES and violated neither its basic state-centrism and rootedness in territoriality, nor its focus on segmentary and stratificatory differentiation. The FDM depends on a different type of differentiation, with quite radical consequences. On the unit level, functional differentiation separates modern states from premodern ones, and postmodern states from both. Whether functional differentiation strengthens or weakens the state is very much still a matter of argument, but it certainly changes it. On the system level, functional differentiation questions both state centrism and territoriality. It draws mainly from globalization and international political economy (IPE), the former not really emerging in IR until the 1990s, and IPE, as already noted, being a subject area notoriously avoided by the founding fathers of the ES. As noted in Chapter 1, the FDM opens up a view of international society where the territorial state system itself is being broken down, especially by the global market, but also by other transnational forces, social, political, legal and technological. In this model, postmodern states project their domestic functional differentiation out into GIS, in the process both changing its binding logic and differentiating, and in some ways liberating, the types of actor in play. This process quickly becomes a two-way street as a more functionally differentiated GIS feeds back into both leading-edge states and all of the others. The FDM thus opens up to the transnational and interhuman domains much more than the other three models.

As with the RSM and HPM models, the FDM involves a more elaborate differentiation than the like-units model. As befits its link to globalization, the FDM shares with the LUM the global-scale, universalist perspective: functional differentiation is a characteristic of systems. But like the RSM,

162

the FDM can be differentiated spatially (some regions might be more functionally differentiated than others), and like the HPM it can be seen in stratificatory terms (if functional differentiation correlates with power and authority). Functional differentiation might well be more developed within some regions (for example, the EU) or amongst some subglobal groupings (the OECD) than it is globally. And perhaps more important, some states are much more functionally differentiated internally than others, and it is these leading-edge states that initially project their domestic structure out into GIS. The FDM can, with some difficulty, be set out as a fully developed ideal-type model, but empirically it exists only in both synergy and tension within and alongside the other models.

Although Bull was part of the early ES's general neglect of IPE, one can find lines in his discussion that open up some space for it, particularly his idea of 'neo-mediaevalism' (Bull, 1977: 248–56, 264–76). Bull saw this as an alternative *to* the states-system, rather than a variation *within* it. That is perhaps true if one is thinking in terms of a pure idea-type model, less true if one is thinking about the hybrid empirical realities of the present day, where all forms of differentiation are present together, with none being dominant overall. Bull was not keen on the neo-mediaeval model. His assessment of the technological unification of the planet – that it was becoming a global city – was pretty good, but his strong state-centrism overwhelmed his ability to get a clear view of how NSAs of various kinds might come to be players in GIS. He grasped the interdependence between TNCs, but did not really get the importance of global capitalism as a powerful reshaper of GIS. Neo-mediaevalism thus opens some space for the FDM, but does not capture anything like the full significance of functional differentiation as an alternative type of social structure.

Because the FDM questions the position of the state in a way that the other models do not, we need to take a somewhat different view of primary institutions than we have done in the previous three chapters. As in those chapters, the state-centric framing remains relevant: it still matters which states accept, or don't, which primary institutions. But in this chapter, we need also to think differently about primary institutions, seeing them in addition as a form of differentiation that to some extent transcends the segmentary and stratificatory differentiations that underpin the other three models and in so doing opens up legitimate space within international society for actors other than states.

1   The Model

As just noted, the FDM in some senses comes out of IPE and globalization thinking in IR. But this link is at best partial. IPE and globalization are both mainly about interaction capacity, both physical and social, and the shrinking of time and space that has been accelerating since the nineteenth century (Buzan and Little, 2000: 80–4; Buzan and Lawson, 2015a: 67–96). They are also about the idea from classical liberal theory that the economic sector is a quasi-autonomous and analytically separable structure at the global level. They are therefore rooted in the implicit assumption that the economic and political sectors are functionally differentiated in GIS, and the explicit one that the rapid development of both interaction capacity (physical and social) and the global economy are forcing deterritorialization in a major way. These approaches question state-centric, territorialist models of IR, but neither of them makes much explicit use of differentiation theory, and neither goes far towards exploring the full implications of a functional differentiation model of GIS.

Functional differentiation is a big idea in sociology, but one that has so far had limited impact on IR theory (Donnelly, 2009; 2012; Buzan and Albert, 2010; Schouenborg, 2011; 2017; Albert, Buzan and Zürn, 2013). The two points of possible theoretical contact are both on the margins of the IR discipline: Luhmann's concept of world society, and the Stanford School's idea of world society, already mentioned in Chapter 3 in relation to the isomorphism of the LUM. Luhmann's approach represents a radical departure from both standard IR and sociological theory. Most normative IR theory, including the ES, has its roots in classical sociological theories that are in one way or another based on the idea that society is about various types of normative cohesion (shared norms, rules, institutions, values; common identities and/or cultures). Luhmann's concept seeks to replace a normative understanding of society with one based on processes and structures of communication. It sees a world of communicative function systems each defined by its own binary code: true/false for science, legal/illegal for law, profit/loss for the economy, winner/loser for sport and suchlike, and each serving as an environment for the others (WSRG, 1995: 8–9; Albert, 1999; Diez, 2000). Luhmann's idea of world society represents a pure form version of the FDM. But it does so in a way that is too alien from ES thinking to provide more than some useful concepts such as *function systems*, and a glimpse of what a full functionally differentiated GIS might look like (Buzan, 2004a: 70–2). The Stanford School approach is closer to ES ways of thinking (Navari, 2018). Its idea of a world society sees a GIS already composed of a variety of actors in addition to states (IGOs, TNCs, individuals) and that 'legitimated actorhood operates at several levels' (Meyer et al., 1997: 168). This includes a lot of functionally defined collective actors that within the context of GIS are 'entitled to promote functionally justified differentiation'

(Meyer et al., 1997: 171). Neither of these provides the strong link to mainstream IR theories that, for example, realism did for the LUM. But they do provide some clues about how to construct an FDM of GIS.

To tease out the key assumptions behind the FDM, it helps to start from the basics of functional differentiation as set out in Chapter 1. Both Luhmann and the Stanford School focus on the global system/society level, and although in different ways, both see an increasing division of GIS into legal, political, military, economic, scientific, religious and such-like distinct and specialized subsystems or sectors of activity, each with its own suite of distinctive institutions and actors. So the key to the FDM is that functional differentiation has begun to play a substantial role in defining the social structure of an international system/society, and that this brings a diverse set of actors from across the three domains into GIS. By so doing, and like the HPM, it raises hard questions about what membership in GIS means. In the LUM and the RSM, membership in GIS is basically about states. The FDM opens the door to many kinds of NSA being able to claim legitimate standing as 'members' within a more complex social structure. In a fully formed ideal-type FDM, functional differentiation would be the dominant form, subordinating whatever remained of segmentary and stratificatory differentiation. In an emergent FDM, functional differentiation exists and works alongside the other two forms, mainly still in subordination to them.

But as noted in Chapter 1, because functional differentiation applies both to the states and to the GIS as a whole, the FDM has an additional complexity not found so strongly in the other models. As argued by Galtung (1971), the core–periphery aspect of the HPM also has elements of this two-level structure. He lays out the way in which members of the core and members of the periphery each contain domestic reproductions of the core–periphery structure of the system as a whole. There are core-like elites within the periphery, and periphery-like exploited classes within the core. He sees this as a fairly uniform pattern, and in that strictly analytical sense, the domestic structure is a comfortable fit with the GIS one. The two-level issue in the FDM is not so easy to handle because functional differentiation at the global level might be heavily shaped by functional differentiation within the units. Ideally, one would want to think of functional differentiation within GIS as both generated at the global level and fairly evenly distributed there. But the reality is that the variation amongst states can be, and is, large. Advanced, 'post-modern', liberal capitalist societies might be internally dominated by functional differentiation, whereas in 'modern' authoritarian states and absolutist monarchies stratification remains dominant. If those states that are the most functionally differentiated are also the most powerful ones in GIS, then they will project their domestic structures into the rest of the system, giving the FDM a potentially imperial or at least core–periphery character close to the HPM.

Either route to an FDM produces a GIS with multiple types of members – states, IGOs, INGOs, TNCs and individuals – whose legitimacy and relationships within GIS are defined by functional differentiation. This is the big difference between the FDM and the other three models. Both the LUM and the RSM suppose that states are the only legitimate members of GIS, and other entities participate in it only on their sufferance. HPM allows for a wider differentiation of types of states than just on the basis of power, but it is still mainly state-centric. As noted in Chapter 1, in a GIS with multiple types of legitimate member, recognition is based not on likeness, but on difference: an acknowledged position with a division of labour in which states govern, IGOs regulate, firms do business, INGOs lobby and individuals have rights. Each type of unit would be acknowledged by the others as holding legal and political status independently, in their own right, not as a gift from any of the others, but linked to their position within a functionally differentiated structure. Individuals, firms and other transnational NSAs would thus become subjects of international law in their own right. In this sense, the FDM does not necessarily privilege one domain over the others.

In order to grasp the general character and features of the FDM, one needs to start by looking at primary and secondary institutions from a different perspective: not just as areas of normative convergence amongst the states-members of GIS generally, and the great powers in particular, but as both statements and embodiments of functional differentiation within GIS. In this perspective, classical pluralist primary institutions such as sovereignty, nonintervention, territoriality, diplomacy, the balance of power, great power management and war can be seen as markers by which the political sphere is differentiated from other spheres. This differentiation is embodied in secondary institutions such as the UN General Assembly and the UN Security Council. Although it is also one of the classical pluralist primary institutions, international law extends functional differentiation by creating a legal domain within GIS that has its own rules, procedures, discourses and secondary institutions. The latter take the form of the many international courts now in existence, such as the International Court of Justice (ICJ), the International Commission of Jurists and the International Criminal Court (ICC). One does not have to accept the communicative assumptions of Luhmann's theory to see how thinking in this way opens up the idea of differentiated function systems as a way of understanding GIS.

The newer, often more solidarist, primary institutions extend this expression and embodiment of functional differentiation. The market confirms the differentiation of the economic sector implicit in globalization and IPE, and more deeply in liberal theory from Adam Smith onwards. This differentiation is consolidated in a host of secondary institutions, both the well-known state-centric ones such as the WTO, the IMF, the World Bank and its various affiliated organizations, the International Labour Organization (ILO) and a host of regional development banks, including China's new Asian Infrastructure Development Bank (AIIB), but also ones stemming from the NSAs within the economic sector itself, such as the Bank for International Settlements (BIS). Similar patterns can be found for emergent primary institutions such as human rights and environmental stewardship. Human rights are expressed and institutionalized in, *inter alia*, the 1948 Universal Declaration of Human Rights (UDHR), Amnesty International and the International Federation for Human Rights (FIDH). Environmental stewardship is expressed and institutionalized in, *inter alia*, the United Nations Environment Program (UNEP), the Intergovernmental Panel on Climate Change (IPCC), The International Union for Conservation of Nature (IUCN), the 1972 Stockholm Conference, the Rio Summit of 1992, conferences in Copenhagen (2009) and Paris (2015), Greenpeace and the World Wide Fund for Nature (WWF). And one could push on to ever more forms of differentiation expressed and embodied in this way. There is, for example, what might be called a medical or health sector in which there are state-centric secondary institutions, such as the WHO, and secondary institutions from global civil society (GCS), such as Médecins Sans Frontières (MSF). A case might be made for many other substantive functional differentiations within GIS. Stroikos (2015) makes the case for a nuclear one, and the secondary institutions supporting this include the IAEA, the Nuclear Energy Agency (NEA) and the World Association of Nuclear Operators (WANO). Something similar might be argued for a primary institution of development supported by the UNDP, Oxfam International and Cooperative for Assistance and Relief Everywhere (CARE).

In terms of some of the 'new' spaces discussed in previous chapters, there are also specific government and nongovernmental organizations set up to functionally manage these. The International Civil Aviation Organization (ICAO) regulates airspace, the United Nations Convention on the Law of the Sea (UNCLOS) and its associated organizations handle sea space and the nongovernmental (although maintaining links with the US government) Internet Corporation for Assigned Names and Numbers (ICANN) is tasked with making the Internet (cyberspace) run. And then, lastly, there is the International Organization for Standardization (ISO), a nongovernmental organization that has as its very raison d'etre to set international functional standards. Arguably, the advanced division of labour in most functional issue areas, and indeed the level of market integration across the globe, would not be possible without this organization's work.

Elaborating the FDM in this way quickly leads to functional differentiation that is expressed and manifested by institutions that fall wholly outside of the state-centric primary and secondary institutions. As suggested by Buzan (2004a: 118–38; 2018a) the transnational and interhuman domains will also have their own institutional drives and logics. That being the case, it should be no surprise that the FDM includes a range of differentiations wide enough to account for the fact that its membership runs a lot wider than just states. Putting TNCs, INGOs and individuals into play as members of GIS allows them also to generate expressions and embodiments of functional differentiation, potentially to an almost infinite degree of complexity. There is a vast array of functionally specific entities that range from hobbyist clubs and sporting associations through mafias and religious institutions to firms and interest lobbies and professional associations (Risse-Kappen, 1995; Boli and Thomas, 1999; Noortmann, Arts and Reinalda, 2001: 303; Risse, 2002). Within the FDM, there are powerful incentives for NSAs of a similar type to agree pluralist type rules of recognition and conventions of communication amongst themselves and work out practical measures of coexistence. Cartel agreements amongst firms or mafias not to compete with one another in certain markets or territories are parallel to rules of nonintervention and spheres of influence amongst states. Moreover, Bitcoins are an interesting example of a functional solution to the trust problem in finance that straddles the civil and uncivil (when used for illicit transactions) domains of GIS, one that directly challenges states' traditional monopoly on issuing legal tender. Similarly, it is not difficult to find elements of solidarism in transnational societies. Games (chess, go/weiqi, bridge, etc.) and sports (football, golf, tennis, cricket, etc.) clubs cooperate in setting up system-wide rules, standards and tournaments. Firms agree on common standards for everything from screws to software systems. Stock exchanges make their buying and selling practices interoperable. As with states, therefore, other types of functionally differentiated collective units have choices about how they relate to each other, and these choices can range from zero-sum rivalry, through pluralist modes of coexistence to more solidarist modes of cooperation in pursuit of joint gains and interoperability. The range of functional differentiation stretches right across the spectrum from states on one end to organizations coming purely out of GCC on the other, with everything in between.

This perspective opens up a quite radical view of GIS. The ES discussion of GIS has mainly confined itself to thinking about the structure of international society in state-centric terms. At best (Clark, 2007), and in various discussions of human rights (Donnelly, 1998; Wheeler, 2000), it has acknowledged that the institutional structure of the society of states can be and sometimes is shaped by upward pressure from world society. But the ES has never really confronted the question of what the institutional structure of world society does, or could, look like. Pursing the FDM necessitates opening up this question.

A snapshot view of contemporary GIS certainly does not show anything close to a fully developed FDM. What it does show is a mix in which functional differentiation plays a significant role. The contemporary GIS contains all three forms, with the dominant segmentary one (territorial states, sovereign equality, anarchy) being questioned by both stratificatory elements (the return of empire, hegemony, core–periphery) with functional differentiation playing around and through these as just discussed. As the globalization and IPE perspectives suggest, it is in the economic sector that functional differentiation is best developed in the contemporary GIS. And that in turn reflects a longstanding stratificatory structure, in place since the nineteenth century, in which Western powers and their affiliates have held a dominant position (Buzan and Lawson, 2015a). As Albert, Buzan and Zürn (2013: 243–4) put it:

The existing normative framework of international society is largely a projection of those Western powers within which functional differentiation (aka modernity) initially took the dominant role. This process was led by northwest Europe from the 19th century, and since 1945 by the United States, which added its own twist to the liberal formula. What we have, therefore, is a liberal form of international society in which a whole group of liberal states have both successively and in parallel projected their interior functional differentiation out into international society. This quite substantial group – the West and its various close associates – feels relatively comfortable with this arrangement because it is in broad harmony with their domestic arrangements. It is a kind of collective hegemony reflecting their preferred mode of differentiation. For states that do not share this domestic pattern of differentiation, an international society featuring functional differentiation is deeply threatening.

This hybrid view of GIS is discussed in more detail in Chapter 7.

In dynamic perspective, the FDM presents a complex and somewhat confused picture. One could argue that functional differentiation in international society has a long and deep history. The main line here would be the differentiation between religious and political spheres. At various times and in various places, religious institutions and practices functioned autonomously from the political system. Think of the Oracle at Delphi, the various branches of Christianity that had separate and autonomous institutions, most obviously the Catholic and Orthodox hierarchies, and autonomous practices and hierarchies within Islam, Buddhism and Hinduism. At times, of course, the religious and the political fused in a variety of god-king arrangements, but often they were functionally differentiated as in the biblical injunction to 'render unto God what is God's and unto Caesar what is Caesar's'. This differentiation was part of a system going back to the beginning of civilization in which segmentary and stratificatory modes of differentiation largely characterized polities.

But there is not all that much linkage between this classical story about religion and politics and the modern one that links differentiation to the revolutions of modernity that took off during the nineteenth century.[1] The sociological analysis of modernity suggests that since the middle of the nineteenth century, functional differentiation in a wider sense has been increasing in strength, especially within the leading-edge capitalist states. This differentiation is perhaps most strikingly about the separation of economics from politics but is more broadly about the replacement of a stratificatory hierarchy based on genealogy by a functional differentiated society based on technical skill and merit. This modern story certainly carries a strong sense of evolution, but this is of quite recent provenance, is quite messy and is very far from being fully worked out. One can argue that the many totalitarian movements of the twentieth (and twenty-first) century were partly a reaction against the perceived problems of modernity (the sense of uprootedness, loss of traditional culture and social standing) and an attempt to reimpose stratificatory differentiation on functional differentiation that had been judged to have gone too far. This was particularly an aspect of fascist or right-wing totalitarian movements. At the other end of the political/totalitarian spectrum, communists celebrated a future/utopia in which the division of labour was no longer the source of parallel divisions in society, and anarchist thought took this to the logical conclusion that functional entities, worker collectives, would be entirely self-organizing and the stratificatory superstructure of the state finally made obsolete. From a macrohistorical perspective, we are still in the early phases of the unfolding of modern functional differentiation. A mere two centuries of modern development give us mainly turbulence and not yet much in the way of reliable patterns.

---

[1] The main link being those who argue for a link between religion, mainly Protestant Christianity, and the emergence of modernity in Europe.

Since the states and societies that modernized earliest have dominated the system, they have over the past two centuries projected their own form outwards and imposed it onto GIS as a whole, most obviously and strongly in the form of globalized industrial and postindustrial capitalism. Initially, this was done directly in the form of spheres of imperial preference. But since 1945, US leadership has promoted global capitalism in hegemonic core–periphery form. That said, however, there is very little to suggest that there is any neat and tidy evolution happening in which functional differentiation is steadily overwhelming the segmentary and stratificatory forms. Instead, what is evolving is a highly complicated mix in which all three are in play and deeply interwoven with each other. Whether this mix is itself transitional towards a GIS dominated by functional differentiation, or whether it is stable enough to endure in its own right, is difficult to assess. Current developments show crosscurrents and contradictions. On the one hand, we argued in Chapter 5 that stratification (hierarchy) was giving way to functional differentiation in terms of the merger between great power management and global governance. But against that, we also argued that there has been a marked consolidation of formal state privilege over firms and NSAs since the nineteenth century. At the time of writing (2017), it is beginning to look as if the leading-edge states of the Anglosphere that created a globalized and functionally differentiated GIS are starting to react defensively against its consequences for their domestic social (migration), economic (inequality) and political (delegitimation) orders.

In IR terms, this complex mix of differentiations might well not be unusual, notwithstanding the theoretical position from classical sociology that one of the three forms of differentiation should always be dominant. A case can be made that premodern international relations has throughout several millennia been mainly a struggle between segmentary and stratificatory differentiation. Functional differentiation on a global scale, and much more elaborate than that between religion and politics, is a recent addition into this mix, making it considerably more complex. Perhaps, however, this addition does not change the basic idea that for IR, with its distinctive two-levels-of-society mix (i.e., society *within* the collective units and the larger international society formed *amongst* those units), it is normal to have more than one type of differentiation in play at the same time, without a clear pattern of one mode of differentiation necessarily being dominant (Albert, Buzan and Zürn, 2013: 232–4).

Taking all this into account, what does the FDM suggest about criteria for assessing whether international society is getting stronger or weaker? In order to think about this, we have first to consider the difficulty raised by Buzan and Albert (2010: 320–2) that there is no settled agreement about this issue in sociology itself, where some see functional differentiation as necessarily weakening society by breaking apart its traditional forms, while others see it as providing a new type of social cohesion (a debate that mirrors some of the political arguments put forward by the totalitarians and antiglobalizationists previously discussed). On top of that, there has not been much discussion about how this issue transposes into IR, with its broader notions of international and world society.

It is helpful to view this question in the light of classical sociology's two ideal types of society: *Gemeinschaft*, in which society is a traditional, historical construct of community in terms of shared values and culture; and *Gesellschaft*, in which society is something instrumental, contractual, and more purposively constructed. In a nutshell, the sociological argument goes like this. On the one hand, if society is viewed as *Gemeinschaft*, then functional differentiation is corrosive of it. The process of modernization necessarily divides and fragments a *Gemeinschaft* society into new and often bigger functional structures. If this is the case, then increasing functional differentiation necessarily weakens, or decomposes, society. On the other hand, society can be viewed as *Gesellschaft*, in which case functional differentiation can be seen as an emergent form. From that perspective, more functional differentiation is not necessarily weakening to society, though it is not necessarily strengthening it either. To strengthen society, functional differentiation has to embed both a degree of respect and understanding among the functional sectors, and an understanding that functional differentiation creates a deepening interdependence in which the well-being of each depends on maintaining the stability of the whole assemblage. On this basis, one can create a reverse story in which rather than *Gemeinschaft* societies being broken down by *Gesellschaft* ones, contractual *Gesellschaft* ones could, over time, evolve into affective *Gemeinschaft* ones. This makes the assessment of weakening or strengthening in relation to functional differentiation particularly difficult. If it just wrecks a *Gemeinschaft* society, then it is weakening. If it both wrecks the *Gemeinschaft* society and puts something new in its place, then the question of weakening or strengthening is complicated and multifacetted, requiring difficult and nuanced assessments about different types of strength and weakness.

When this logic is transposed to IR, the structural difference between society at the unit level and society at the system level becomes a major issue. Most unit society stories can be told as evolutions from *Gemeinschaft* to *Gesellschaft*. But as is abundantly clear from almost any IR textbook, and from Bull's nicely chosen term 'anarchical society', GIS has no *Gemeinschaft* foundation. Where *Gemeinschaft* plays in the ES formulation is captured by Wight's (1977: 33) idea, already noted, that 'We must assume that a states-system will not come into being without a degree of cultural unity among its members'. The classical ES mostly thought that international societies needed to begin amongst polities that shared a culture, such as the ancient Greeks, the early-modern Europeans and the Chinese of the 'warring states' era before 221 BC. Only then could shared values be found on which to base the institutions of international society. Whether correct or not (for argument against it, see Buzan, 1993; 2010a), such a view would effectively confine international societies to the scale of a single civilizational zone, such as Christendom, Islam or Confucianism. For the ES, however, the problem of the modern GIS was precisely that it had expanded far beyond its cultural home base and therefore lacked much if any shared culture on which to base institutions (Bull and Watson, 1984a). Moreover, this expansion had been carried out by a coercive process of colonization and decolonization that had left as its legacies both a small, partly Westernized elite and a 'revolt against the West' in most decolonized states. The result was a GIS no longer under the thumb of Western imperialism, and in which decolonized states both formed a majority and were both able and keen to mobilize their indigenous cultural resources towards political ends both domestically and internationally. Whether or not modernity itself might count as a shared culture then becomes a crucial question in relation to the strength or weakness of GIS. As noted in Chapter 3, the expansion of European international society to global scale was thus thought of as weakening GIS by reducing its cultural coherence. Alternatively, one could see GIS as a pure form of modern *Gesellschaft* emergence, not necessarily having any link to a prior *Gemeinschaft*.

While the classical ES was inclined to idealize the colonial GIS of the nineteenth and early twentieth centuries, it nevertheless saw clearly enough the absence of *Gemeinschaft* society in the post-1945 world. In this sense, there was not much at the global level for an increase in functional differentiation to decompose, and the path for it to 'emerge' and provide new forms of social cohesion was relatively clear. The United States led the way with its project to create a global liberal international economic order as a bulwark against great power war in general and the Soviet project in particular. Extending functional differentiation to a global scale was thus a hegemonic project that in some ways took the place of the stratificatory global structure created during the European-centred imperial era. Functional differentiation was not, however, only a hegemonic imposition from the West. It was also the key to development, and therefore to wealth and power, for all states and societies. However much controversy there might be about whether modernity required democracy, capitalism or human rights, there was relatively little controversy, especially after the Chinese turn in 1978 and the Soviet collapse in 1991, that modernity, and therefore functional differentiation, was the key to wealth and power. It is noteworthy in this regard that during the nineteenth century both Japan and China focused their responses to the dual challenge of modernity on acquiring wealth and power, using slogans such as 'rich country, strong army' (Schell and Delury, 2013). That said, it was also clear that the durable distinction between developed and developing countries was a powerful marker for both the absence of a globally shared culture of modernity and the presence of stratification based on level of development.

This rather complicated history left the classical ES with two apparently contradictory views of GIS. On the one hand, given decolonization, it was left with a rather Hobbesian perspective on GIS in which polities start out as different, mutually alienated and mutually threatening members of an international system. At the international level, therefore, there was little or no *Gemeinschaft* society to be threatened or decomposed by the rise of functional differentiation, and international society was necessarily emergent and *Gesellschaft*. On the other hand, the ES's understanding of international society that we are building on here was initially, and remains, heavily dependent on a shared values/culture idea of society that is close to the *Gemeinschaft* understanding of what society is. Implicitly, therefore, the ES conception of GIS has to be a version of the idea that *Gesellschaft* societies can, over time, evolve into *Gemeinschaft* ones.[2] It depends on the growth of both shared values and consciousness about interdependence amongst the members of GIS, whether those units are 'like' or whether they are of different types. At its most basic, that consciousness works in a pluralist way, where the shared interest is in finding rules of coexistence to allow relief from the Hobbesian condition of the permanent war of each against all. Once the rules of coexistence become stabilized, then there is the possibility of extending into a solidarist logic of cooperation, mainly rooted in functional differentiation, in which the members of GIS aim to pursue joint projects that might range from setting up and managing a global economy, to protecting the planet from global warming or space rocks, to the pursuit of human rights. So, while the ES's conception of contemporary GIS is almost entirely one of *Gesellschaft* and emergence, it is by definition aimed at constructing a *Gemeinschaft* society defined by a shared culture of modernity.

---

[2] This is of course contrary to the classical view in which *Gemeinschaft* is the original organic form of society that is undermined by the *Gesellschaft* generated by modernity.

Where, then, does all this leave us regarding the question of what the FDM tells us about the criteria for assessing whether international society is getting stronger or weaker? One might, more or less comfortably, set aside the problem of decomposition at the global level on the grounds that there is little or no *Gemeinschaft* society at that level to be sundered by the emergence of functional differentiation. Even at the regional level, this is not an important issue. Regional level decomposition/weakening would depend on there being strong *Gemeinschaft* regional or subglobal international societies, and as argued in Chapter 4, this is not an obvious feature of GIS. Quite a few regional international societies cultivate a *Gemeinschaft* image by taking on civilizational, ethnic or cultural identities: Islamic, European, Arab, Latin American, Scandinavian. But these regional/subglobal constructions are either marginally differentiated from the wider social structure of GIS (Arab, Islamic, Latin American) or, where more substantially differentiated (Europe, Scandinavia), mainly *Gesellschaft* developments based on functional differentiation.

At the unit level, however, the decomposition issue is far from marginal. There are at least three stories from contemporary IR that can be understood in terms of *Gemeinschaft* societies being threatened and weakened by *Gesellschaft*, developments in terms of functional differentiation. The first one is, ironically, about the decomposition in the Western states that have been and still are the leading edge of functional differentiation in the GIS. Here the story, still ongoing, is about the impact of neoliberalism and globalization on Western states and societies. This ranges from increasing concern about the rise of extreme inequality, and the breakdown of social mobility, to rising unemployment and fear about the cultural and civilizational impact of immigration of people from different cultures and races. If the societies at the leading edge of functional differentiation themselves fall into a decomposition crisis, then that would certainly weaken functional differentiation within GIS as a whole, and thus probably degrade the development of a *Gesellschaft* GIS based on functional differentiation. The shocks of Brexit and Trump in 2016 suggest the possibility that the Anglosphere core itself has revolted against globalization, and that the EU project might be in deep trouble. At the time of writing, however, these developments are still too recent to enable us to assess their longer-term significance.

The second and third unit-level decomposition stories are both about authoritarian states whose stratificatory domestic structures are challenged by the spread of functional differentiation. In this category, one finds both traditionally authoritarian states such as Russia, China, Egypt and Turkey and weak and failed states such as Somalia, Afghanistan, Haiti, the Democratic Republic of the Congo, Syria, Iraq and such like.

Differentiating between these two groups requires that there be a meaningful distinction between, on the one hand, states/societies in which there is a deeply ingrained political tradition of the dominance of strong stratification; and on the other hand, states/societies in which authoritarian stratification is not so much a deeply rooted tradition as a shallow response to weak social structures and the immediate alternative of chaos. This distinction is clear enough in principle. Empirically, there is, for example, plenty of evidence that polities within the Confucian tradition have a strong bent towards hierarchical political orders (Fairbank, 1968; Kang, 2003; 2003–4; 2005; Callahan, 2009; Pines, 2012; Harris, 2014: locs. 362–74, 1289; Chen, 2015). But it may well be less clear in practice. Both Russia (in the years around 1917 and 1990) and China (1911–1949) have been through periods where they were weak or failed states. Countries that are assemblages of tribes and clans, such as Somalia and Afghanistan, might also be said to have authoritarian traditions at the level of their component units, though whether concepts such as 'authoritarian' are valid for the traditional political structures of such units is no doubt an arguable question. For weak and failed states, the decomposition problem is the existential one of whether they can hold themselves together convincingly enough to retain diplomatic recognition as members of GIS. For states with culturally embedded authoritarianism, the question is whether such states can retain their stratificatory politics while at the same time adopting functional differentiation as the necessary means to produce wealth and power in modern terms. The Chinese Communist Party's project to prove that capitalism (a.k.a. 'market socialism') can work without leading to democracy provides a fascinating and poignant case study of this decomposition dilemma for traditionally authoritarian societies.

Weak and failed states can be seen as abrasions or even tears in the fabric of GIS, leaving it weakened. Such states may become in some sense wards of GIS, unable by themselves to sustain the requirements of either juridical or empirical sovereignty (Bain, 2003). This comes close to reducing the membership of GIS by making some of its members dependent on outside support in ways that can bring into question the principle of sovereign equality. Traditional authoritarians, especially when they are powerful, do not leave rents in the fabric of GIS but become sites of resistance to increasing the range and depth of shared values. If they are great powers, they will undermine the effectiveness of great power management by leaving that elite club internally divided. That was the case during the Cold War and seems to be emerging again as Russia and China team up to make life difficult for the United States, and vice versa. While the strength of GIS is not entirely dependent on the great powers, strong division amongst them will weaken it.

That leaves the question of whether an emergent functional differentiation can in itself strengthen or weaken GIS, and if so, how? This is pretty much virgin territory for the ES, which, while it has thought quite a lot about the structure of interstate GIS, has thought hardly at all about the structure of world society, i.e., the transnational and interhuman domains of GIS, either in themselves or in how they relate to the interstate domain. As we have shown, the FDM takes us deeply into those domains. Only with some sense of the social structure in the transnational and interhuman domains can we assess how the advance of functional differentiation might strengthen or weaken GIS. So, a full and confident answer to this question would require a lot more theoretical and empirical research into the transnational and interhuman domains than we can do for this book. At this point, the best we can offer is some guidelines to help structure that research. As readily becomes clear, functional differentiation plays into all five of the strengthening or weakening criteria discussed for other models:

- Functional differentiation can impact on the membership of GIS in two ways. First, it can reduce the number and/or proportion of states and peoples who have full membership of the international society by pushing some states into decomposition crises that make them more wards than members of GIS. This would count as weakening GIS. Second, functional differentiation could increase the types of entity that count as members, or at least have formal standing within, GIS. The effects of this are complicated to assess. It might well increase the number of members, but it might at the same time change the composition and meaning of membership. A fully developed FDM might even have eliminated states altogether, thus representing a very different form of international society from the Westphalian one. The issue then would be not so much strengthening/weakening of an existing form of GIS but a transition to a new form. This potential for change in the composition of the membership of GIS to a wider and more differentiated mix is the main difference between the FDM and the other models. Rather than having states as the only legitimate members, the FDM allows, and indeed almost requires, a range of members stretching from states, through a variety of transnational NSAs, to people. While a fully functionally differentiated membership of GIS is not yet in place, there are significant developments that move towards it. These include the widespread embedding of a great variety of INGOs into IGOs, the quasi-autonomous role of TNCs in the world economy and the increasing weight of the norm that human beings have rights that transcend the sovereignty of their states. In terms of strengthening and weakening, this development could cut both ways. On the positive side, it could have profound benefits for the legitimacy of GIS by deepening and broadening the social constituencies that it represents. The normative linkages between GCC and the institutional structure of state-centric GIS shown by Clark (2007) can only be strengthened when GCC becomes a formal part of the membership and not just an external lobby. On the negative side, there is the simple logic of numbers: it is generally more difficult to reach a decision or get a consensus within a larger group of members than within a smaller one, and perhaps that difficulty increases when the members are not just like-units but diverse types.

- It can impact both positively and negatively the number of primary institutions that are commonly held. The most obvious negative impact would be by creating tension or even conflict between those states with more stratified domestic structures and those with more functionally differentiated ones. Drawing on the RSM, this could also manifest itself as tension between different subglobal or regional sections of GIS, premised on their respective acceptance of functional differentiation internally. In addition, there is the scenario discussed in Chapter 4, where a fragmentation of the primary institutions of interstate society is matched by a buildup of primary institutions in the transnational and interhuman domains. This could cut both ways. The most obvious positive impact would be by expanding the number of primary institutions in line with the ever-more finely detailed functional differentiation of GIS and its extension into the transnational and interhuman domains, as previously suggested. An option could also be the agreement on certain *foundational* primary institutions across the three domains, putting in place the basis for further specialization of primary institutions in each domain. This latter option would probably be incompatible with the current foundational primary institution of sovereignty, subordinating NSAs and individuals to the state.
- It seems likely that functional differentiation will tend to increase the elaboration and uniformity of practices within already agreed institutions (this logic is forcefully represented by the ISO). Once the principle of functional differentiation gets established, it generates a structural pressure for interoperability and shared standards in metrics ranging from screw threads to measures of inflation. Such developments can readily be observed in the economic sector, and functional logic naturally lends itself to ever-finer degrees of elaboration. It is an interesting empirical question as to whether or not such elaboration will increase the opportunity for fragmentation of practices within GIS.

- To the extent that functional differentiation is successful, it holds the prospect of strengthening GIS by bringing more solidarist, cooperative primary institutions into play. The division of labour generates interdependence and therefore tends naturally to elaborate towards cooperative and therefore solidarist ventures such as sport and the economy. As proposed in Chapter 4, this is not because increasing cooperation equals a strengthening of GIS, but rather because cooperation can promote an increase in the volume, scale and range of social interactions and functions shared and a complementary uniformity of institutional practices. However, it is important to emphasize that pluralist international societies also have the potential to be very strong or thick according to this standard (for example, the communist bloc during the Cold War). It is only that solidarist primary institutions, other things being equal, seem to contain a natural momentum towards this outcome.

- Whether and how functional differentiation plays into the binding forces of GIS are quite tricky questions. In principle, the logic of division of labour and increasing interdependence, if it is not causing a decomposition crisis, should strengthen the social cohesion of GIS. This, however, might only work if this structure is fairly evenly distributed across GIS. Functional differentiation would be strongest if accepted consensually, and weakest if seen as being imposed coercively, with calculated acceptance of it somewhere in the middle. Given the core–periphery character of the emergent FDM, and its negative impact on states with stratificatory domestic structures, this can only present a rather mixed picture in the contemporary GIS. However, the very notion of function also seems to carry an instrumental or utility logic along the lines of 'if it works, keep it, if it doesn't, discard it'. This is close to the *Gesellschaft* argument. In that sense, the FDM appears to be inherently wedded to calculated acceptance, not unquestioned belief. To the extent that this is true, all functional social structures are essentially precarious if not supported by either belief (as in the case of those who believe in the market) or by complementary social logics emanating from the LUM, RSM and/or the HPM. In a rather convoluted fashion, this also opens up the space for thinking about the functional division of labour between nominal equals being supported by a higher-order logic coming from another model: what we in the previous chapter termed a privilege–equality nexus. The models, like primary institutions, can be hierarchically organized. Whether or not these hierarchies are contested is the key to understanding strengthening and weakening.

2   Strengths and Weaknesses of the Model

As in the preceding three chapters, this section asks three questions about how the model relates to GIS:

• How well does it capture the actual nature of the units?
• How well does it capture the actual nature of the structure?
• How well does it capture the binding forces?

Capturing the Units

As argued in Chapter 3, the ES has a rather more ambitious and compli-cated aim than realism because it needs to get to grips with the complex-ities not just of an international system but of international society. The LUM emphasized segmentary differentiation into states/polities, and while its simplification fits within the pluralist view of the ES, it does badly when it comes to solidarist perspectives on GIS and has difficulty with weak and failed states. The RSM opens things up a bit, and the HPM does so even more by explicitly bringing in NSAs. The FDM carries this momentum forwards by bringing into the formal as well as informal membership of GIS both NSAs and people. The price of this, as noted, is to make the membership structure of GIS much more compli-cated, and in some ways more difficult to assess. Amongst the problems to be solved would be how to determine the relative autonomy of NSAs and people from states and therefore their standing within GIS. Rather than the relative simplicity of defining membership on the basis of *similarity* of form and function, the FDM requires that membership be defined on the basis of *differences* in form and function, accompanied by some notion of a division of labour and an apportionment of rights. The social contract of GIS in the FDM is much more complicated than it is for state-centric models. However, as Bull (1977) recognized, mediaeval Europe, and other historical assemblages such as the German Confeder-ation (Haldén, 2011), provides hints to how this might be worked out in practice.

The FDM certainly does not solve the problem of how to deal with weak and failed states as members of GIS, but it does perhaps put it into a clearer perspective. In many ways, the FDM sets out the specifics of why it is that some states cannot quickly or easily develop the internal robustness necessary to function in a highly dynamic and intrusive GIS. It also offers some leverage on how GIS copes with this problem by making room within the state-centric model for the activities of NSAs and people. In principle, the FDM takes the whole idea of GIS away from its state-centric tradition and opens it up to a wide variety of units and constitutional arrangements. This is a potentially powerful theoretical move in understanding GIS, albeit one requiring steaming boldly into uncharted waters. There seems to be little prospect of anything like a fully fledged FDM emerging in the foreseeable future. But this model, along with the HPM, does offer a clear pathway to thinking about the standing of NSAs in GIS, which is something that the ES has neglected and needs to develop.

Capturing the Structure

The FDM neither attacks the basic framing of primary institutions set out in the state-centric models nor solves any of the problems of how to differentiate between emergent and sectional primary institutions, or how to address divergent practices within institutions. Instead, it does three things. First, as previously argued, it opens the door to extending and refining the list of primary institutions that define GIS. By allowing TNAs and people into the picture, the FDM opens up a picture of GIS that is potentially much more functionally differentiated than the state-centric LUM and RSM by themselves allow. It picks up and strengthens the core–periphery aspects of the HPM with which it has many synergies. Second, and consequently, it requires that much more thought be given, and empirical research be done, about what such institutions look like in the transnational and interhuman domains, or at least what difference it makes when one sees primary institutions not just as an interstate phenomenon but as an expression of a GIS with a much more diverse and differentiated membership. Amongst other things, this might clarify how primary and secondary institutions play together to institutionalize GIS in a deep and quite finely detailed way. Such work could fruitfully pick up and develop Spandler's (2015: 611) and Navari's (2016) structurationist suggestions that both primary and secondary institutions help constitute international actors, and that actors in turn institutionalize international society. Third, the FDM also raises the question of whether having a larger and more diverse membership makes it more difficult to reach consensus on the set of primary institutions that define GIS. In principle, larger numbers and a great diversity of actors point to greater difficulty in obtaining consensus. In practice, however, as the many examples given in this book of NSAs being part of the institutionalization of contemporary GIS suggest, this may not be a difficulty. The apparent tension between the theory and the actuality here needs empirical investigation as part of how the structure of the FDM model works. Because of the ongoing sociological dispute about whether functional differentiation generates decomposition of traditional *Gemeinschaft* society or emergence of modern *Gesellschaft* society, it is unclear how the FDM plays into the solidarism–pluralism equation. One could, perhaps, investigate the hypothesis that increasing functional differentiation should increase solidarism through a widening and deepening of interdependence.

Capturing the Binding Forces

The FDM raises similar questions to the other three models about the mix of coercion, calculation and belief as the glue of GIS. What it perhaps adds to the mix is the structural logic of functional differentiation itself, which as argued in the previous question might shift the focus away from whether or not like-units share norms and values, and towards the issue of how awareness of functional differentiation, with its consequent division of labour and interdependence amongst different types of units, might itself act as a binding force for GIS, not least by both conditioning, and putting into the foreground, the logic of calculation. Functional differentiation is at least initially associated with a move away from *Gemeinschaft* societies based on belief to *Gesellschaft* ones based more on calculation. In this phase, perhaps more than for the other models, calculation can underpin strength in the FDM, though this probably does not question our general view that belief remains the strongest binding force for social structures. If *Gesellschaft* societies eventually generate *Gemeinschaft* ones, then belief would come back into play.

3   Conclusions

The FDM is more difficult to bring into clear focus than the other three models. That is partly because the model itself contains unresolved elements, such as the debate over decomposition versus emergence, and partly because we have no pure cases of a GIS where functional differentiation has become dominant. Even the EU, which is the most advanced liberal solidarist international society we have ever seen, is, as its current crisis shows, very far from transcending the logics of segmentary and stratificatory differentiation and may even be sliding back towards them. To the extent that an FDM exists in contemporary GIS, it is woven around and through the other three models. There are also awkward questions about whether the functional differentiation we see in contemporary GIS is mainly imposed coercively, or by a logic of calculation, rather than by more deeply rooted beliefs. Bringing in NSAs and people into GIS extends the range of what might count as primary institutions and opens the need to think much more than has been done so far about primary institutions in relation to the transnational and interhuman domains. The FDM thus opens up some quite large changes to the whole conceptualization of GIS. These include a bigger and more diverse membership, a wider range, finer detail of primary and secondary institutions and an understanding that such institutions are not just areas of normative convergence amongst the states-members of GIS, but also both statements and embodiments of functional differentiation within GIS. The FDM also offers a mixed picture on the question of whether GIS is strengthening or weakening, with elements pulling in both directions. It clearly caters to solidarist lines of thinking within the ES much better than the other models, but also constructs a larger and more diverse membership amongst which consensus might be more difficult to find. It has synergies with the HPM both in the core–periphery structure and in the general position of NSAs within GIS. The complexity of the FDM means that it has the opposite character to the LUM, which offers too simple a picture of GIS. Our four models of GIS have moved from simple through increasing degrees of complexity, with the FDM being the most complex of all. Neither simplicity nor complexity is grounds for dismissing a model or a concept. Both have their virtues and their vices. But simplicity and complexity do have consequences, and we need now to try to combine the models to arrive at a composite picture of contemporary GIS and its dynamics.

7 Aggregating the Models
The Complex Differentiation of Contemporary Global International Society

1 Introduction

In the previous chapter, we suggested that a hybrid view, in which all of the models played alongside and through each other, was perhaps the most appropriate way to understand the structure of the contemporary GIS. This chapter expands on that idea by assembling a broad historical account of international society, both modern and premodern, in terms of the mixing and interplay of the four models. We argue that a mixture of models is the general rule, with a trend towards increasing complexity. We then turn to the core question of this book about how to determine whether an international society is strong or weak, and how to identify whether the trends are towards stronger or weaker. We begin by reviewing and aggregating the criteria for strengthening and weakening that were generated by the four models and then apply this aggregated set to the concrete question about the condition and direction of the contemporary GIS. This question turns out to be surprisingly complicated, with many factors in play, some pulling in one direction, some in another.

2 Weighing the Four Models

In the perspective of the ES, GIS is, like any social structure, in a continuous process of reproduction and renegotiation. In the classical view of the 'three traditions', this process was understood as an ongoing state of flux amongst Hobbesian (international system), Grotian (international society) and Kantian (world society) elements, with the balance always open to change. In our structural approach, that same essential fluidity is understood in terms of the interplay amongst the four models, where the pattern of dominance among them changes with time and place. Neither perspective assumes that there is any teleology in play: the balance amongst the elements shifts in response to a complex array of driving forces and is indeterminate. To balance this fluidity, both perspectives assume that the process of change is generally sticky and slow moving. Revolutionary upheavals in normative structure are not impossible (Armstrong, 1993; Schouenborg, 2012), but the expectation is that changes in the structure of GIS are mostly evolutionary, as charted by Mayall (1990), Holsti (2004) and Buzan (2014a) in their studies of the rise, evolution and decay of primary institutions.

In earlier chapters, we have sketched out static and dynamic pictures of what GIS looks like in terms of each of the four models. There is no need to repeat that here, though we draw heavily on the histories and interpretations established in the preceding chapters. Now we need to aggregate those stories to see what sense of flow and interplay they give us about the structure of GIS. We focus mainly on the period from the nineteenth century to the present, because only in the nineteenth century did a truly global international society in the modern sense come into existence. In what follows, we track the relative weight of the four models through four periods: premodern international societies; the first global international society (version 1.0) running from the nineteenth century up to 1945; the transformation to GIS after 1945 (version 1.1); and what seems to be the transition to a version 1.2 since the economic crisis of 2008.

Before the emergence of the Westphalian model of international society in seventeenth century Europe, almost all international societies everywhere were mainly versions of the hierarchy/privilege model (HPM). Even the ancient Greek society of city-states, which stands as the main exception to this rule, had its own great powers and had to deal with external, hegemony-seeking empires, particularly Persia. Accompanying the principles of the HPM were also some basic elements of the functional differentiation model (FDM). These mainly took the form of differentiation between religion and politics that was quite common in agrarian civilizations, though sometimes becoming merged in god/emperors. At least up through the eighteenth century, even while it was evolving the principle of sovereign equality pointing towards the like-units model (LUM), the Westphalian international society in Europe also had not only significant elements of the HPM within it, mainly in the form of the aristocratic rankings of the various princes, kings and emperors, but also the classical elements of FDM in the differentiation between church and state. Significant traces of these remained even during the nineteenth century, although aristocratic hierarchy was increasingly displaced during that century by a new HPM differentiation between great powers and the rest, and religion was pushed more to the margins of political life.

At first glance, one might think that the regional/subglobal model (RSM) was also strongly in play during this period, but this model is difficult to apply until the middle of the nineteenth century. Up to that point, there was no GIS to speak of, and only rather superficial global interactions. To be sure, from the sixteenth to the eighteenth centuries, European powers were steadily imposing themselves on the Americas, by repopulating them, and on South Asia and Indonesia (by imposing their rule on the indigenous populations). But for most of Africa, the Ottoman Empire and East Asia, European political penetration remained shallow. In order to get economic access, Europeans had to negotiate, and some-times fight, as best they could against the local powers, and were far from always successful in doing so. While there was in some sense a global-scale international system, inasmuch as most of the major centres of population on the planet had some contact with some others, there was no real GIS in the sense of a common set of rules, recognitions and institutions, only a patchwork of individually negotiated bargains. Thus although there were distinctive international societies scattered about the planet during this time, there was no *global* international society for them to be regions or subsystems within. They are perhaps best seen as 'worlds' in their own right, often having thin and light contact with other such societies, but not being part of a coherent whole. So although there is in one sense a clear geographical differentiation in play among these 'worlds', we cannot see either the European or other international soci-eties at this time as regional or subglobal international societies of some bigger GIS. Whether the RSM criteria could be applied within some or all of these 'worlds' would require closer empirical study than we have space for here.

Nevertheless, during these three centuries the Europeans were steadily expanding their reach and influence and slowly becoming the agency that would tie together a truly global international society. This process culminated during the nineteenth century, when the revolutions of mod-ernity quite quickly gave the Europeans and the Japanese a huge power advantage over everyone else. Using that advantage, the Europeans quickly achieved dominance over, and heavy penetration of, both the last bastions of classical civilization (the Ottoman Empire, China and Japan) and Africa (where the obstacles to them had been mainly medical and geographical) (Headrick, 2010). The Europeans quickly built the first GIS on their own terms. Not surprisingly given the huge power difference between those who had harnessed the revolutions of modern-ity and those who had not, this version 1.0 GIS took the form of a strong blend of LUM and HPM. It was not regionally or subglobally differenti-ated except inasmuch as the empires built by the Europeans, Americans, Russians and Japanese could be seen as forms of subglobal differenti-ation. But the main point was a broadly two-tier GIS in which the LUM applied amongst the 'civilized' and mainly white states, and the HPM applied between the 'civilised' states and the rest. On the back of Western and Japanese power, this two-tier racist and colonial international society became the dominant form of the first truly global international society. But it was not a pure split between a LUM core and a HPM core–periphery. Within the core, there were also significant elements of HPM, especially in the rights and status accorded to great powers. Under the influence of the revolutions of modernity, the core was also beginning to generate modern functional differentiation and to project this into the periphery. Again, the RSM did not really apply at this time, because the imperial powers dominated the political sphere. 'The rest' did not have sufficient power or political agency either to form or to defend their own international societies.

The version 1.0 GIS therefore was, right from its nineteenth century beginning, born as a complicated and contradictory mix of the models. At its inception, it already contained a massive central tension between LUM and HPM. The LUM part, based around sovereignty and territoriality, was a powerful and distinctive inheritance from early-modern (Westphalian) Europe. That tradition was reinforced during the nineteenth century by the new political ideologies of nationalism, popular sovereignty, liberalism and socialism, and in the twentieth by the shift to human equality. Because it was carried by the core states and societies, the LUM logic defined the 'standard of civilization' that was projected onto 'the rest', steadily reshaping their aspirations towards achieving independence and equality with the framing of the LUM. The HPM part drew its power from two sources. First, was the strong carryover of HPM thinking from premodern societies. This applied as much to the aristocratic traditions of Europe as it did to similar dynastic traditions in most other parts of the world. This, however, was a waning asset, subject to continuous subversion and erosion by the ideologies of progress that were part of the revolutions of modernity. Conversely, the second source of support of the HPM, the opening of a huge mode of power gap between core and periphery, drew directly on those ongoing revolutions. The vast difference in military, economic, scientific and organizational capability that opened up between core and periphery during the nineteenth century easily lent itself to the 'standard of civilization' and the formal vertical differentiation logic of the HPM. Up until 1945, the logic of the HPM, and the two-tier colonial GIS that it supported, was also reinforced by the fourth ideology of progress, 'scientific' racism. At its apogee in the fascist movements of the 1930s, stratification by race became an essentialized and hugely destructive component of HPM thinking.

As if this massive tension between LUM and HPM was not enough, the version 1.0 colonial GIS also contained an element of the FDM. In part, this was a continuation of the traditional differentiation between politics and religion that was common in agrarian societies, although with the difference in the West that religion was steadily taken out of politics and moved to the private sphere of individuals. But the main trend of FDM, as for the LUM, was strongly linked to the revolutions of modernity being projected into the periphery by the core. These revolutions were substantially defined by functional differentiation, and even during the nineteenth century there were clear signs of this, ranging from the separating out of economics from politics in liberal ideology to the rise of functional IGOs and INGOs covering a growing range of globalizing activities from postal services and telecommunications to sport, law and religion. For the RSM, as already noted, the two-layered structure of the version 1.0 colonial GIS, with its strong hierarchy between imperial core and colonial periphery, did not give much scope. This basic structure of the version 1.0 GIS, with a central tension between the LUM and the HPM elements, the FDM bubbling up in the background and the RSM hardly registering, remained in place until the Second World War.

As Buzan and Lawson (2014a) argue, the years from 1929 to 1949 constitute a primary benchmark date (1942 as the tipping point) in international relations. These twenty years encompass, *inter alia*, global economic crises, major revolutions, world wars and transformations in civil and military technology. Amongst the many big changes at that time were several to the structure of primary institutions defining GIS. Colonialism and racism (human inequality) were delegitimized, and replaced by human equality, human rights and development. 'Development' was the postdecolonization form of metropolitan responsibility to colonized peoples, imposing obligations of aid on what were, in economic terms, still the core powers of GIS. This shift in the normative structure of GIS quite swiftly dismantled the formal two-tier, divided-sovereignty practices of the version 1.0 GIS, and globalized what had previously been the formal structure of the core: sovereign equality plus the legalized hegemony of the great powers. The Western empires were dismantled between the mid-1940s and the mid-1970s, and the Soviet one in 1991. The core–periphery structure remained in place in many respects, particularly economically, with new stratifications based on 'development' and formalized within the UN system. But much, though not all, of its formal hierarchical political structure was abandoned. What had been an international society that was global mainly because a few empires had divided up the world, became a GIS on the basis of the sovereign equality of states and peoples, with all now participating in it consensually in their own right.

Despite significant continuities of the core–periphery structure, this was a big enough transformation to count the GIS after 1945 as version 1.1. The essential change was a major collapse in the formal political hierarchy element of the HPM represented by colonialism, and thus a major shift towards the LUM, albeit including its privileging of the great powers (some now superpowers). This shift greatly reduced, though by no means eliminated, the central tension within the version 1.0 GIS between the HPM and the LUM.

The collective crises of the benchmark period from 1929 to 1949 impacted on the FDM in contradictory ways. On the one hand, the influence of the FDM was significantly strengthened by the leading role of the liberal-democratic powers of the Anglosphere as the main victors of the Second World War. These capitalist powers pushed to expand the role of functionally specific IGOs, INGOs, as well as TNCs, within GIS, and generally to promote the differentiation of the world economy into a functional sphere attended by its own IGOs covering trade (General Agreement on Tariffs and Trade [GATT], WTO) and finance (IMF, World Bank). Their wartime victory enabled them to incorporate Japan and Western Europe, including most of Germany, into the Western, liberal-democratic, capitalist sphere. That in turn enabled them to intensify the development of a global economy in many, but not all, parts of the planet.

Yet on the other hand, because the Soviet Union, joined in 1950 by communist China, was also a victor in the Second World War, it was able to set up a bloc of communist powers that stood against the Western project to build a global economy. The resulting Cold War was thus in a sense about to what extent the FDM would be allowed to influence GIS beyond the Western sphere. The logic of functional differentiation necessarily operated powerfully *within* all modern and modernizing states and societies, including communist ones. While the communist states were happy to participate on the fringes of global FDM, as in sports, they were resistant to global FDM if done on Western liberal-democratic and capitalist terms. This rift dominated GIS for more than thirty years. It began to unravel in the late 1970s, by which time the Western model of political economy had decisively demonstrated its superiority over the Soviet one in generating wealth and power. When Japan's economy surpassed that of the Soviet Union, the writing was on the wall for command economies as a viable pathway for modernity. In the late 1970s, China abandoned the command economy and opted to pursue export-led, capitalist development within the Western world economy. China's move followed in the line of Japan's developmental state model, and set out to prove that capitalism did not require democracy as liberals predicted it would. In this sense, China's leaders took more seriously than liberals did the functional differentiation separating economics and politics. The Soviet experiment in command economy collapsed a decade later, ending any major resistance to globalizing the economy, and thus increasing the influence of the FDM in GIS. The 1990s and early 2000s period of neoliberal ascendency represented a high point for global functional differentiation in the economic sphere.

With the onset of widespread decolonization after 1945, space also opened up for the logic of the RSM. With decolonization, the periphery regained fully independent political agency. Many regional IGOs were formed, and there was political space, especially within the UN system, for regions and subglobal groupings to differentiate themselves within GIS if they so wished. Up to a point they did, though ironically the main regional developments were within the former core of the West, particularly the EU. As we argued in Chapter 4, the RSM has not as yet posed any fundamental challenge to the LUM. Whether this will remain the case as Western power declines is an interesting and important question.

From 1945 until the first decade of the twenty-first century, version 1.1 GIS can be compared to the 1.0 version in the broad-brush terms of our four models as follows:

- The LUM became more influential, not just politically with decolonization, but, more slowly and patchily, also economically, as South Korea, Taiwan, Singapore, China, Turkey, India and others began to move up the development hierarchy. In effect, the core has been expanding and the periphery shrinking.
- The HPM became less influential despite a brief burst of so-called unipolarity when the United States became the sole superpower after the demise of the Soviet Union. While formal hierarchy amongst states has declined, that between states and NSAs remains robust even as NSAs have greatly increased their presence within GIS and their informal statuses and privileges.
- The FDM became more influential, first within the Western sphere, and, after 1990, globally.
- The RSM came into play, but modestly, and from a very low starting point.

At the time of writing, we seem to be in a transition period towards a version 1.2 of GIS. The global economic crisis starting in 2008 has brought into question the political sustainability of the neoliberal model of the globalized economy. The instability of this model in terms of recurrent financial crises extracts a high economic price, and it is unclear whether the large inequalities it generates are politically manageable within the frame of likely rates of economic growth. At the same time, the Western core has gone into relative decline, both economically and in terms of political leadership. The rise of China and India brings into play great powers that still see themselves as developing countries, have big historical chips on their shoulders and are so far without a clear vision of what kind of GIS they want. The 2016 votes for Brexit in the United Kingdom and for Trump in the United States might well point to the end of the Anglosphere leadership of GIS that has prevailed since 1945. All of this might suggest a resurgence of the LUM and some rollback of the FDM. But it is unclear how much the global economy can be wound back without causing large losses in wealth and power. At the same time, a variety of other functional issues of shared fate create strong pressure for functional management at the global level. These range from climate change and global disease control; through protecting the Internet and controlling transnational criminals and terrorists; to managing planetary defence against space rocks, controlling mass migration and dealing with the spread of weapons of mass destruction.

The justification for thinking that GIS is currently in transition to version 1.2 is that the era when the West dominated the core, and the core dominated the periphery, is coming to an end. The version 1.0 GIS was dominated by a handful of Western powers in imperial style. Version 1.1 was still dominated by the West, but mainly through its ongoing economic – and, up to a point, cultural (i.e., soft power) – primacy. Version 1.2 would mark the end of the Western ascendancy within GIS and the onset of a more politically, culturally and economically pluralist world, in which the West would no longer define the economic and cultural core, and liberal democracy would no longer define the hegemonic teleology of GIS. But version 1.2 would still be a recognizable relative of the state-centric GIS set up during the nineteenth century. In this world, power, wealth and legitimacy will be more evenly spread, and no state will be able to amass sufficient material resources or ideational legitimacy to play a superpower role. Arguably, the idea that any state, or any single civilizational group of states, has the right to lead GIS will itself become illegitimate. Version 1.2 GIS will be pluralist in a deep sense. It will be a world of great and regional powers playing alongside a wide range of NSAs, some of them also quite powerful. Rising powers such as China and India will join older dissidents such as Russia in asserting their own cultural and political values, and the West, although it will remain strong and influential, will no longer be able, or indeed willing, to set the terms of a liberal 'standard of civilization' applicable to all. The revolutions of modernity will have spread decisively beyond the West. This spread will not, however, create a culturally and politically homogeneous membership for GIS. The spreading of wealth and power, and the benefits and problems associated with them, will generate a substrate of the shared ideas of modernity, including sovereignty, territoriality, nationalism, human equality, development and scientific progress. But it will also empower a wide range of cultural and political differences. The spreading of modernity, following the logic of uneven and combined development, will continue to generate many different varieties of capitalism, each with its own political and cultural norms.

This emerging structure will not be *multipolarity* as classically understood because, lacking any superpowers or any aspiring to be superpowers, it will not feature a realist-type struggle for domination of the whole system. It will be something much more complicated than that, and has already been given many labels: *plurilateralism* (Cerny, 1993), *heteropolarity* (der Derian, 2003), *no one's world* (Kupchan, 2012), *multinodal* (Womack, 2014, *multiplex* (Acharya, 2014), *decentred globalism* (Buzan and Lawson, 2015a), and *multi-order world* (Flockhart, 2016). Our preferred label is *deep*, or *embedded*, *pluralism*, where *deep* means a diffuse distribution of power, wealth and cultural authority; and *embedded* means that cultural and ideological difference is not only tolerated, but respected and even valued as the foundation for coexistence. Whichever label is preferred, the emerging global structure is likely to be a mixture of globalization and regionalization. Such a return to a two-tier GIS has echoes of the version 1.0 GIS, but in version 1.2, the layering will reflect the logic of the RSM and FDM rather than the HPM. Globalization will take the form of an ongoing global economy on which all depend, a strengthening role for NSAs both civil and uncivil and a variety of shared fates needing to be managed. Regionalization will take the form of cultural and political clustering, some great power hegemonism and great power regional competition over spheres of influence. If the great powers behave responsibly about shared fates, then perhaps some kind of capitalist concert can manage what will be an increasingly pressing agenda of global problems.

Deep pluralism points towards a two-tier international society in which the global level is mainly concerned with handling shared fate issues, and the regional level is mainly concerned with promoting and defending regional political and cultural differentiation within the context of some form of ongoing global economy. In terms of our four models, this suggests that version 1.2 GIS will be an even more complicated mix than the earlier versions. The LUM will continue to be strong globally, though it is possible that empire-minded great powers such as Russia and China might try to undermine it within their regions. The HPM might be strong within some regions but seems unlikely to be resurgent at the global level, where cultural and political pluralism, and the more even spread of wealth and power, works against it and for the LUM. That said, it is a big but open question as to whether the HPM between states and NSAs will continue to hold. Some uncivil NSAs such as Islamic State have already dropped out of state jurisdiction, and some TNCs are powerful enough to defy or control some states. A breakdown or even a substantial weakening of this aspect of GIS might be a sufficient redefinition to justify a jump-shift to version 2.0.

On our analysis, version 1.2 GIS should be more defined by the RSM than has been the case so far, though this regionalization may well not be voluntary in some cases. Given the current crises in the EU and other regional IGOs, this is a bold prediction, but that is where the logic points. Given the global spread of modernity, increasing functional differentiation seems unstoppable within states and societies, and also in many ways at the global level. Shared fate issues, including the stability of the global economy, will make the FDM a continuing influence on GIS, though probably not a defining one.

Near the beginning of this work, in Chapter 2, we mooted a fifth formative submodel for GIS which we called *engagement among equals*. This model was offered as a possible pathway to the formation of a GIS within the larger *polycentric* model. We did not develop it much, because history mainly went down the *monocentric* pathway to GIS. But looking ahead, an *engagement amongst equals* model might be a useful guide for thinking about the evolutionary dynamics of version 1.2 GIS. In a world in which power, wealth and cultural and political legitimacy are widely distributed across both state and non-state actors, the next phase of evolution of GIS will almost certainly take a deep pluralist form. With some luck and some skill, it might also become embedded pluralism in which tolerance of difference has to be combined with common interest in dealing with a whole set of inescapable shared fate issues.

To conclude this exercise, it is important to restate the fact that a truly global international society is a quite recent development. Although its construction was under way during the early centuries of the European expansion, it was not fully realized until the middle of the nineteenth century. Before that, there was no GIS, but a collection of largely separate worlds with degrees of contact with others ranging from zero to sustained conflict. Within that framing, it seems to be the case that international societies, whenever and wherever found, usually operate with the logic of more than one model in play. Classical agrarian international societies tended to look mainly like versions of the HPM, but with religion in play they also contained significant elements of the FDM. Historically, the LUM is relatively rare, but it features enormously in ES thinking because it was the distinctive form that emerged out of Westphalian Europe, was then imposed on the rest of the world and has been gaining strength ever since. But this too has never operated in a pure fashion. During the colonial era, it was accompanied by strong elements of HPM both within the core, and much more so between the core and the periphery. Since the nineteenth century, the logic of the FDM has been growing within it, and since 1945, the RSM has also come significantly into play. So Adam Watson (2001: 467–8) was not wrong to criticize the ES for focusing too much on the LUM and not enough on hegemonic (i.e., HPM) forms of international society. Historically, HPM has perhaps been the dominant form of international society. But from our perspective, his critique was too narrow. First, there are other logics than LUM and HPM in play. Second, the choices are not mutually exclusive: most international societies contain mixtures from two or more of the models. If there is any sense of direction about this voyage through the three versions of GIS, it is that the mixture amongst the four models is getting ever more densely interwoven and complicated. That complexity will increase even more if, as we suggest, the RSM becomes more influential. A development along those lines would mean more differentiation at the regional level of international society, and a redefinition of the aims and purposes of international society at the global level.

If GIS is nearly always a mix amongst two or more of our models, and if the trend is towards greater complexity, how we can know whether GIS is getting stronger or weaker, or just different?

3   The Strengthening/Weakening Question

In this section, we start by aggregating the criteria for strengthening and weakening that were rather crudely sketched in the previous four chapters. Then we move on to consider each criterion in more depth and detail. Do these criteria contain more depth and nuance than we first identified? When taken together, to what extent do they overlap or play into each other?

We group these criteria in terms of how they relate to the units, structures and binding forces of GIS and note from which model(s) the criteria are derived. There are three criteria that relate to *units*:

1. Increasing the number or proportion of state members of GIS strengthens GIS while reducing either weakens it (LUM).
2. Weakening the units taken to define GIS weakens it, and strengthening the units strengthens it. The weakness/strength of states here is in terms of their degree of sociopolitical cohesion, not their level of material power (FDM).

3. Increasing the types of unit counted as members can cut both ways. On the one hand, bringing in NSAs and/or individuals can strengthen the legitimacy of GIS and broaden its social base. But on the other hand, multiplying the types and numbers of actors in play within GIS makes its decision-making more complicated (FDM).

There are a further seven criteria relating to *structure*:

4. Increasing the number of PIs defining GIS strengthens GIS, while decreasing the number weakens it (LUM, HPM, FDM).
5. Increasing the number of disputes over defining the PIs that constitute GIS weakens it, while decreasing such disputes strengthens it (LUM, FDM, HPM).
6. Fragmenting the core meaning of PIs weakens GIS (RSM, HPM), perhaps especially so if the PIs at issue are 'master' or 'foundational' ones, less so when they are 'derivative' (RSM), while consolidating the core meaning strengthens it.
7. The emergence of distinctive PIs at the regional or subglobal level might weaken GIS by fragmenting it but could also strengthen its legitimacy if it is seen to allow variations that do not contest its basic structure (RSM).
8. Increasing the uniformity and elaboration of shared practices within the PIs, beyond core meaning, that define GIS strengthens it (LUM, FDM), while fragmenting them weakens it (RSM, HPM). These practices are what was referred to as a PI's 'protective belt' of ideas in Chapter 4.
9. Increasing the proportion of solidarist to pluralist PIs within GIS strengthens it according to the LUM and its inherent logic of convergence. However, whether solidarist PIs have this effect in general has turned into a very complicated question indeed. The RSM and HPM are basically agnostic about the effects of solidarist PIs, recognizing their Western normative baggage. For these two models, the crucial standard for assessing strength or thickness is the volume, scale and range of social interactions and functions shared, as well as the relative absence of PI fragmentation (including regionally and subglobally). International societies dominated by pluralist PIs can do well according to this standard. Meanwhile, the logic of cooperation and interdependence entailed in solidarist PIs seems to create a natural momentum towards further specialization and hence will likely strengthen the FDM dimension of GIS. Whether the latter strengthens or weakens the overall cohesion of GIS seems to depend on a number of auxiliary principles we discussed in the previous chapter. This criterion therefore also cuts both ways.

10. Although it overlaps and integrates some of the preceding criteria, cultural cohesion also needs to be listed here. It plays in the LUM on the basis of Wight's influential hypothesis previously discussed about the linkage between shared culture and international society. It plays in the RSM in the form of cultural regions such as Europe and Latin America and culturally coherent subglobal groupings such as NATO and the OECD. It plays in the HPM in the form of cultural foundations, or not, for legitimizing hierarchical differentiations. And it plays in the FDM in terms of the vexed question of whether functional differentiation decomposed societies or provides emergent new foundations for them in division of labour and interdependence.

And there are a final two criteria relating to *binding forces*:

11. Structures supported by belief are stronger than those supported by calculation, which are stronger than those supported by coercion (LUM, RSM, FDM). This is particularly important for relations of hierarchy/privilege (HPM).
12. Arrangements of privilege/hierarchy cut both ways in terms of strengthening or weakening GIS, the key issue being whether they are legitimate (in which case they make GIS stronger) or not (in which case they weaken it).

Where relationships of privilege/hierarchy are more formal, this should strengthen GIS; where they are less formal, those relationships weaken GIS due to the potential for ambiguity and fragmentation in the interpretation of primary institutions (HPM). There appears to be a Western, perhaps legalistic, assumption that formal arrangements are per definition more legitimate, entailing belief, but that is far from always the case.

How does the contemporary GIS, and our mooted version 1.2 characterization of it, with its complicated mix of the four models and its transition towards deep pluralism, score according to these criteria?

Criterion 1:   State Members

This is a straightforward criterion that can fairly easily be measured by indicators such as membership in the United Nations General Assembly (UNGA) or mutual diplomatic recognitions. By this measure, contemporary GIS is strong and has only a little room for improvement. With the exception of Taiwan, the Israel/Palestine problem and a few small enclaves here and there, such as Abkhazia, nearly all states accord each other diplomatic recognition and/or have a seat in the UNGA. This is a notable improvement from the situation before 1945, when a majority of the world's states and peoples were denied such recognition. In 1946, the UNGA had fifty-one members. By the mid-1970s, decolonization, mainly of Asia and Africa, had trebled this number, and with the new states created after the dissolution of the Soviet Union and Yugoslavia during the 1990s, the number is approaching two hundred. Nearly all states and peoples are now members of GIS, so any further changes will be either marginal strengthening or, if some states and peoples leave or are pushed out, weakening. This criterion would not change much in a version 1.2 GIS.

Criterion 2:   Weak/Strong States

This is a much trickier criterion to measure. The general idea of states being spread across a spectrum from weak to strong in terms of socio-political cohesion, and that cohesion being consensual rather than coercive, is clear enough. Actually measuring this without political bias is much more difficult. In its survey of 178 states, the *Fragile States Index 2016* labels 126 of them as fragile in some degree, with 16 of those in its top two categories of fragility, and the other 52 as in varying degrees stable (Fund for Peace, 2016). But the criterion of consensual is easily conflated with democracy, and it is far from clear how to deal with countries such as North Korea, where it is impossible to tell whether the people genuinely love their government or are fiercely coerced into appearing to do so. Authoritarian governments in Russia, China and elsewhere can be quite popular, though both appear on the wrong side of the *Fragile States Index*. Yet there is a world of difference between a state such as China, where an authoritarian government has the support both of a mass party and a large part of public opinion, and might well win an election if it dared to hold one, and squalid, repressive, ineffectual dictatorships such as those in Gabon or Turkmenistan. Despite these difficulties, it is clear enough that there is a lot of room for improvement in this criterion. The suggestion in the *Fragile States Index* that more than two-thirds of states are on the wrong side of the fragile/stable line, with 38 of those very much on the wrong side being probably a broadly correct indicator of the current state of play. In its 2006 survey covering 146 states, the numbers were 106 on the fragile side and 40 on the stable side, which suggests not much change in the proportions over the last decade. So, by this criterion, while contemporary GIS has been strengthened by bringing most states and peoples into membership, it has been weakened because many of its members are weak or failed states. The concern in the classical ES about decolonization weakening GIS by bringing in a lot of weak states was not wrong and has not gone away (Bull and Watson, 1984a). Considerably fewer than half of the states-members of

GIS are strong and stable as states. This is a deep problem, unlikely to be solved quickly despite successful modernizing programmes in China and some other countries, or the solution of further partitioning existing states (compare unsuccessful South Sudan with the relatively more successful but still unrecognized Somaliland). So, this component of weakness would continue to play in version 1.2 GIS.

Criterion 3:   Types of Unit

We have argued that the formal hierarchical privilege of states over other types of actor remains strong, with states still holding the legal and political high ground within GIS and acting as gatekeepers on the type and level of participation allowed to NSAs. This means that formally, GIS remains largely a society of states, with other types of unit operating only within that framing, subject to the permission of states. On the other hand, we have also argued that NSAs have increasingly infiltrated diplomacy and other primary and secondary institutions of GIS, and that the more powerful of them can influence or even capture states. Thus, while NSAs have only subordinate formal ranking within GIS, their informal standing and status can be quite high. This is captured in the literature on global governance (e.g., Rosenau and Czempiel, 1992; Karns and Mingst, 2010; Bukovansky et al., 2012; Weiss, 2013; Smith, 2014), which emphasizes the practical extent to which smaller states and NSAs actually provide much of the global governance that used to be thought of as the province of great powers through the institution of great power management. But as Cui and Buzan (2016) argue, it is increasingly a blend of great powers, smaller powers and a variety of NSAs that provide the services of global governance.

Evaluating this development in terms of the strengthening or weakening of GIS is quite complicated. By keeping NSAs legally subordinate, GIS has largely avoided the problem of new types of formal members increasing the number of actors and the variety of interests in play to such an extent as to render decision-making within GIS potentially almost impossible. The active engagement of many NSAs in GIS thus strengthens it by bringing in new resources without diluting its political structure to the point of dysfunctionality. Indeed, the global governance literature sees such activity as getting around the dysfunctionality of great power rivalry and inertia. However, here we do run the risk of seeing more problems than is actually called for. Mediaeval Europe and the German Confederation are interesting case studies of how to make decision-making work with diverse types of actor, as are a number of other examples from non-Western history (Schouenborg, 2017). Whether such wider participation strengthens the legitimacy of GIS is difficult to say. By analogy with criterion 1 about numbers and proportions of states participating in GIS, wider societal participation should strengthen GIS. But against it is the argument that since most of the NSAs in play are Western ones, their participation plays into the politics of inequality and postcolonial resentment that weaken GIS (Clark, 2007: 183; Hurrell, 2007a: 111–14; on non-Western INGOs, see Davies, 2013). This criterion thus gives a mixed picture of contemporary GIS. In some ways, it has the best of both worlds by having substantial NSA participation without having opened formal membership to them. NSA participation no doubt increases legitimacy in some ways, but the uneven provenance of NSAs offsets this. Opening GIS to formal membership for NSAs alongside states would certainly be a very big structural change. But it is not clear that such a move would strengthen or weaken GIS, for a lot would depend on the nature of the NSAs included and excluded and on whether the necessary reforms to decision-making procedures were effective or not.

It is difficult to say how this criterion would play in a version 1.2 GIS. There is little sign that GIS is moving towards a formal opening up of membership to NSAs, and if it did that would mark a jump to version 2.0. To the extent that the existing array of NSAs is predominantly Western, and broadly linked to liberal agendas, it might be expected that NSAs' influence in the more pluralist world order of version 1.2 GIS would weaken. This would happen because of a relative decline in both the material resources and the ideational legitimacy backing them. Almost by definition, authoritarian societies are less likely to generate a robust sector of NSAs, meaning that in a world order balanced between democratic and authoritarian states, the authoritarians would not make up for a decline in NSA presence and activity from the democratic states. The main exception here is the corporate sector, where authoritarian states have been keen to cultivate national champion TNCs. It is not clear that the corporate sector has any strong interest in taking on political responsibilities by moving into formal membership of GIS. Version 1.2 GIS might therefore be more state-centric than the later phases of version 1.1.

Criterion 4:   Number of Primary Institutions

This is in principle another quite clear and measureable criterion.[1] Common sense suggests that the more PIs there are within GIS, the stronger its social structure should be, and vice versa. A GIS with only

---

[1] Falkner and Buzan (2017) offer an analytical framework for tracking the rise of new primary institutions and determining when or whether they have 'arrived' at the global level.

one PI does not, on the face of it, look as strong as one with ten. The number of PIs in play is open to empirical investigation, and as already noted there is an established literature looking at the rise, evolution and decline of primary institutions. A reasonable sense of the dynamics can be inferred from Buzan's (2014: 135–63; 2018b) survey of contemporary PIs. He argues that contemporary GIS is built around twelve PIs: the seven 'classical' ones (sovereignty, territoriality, war, international law, diplomacy, balance of power and great power management), four newer ones (nationalism, development, the market, human equality) and one emergent one (environmental stewardship). He argues that three PIs have become obsolete, with their functions being replaced by new PIs: dynasticism (replaced by nationalism and popular sovereignty), imperialism/colonialism (replaced by the universalization of sovereign equality and by development) and human inequality (replaced by human equality). He also argues that two PIs, democracy and human rights, often thought of as emergent, are in fact contested, and best thought of not as emergent but as strong only for a subset of GIS (this is discussed further in the following subsections on points 5 and 6). Buzan's survey suggests that by this criterion, contemporary GIS is quite strong. It has an impressive set of PIs covering a wide range of norms and issues and displays a robust dynamism in both replacing obsolete PIs and inventing and adopting new ones. This seems likely to remain the case within version 1.2 GIS.

Criterion 5:   Disputes over Primary Institutions

While contemporary GIS has a reasonable consensus around the dozen PIs just discussed, there are disputes about the standing of democracy and human rights. There is also the subtler issue of how coherent or not the set of PIs defining any GIS is.

Disputes about whether a particular PI has standing or not are an ongoing part of the evolutionary process of GIS. The market, for example, was contested throughout the nineteenth century and was the core ideological issue between the West and the communist bloc during the Cold War. Only after the end of the Cold War did it become a more or less universally accepted PI. A key difficulty here is distinguishing between PIs that are *emergent*, in the sense that they are heading towards universal adoption; and those that are *contested*, in the sense that some elements of GIS support them while some oppose, with no particular reason to think that they will ever become globally accepted values. With hindsight, it is easy to distinguish the two, but much more difficult looking ahead. During the nineteenth and twentieth centuries, the market looked more contested than emergent, but it won out in the end. Of the three PIs that currently fall into this category, environmental stewardship has successfully arrived, democracy looks likely to remain contested and the fate of human rights will depend on which definition becomes dominant. Environmental stewardship was contested until recently, but at the 2015 Paris conference there was a marked convergence about the practical implementation of 'common but differentiated responsibilities' (Falkner, 2016). This meant that while there was growing international agreement about the necessity for managing climate change, there was now also a growing acceptance that all must contribute to this process rather than just the more developed economies (Falkner and Buzan (2017). No such movement looks likely for democracy, where clear and deep lines exist between political liberals and authoritarians. Liberal claims about democracy as a universal principle and an inevitable evolution will carry less weight as the relative power of the West declines and that of authoritarians such as China rises. Human rights are a more open question. If human rights are defined in the Western way, with priority given to political rights, then this PI will remain contested. But if human rights are defined in the way preferred by China and many developing countries, with more emphasis on human security in terms of welfare, development and survival, then there is more possibility that human rights could become at least partially emergent (Cui, 2014; Ren, 2015; Kozyrev, 2016).

To a considerable extent, then, disputes over PIs in the contemporary GIS have been a consequence of an ascendant liberal West attempting to impose 'universal' liberal values on a partly resistant rest. As the West declines in relative power and legitimacy, GIS will probably become more pluralist, and the force behind liberal universalism weaker. Economic liberalism, in the form of the global market, has become a widely accepted PI. Democracy will remain contested, and to the extent that human rights is defined as human security, some common ground might well emerge, albeit with ongoing disputes over liberal views about political rights. Environmental stewardship is not a liberal institution, arising mainly out of shared-fate logic, and thus avoids this ideological element. All in all, contemporary GIS looks pretty strong in terms of this criterion. It has a lot of consensus on its main set of PIs, some of the disputes look resolvable, and those that remain might well become less pressing as the distribution of power and legitimacy becomes more pluralist.

This seems likely to carry forward into a version 1.2 GIS. To the extent that version 1.2 is defined by the relative decline of the West in general, and the Anglosphere in particular, as the core of GIS, then the disputes over democracy and human rights should become less divisive. There is quite broad consensus territory about human rights in the human security interpretation of it, and in a more deeply pluralist world, democracy will become more a subsystem value and less the universalist teleology of liberal myth. Shared-fate logic seems likely to support both the global market and environmental stewardship.

A more difficult question is the impact on the strength or weakness of GIS of contradictions within the set of PIs that define GIS. As Mayall has argued (Mayall, 1990; 2000), the rise of nationalism, the market and other liberal values such as human rights had a profoundly disturbing effect on the existing structure of GIS during the nineteenth century. The previously discussed classical seven PIs made a relatively coherent set in which each of the institutions was broadly compatible with all the others. Nationalism, the market and human rights, however, changed and often challenged the meaning of the existing institutions, putting pressure on sovereignty and territoriality and changing the purpose of war. As many have noted, human rights has become a new 'standard of civilization' by which the sovereign rights of states might be questioned (Bull, 1984b: 13; Gong, 1984: 90–3; Donnelly, 1998; Jackson 2000: 210–93; Mayall, 2000). From this perspective, the simple increase in the number of PIs is not necessarily an unalloyed good. Ever since the nineteenth century, GIS has been taking on board institutions that did not easily or comfortably fit together. Both nationalism and the market have unsettled territoriality and sovereignty, and the universalism of the market also threatens nationalism. Human equality has redefined sovereignty, and the emergence of environmental stewardship is likewise an uneasy fit with territoriality and sovereignty. It is perhaps quite normal for social structures to contain contradictory values, and such contradictions can serve to drive forward the evolution of societies as they confront and deal with them (Buzan, 2004a: 250–1). But it seems clear that a society with fewer such contradictions is stronger and more stable than one with more. Contemporary GIS has recently taken on two PIs, the market and environmental stewardship, that profoundly disturb some of its existing institutions, and by increasing its contradictions in this way they might be thought to have weakened GIS's structure. There is no sign that such contradictions will disappear in a version 1.2 GIS, and to the extent that version 1.2 is more complicated than earlier versions, there is some chance that they will increase.

Criterion 6:   Core Meaning of Primary Institutions

This criterion follows naturally from the previous one: disputes over primary institutions can erode those institutions' core meaning and/or change some of their associated practices (see criterion 8). This erosion can take at least two forms. One is obsolescence. The familiar example is colonialism after 1945. Another post-1945 example, albeit a derivative primary institution, is wars of conquest. The second form is what can perhaps be termed deep transformation. A principle example would be the fundamental transformation in the meaning of sovereignty when GIS in the nineteenth century moved away from dynasticism and towards popular sovereignty and nationalism. This, figuratively speaking, turned the issue of sovereign legitimacy upside down. Henceforth, legitimacy flowed from the bottom up rather than the traditional top down. This reversal in meaning, implying deep transformation, was also evident in the change from human inequality to human equality.

Are there currently any global PIs at risk of being subject to either form of erosion? This is probably as hard to anticipate as it was for contemporaries to predict the rather sudden and profound changes described in the previous paragraph. However, it is possible to identify some that are under considerable strain. Great power management is such an institution. The idea that there should be management is not challenged, only that it should be the prerogative of a small club of states. One can certainly imagine the move from the traditional oligopoly of the P5 to something like a two-tier division of states, with the ones on top – for example, the G20 – calling most of the shots in GIS, and perhaps with the (formal) involvement of a larger range of NSAs. Deepening global governance and functional differentiation might propel this scenario forward. Another version of this would be 'management coalitions' of small, medium and large states, as well as NSAs, dedicated to managing problems in discrete functional issue areas where they have special competencies or capabilities (Bukovansky et al., 2002). None of this would seem to weaken international society as long as (great power) management remains as an institution, meaning no absolute decline in the number of PIs in GIS.

There are, however, other developments that are potentially more upsetting to the cohesion of GIS and which may be carried forward into a version 1.2, perhaps even marking a change to 2.0. There is the question of the whole status of the transnational domain. If this domain gains in prominence on the back of increasing functional differentiation, calls may emerge for NSAs' formal political incorporation into GIS. This would not only complicate governance and decision-making, as noted previously, but also raise a number of complex questions linked to the current set of PIs. For example, should TNAs engage in diplomacy, and on what terms? Should they be a factor in the balance of power, and should they be able to join alliances? Should they be allowed as parties to international treaties, and what jurisdiction should they enjoy in relation to sovereignty and the monopoly on the legitimate use of force? These are just some of the obvious questions. There is significant potential for both strengthening and weakening here as the number of PIs in GIS either contracts or expands as a result.

Technology and the physical environment pose similar fundamental challenges to the core meaning of institutions. Sea levels may rise, eliminating some land territory in the process, and make 'sea territory' more important for states. This could, in turn, lead to more colonization of sea space, as in the permanent settlement of people either above or subsurface. Presently such sea colonization is mainly a phenomenon associated with houseboats in major coastal cities around the world, but science fiction has been contemplating this scenario for years (notice the 1990s movie *Waterworld*). Technological developments of different kinds could make such colonization more attractive. The same overall argument applies to the other spaces discussed in previous chapters: air space, cyberspace and extraterrestrial space. Sudden physical changes in the planetary environment or in the technologies available for 'accessing' these spaces could spell profound changes for the existing PIs of GIS. Whether any of these scenarios are likely is again very difficult to assess. The safe conclusion is that great power management will remain under some strain in version 1.2, while a number of additional game-changing scenarios are lined up in the background. Overall, then, the core meaning of most PIs in contemporary GIS can be judged as stable, thus contributing to the strength of GIS.

Criterion 7: Regional International Societies

We have argued that regional differentiation was relatively late to emerge in the history of contemporary GIS and that the influence of the RSM has been relatively weak. Since 1945, by far the clearest and strongest examples of regionally differentiated international societies are the EU and the former Soviet bloc. Elements of regional international society can be found in the Middle East, East Asia, Latin America and elsewhere defined by some variations in PIs and more in the practices associated with them. The Soviet bloc was, for a time, a major challenger to the Western-dominated GIS. While it accepted some of the classical pluralist PIs, its ideological position led to quite different practices about sovereignty (the right of the Soviet Union to intervene in the states within its bloc) and to a significant degree of subordination of nationalism to ideology. The Soviet bloc and China of course opposed the liberal PIs of democracy, human rights and the market. This challenge from the regional level has, however, been largely seen off. Capitalism and the global market won the Cold War, and post-Mao China, followed by post-Soviet Russia, abandoned ideological rectitude and embraced strong nationalism. All that remains is the ongoing dispute over democracy and human rights, neither of which ever achieved the status of global PIs. These values are divisive and weaken GIS when pushed as universal values against opposition. But they need not threaten GIS if they are taken as values within and for a regional or subglobal grouping, without universalist pretentions. Up to a point, this has been the case with the EU, which values these institutions for itself and for prospective members, while being less forceful about how others conduct their affairs. This dispute over liberal values was always wider than the East–West split. Elsewhere, regional differentiations have not significantly challenged the social structure of GIS. Even the EU, which produced the most institutionalized and most solidarist international society ever seen, did not challenge GIS in any fundamental way. It led by example, but in contrast to the Soviet bloc did not challenge the structure of international society. So far, then, the emergence of regional differentiation, except during the Cold War and earlier during the fascist period, has not seriously or permanently fragmented the normative structure of GIS. Where challenges were serious, they have been seen off.

That said, we have nevertheless predicted, against this historical trend, that regional differentiation might well play a much more substantial role in version 1.2 GIS than it has done in previous versions. In a more pluralist world, where power, political authority and cultural legitimacy are more decentralized, it is easy to imagine that regional and subglobal differentiation will intensify. If this prediction is correct, then the big question for the strength/weakness of GIS is whether such differentiation will be more along the lines of the EU, strengthening the legitimacy of GIS by allowing local variations that do not contest its basic structure; or more like the Soviet bloc or fascist international society, differentiating from GIS in such a way as to challenge some of its PIs and fragment its coherence. It is easy to imagine that a more regionalized GIS would be divided between democratic and authoritarian forms, but on our argument, this would not weaken GIS because that divide has been long-standing. Democracy has never been a global PI. If, however, some of the regional international societies are organized along hierarchical lines, as might be the case for the regions around Russia and China, then this would be a challenge to GIS that would weaken its normative structure by undermining the principle of sovereign equality. If Russia and China once again start thinking like empires, as both show clear signs of doing, then parts of GIS would move away from the LUM and revert to the HPM, although probably not in the formal way of the version 1.0 GIS before 1945. This, of course, could turn into a strength for GIS to the extent that it was recognized as a legitimate privilege–equality nexus, but we do not currently see much pointing in the direction of that outcome. We have argued that commitment to maintaining some significant form of global market is likely to endure, and that other shared-fate problems will press strongly for a continuation of the quite robust social structure of GIS that currently exists.

Criterion 8:   Shared Practices

The argument here runs in close parallel to that already made in the discussions of primary institutions and regional international societies. On the face of it, increasing the uniformity and elaboration of shared practices within the PIs that define GIS should strengthen it, while fragmenting them should weaken it. Variations in practice around commonly accepted PIs are common, and sometimes substantial. Sovereignty, for example, is universally accepted, but practices around it vary from hard (e.g., China, the United States) to quite soft (e.g., the EU and in some ways the Middle East) in terms of tolerance for intervention. The same is true for territoriality, about which sensitivity is extremely high in some places (e.g., China, Russia, Japan) and rather more relaxed in others (e.g., the EU). Practices are similarly varied in terms of war, with some states taking a highly constrained view (e.g., Japan, Germany) and others prepared to resort to it for a wider range of purposes (e.g., the United States, Russia, Israel). The same can be said for the market, where some countries are relatively open (e.g., the UK) and others much more restricted (e.g., China). In a strict sense, all these variations count as weakening. Yet as with regional differentiation, there is more complexity and nuance under the surface. Tolerating variation can also strengthen and stabilize GIS by allowing a degree of pluralism that increases its legitimacy while not creating such great divergence as to bring the PIs themselves (their core meaning) into question. This principle is recognized in the provisions made within the UN for regional IGOs. It might be argued that deep pluralism is defined by variations of practice, and tolerance of these by others. So long as such variance is recognized as being confined to particular subsets of GIS, and not making a global challenge requiring all to conform to the same standard, variations of practice might well be stabilizing. So-called Asian values are a good example of geographically limited practices and norms that apply mainly to a cultural region and not to the world as a whole. Thus, while greater uniformity of practice does indicate social strength, it is not entirely the case that variation of practice is simply weakening.

It seems likely that deepening cultural and political pluralism will generate more such variation of practice in version 1.2 GIS. Whether this will significantly weaken it will depend on whether the prevailing understanding of GIS shifts to deep pluralism, with its tolerance and respect for differences, or whether it still retains an overhang of universalist liberal solidarist aspiration from version 1.1. Acceptance of deep pluralism would make variations of practice legitimate and stabilizing. But if there is a hangover of aspirations to a universally shared standard, then such variation will be weakening for GIS.

Criterion 9:   Solidarist/Pluralist Primary Institutions

On the face of it, the distinction between solidarist and pluralist PIs looks like a clear marker for strengthening/weakening. A GIS based on logics of cooperation and convergence should be stronger than one based on mere coexistence and toleration of difference. But push a bit deeper, and this conclusion becomes problematic. The whole solidarist/pluralist framing is profoundly West-centric, as we have discussed several times already. It not only draws heavily on Western history but is also open to the ideological objection that it rests on a teleological view of 'universal' liberal values and the desirability of integration and convergence: 'to become one' or to create a world government. In effect, pluralism is the social theory version of classical realism, and solidarism the realization of liberal values. So long as solidarism is understood in this way, it supports a particular type of Western agenda. Arguably, this problem is not insurmountable, however, because the logics of cooperation and convergence do not have to be liberal. It is not difficult to imagine other ideological foundations for them, including, but not limited to, communism, Islam, Buddhism and environmentalism. In other words, humans can cooperate and/or converge around any principles they choose to agree on. Nevertheless, that does not change the fact that however you arrive at the desirability of cooperation, through liberalism, Buddhism or some other ideology/religion, it still seems to be a normative value commitment, not a neutral assessment of what makes social structures strong. Likewise, we should not accept the value commitment, paradoxically also championed by many liberals, that there is inherent strength in multiculturalism, implying pluralism. We need to put this debate on a sound and detached analytical footing, and to us that means understanding social strength or thickness as the volume, scale and range of social interactions and functions shared, as well as the relative absence of PI fragmentation (including regionally and subglobally). When we adopt this standard, we will better be able to understand why some quite uncooperative and conflictual international societies throughout history remained remarkably stable and endured over time. Again, we see longevity as evidence of strength, but not as a direct criterion for assessing strengthening or weakening.[2]

This means that any assessment of the role of solidarist and pluralist PIs in GIS becomes quite complicated. We have granted the possibility that solidarist PIs, to the extent that they promote integration and convergence, may strengthen the FDM dimension of GIS as functional differentiation, other things being equal, seems to flourish under such conditions. However, whether increasing functional differentiation will increase the strength of GIS as a whole is a different question.

Almost by definition, version 1.2 GIS is not heading towards anything like a model of convergence liberal universalism. Rather, it seems to be heading in the direction of a pronounced pluralism, with testy great powers shoving and pushing each other over spheres of influence, and the global commons receiving less attention. In another scenario, there might be a limited amount of functional cooperation on the global economy and a variety of other shared-fate issues such as the environment. It might even develop a post-Western embedded pluralism that is quite genuine and deep in its tolerance and appreciation of difference, though expectations for that can hardly be high. More likely is a continuation of postcolonial resentments, where the past continues to poison the present and the future, perhaps weakening GIS by stimulating fragmentation of not just solidarist PIs such as democracy, human rights and the market but also pluralist PIs, such as the balance of power, diplomacy and great power management. This could also, further down the line, lead to a world where states have resigned themselves to the inevitable consequences of global warming and other shared-fate issues and have withdrawn themselves into semiclosed regional blocs, as was once the objective of some fascist states during the twentieth century (and China and Japan in previous centuries). This could in principle be a very strong social structure, with pluralist PIs regulating the limited interactions between the blocs, as well as pluralist and solidarist PIs shaping the more substantial interactions within the blocs. Arguably, it would be a GIS very vulnerable to a global catastrophic event such as meteor strike, a pandemic or rising sea levels but not necessarily a weak or thin society, and it might have considerable staying power. For the moment, however, the majority of leading states appear to stand firmly behind the idea of managing the global commons somehow, so this latter scenario is not likely in the short to medium term.

---

[2] For a fascinating study of the normative structure underpinning the stability of the Chinese Empire, see Pines (2012).

Criterion 10:   Cultural Cohesion

During the period of Western hegemony, it was possible to imagine, particularly from within the West, that a liberal teleology of modernity was in play that would eventually produce global cultural convergence around liberal (or American) values. In other words, although cultural diversity was obviously present and clearly felt in the periphery, there did seem to be a case for the inevitability of eventual convergence. This was perhaps most famously captured in the future world envisaged by the original *Star Trek* series. Such visions were reinforced by the successful conversions of Germany and Japan after 1945, by the Asian Tigers during the 1990s, by China's shift towards capitalism from the late 1970s and by the implosion of the Soviet Union and its project after 1989. Convergence around liberal-democratic values almost certainly would have strengthened GIS in the same way that it strengthened the West.

But by 2008, this vision was in retreat, and what was in prospect was a world in which particularist cultural reassertion was on the rise. Authoritarians in Russia and China wrapped themselves in the legitimacy of cultural differentiation and strong nationalism. Islamists promoted the Koran as the political constitution for the Muslim world. The BJP in India promoted Hindutva as a national ideology. Britain decided that it did not belong in Europe. And the United States drifted first into unilateralism under the Bush administration and then to Trump's 'America First' withdrawal from global leadership. The victory of capitalism in the Cold War had in an important sense narrowed the ideological bandwidth of GIS and so strengthened the framework of consensual primary institutions. But the removal of zero-sum ideological rivalry between capitalism and command economy did not produce identity convergence. Instead, it opened the door to the rise of identity politics and increasing cultural and political differentiation. This was reinforced by the crisis of neoliberal capitalism over inequality and migration, which sapped its teleological pretentions, and by the diffusion of wealth and power that marked the 'rise of the rest'. What we are looking at ahead is deep pluralism with strong cultural and political differentiations.

This development looks as if it should weaken GIS, especially if seen from a liberal or Western perspective. But that is not necessarily the case. Deep pluralism can itself become a source of strength for GIS provided that the powers accept pluralism as the foundation for common primary institutions. Deep pluralism is an empirical statement about the distribution of wealth, power and authority. It does not necessarily require tolerance and respect for one another (although that is possible too). Within pluralism, the recognition of difference is the starting point for considering what is normal, acceptable practice in GIS. Traditionally, conquering and killing off other states based on cultural difference was considered an acceptable practice in this deep pluralism scenario, though this is now much more constrained by fear of great power war than in the past. If accepted, deep pluralism could become embedded and, probably sustained by a large dose of calculation, open the way for varieties of cooperation on issues of shared functional concerns from the global economy, through the environment, to disease control. This is not an either/or choice between conflict and cooperation: history offers plenty of antecedents for the coexistence of both. If pluralism becomes deep (in the sense of substantial and durable differences amongst the members of GIS), but not embedded (in the sense of transforming the recognition of difference into common primary institutions), then this would weaken GIS.

Criterion 11:   Hierarchy of Binding Forces

This criterion offers the clear proposition that structures supported by belief are stronger than those supported by calculation, which in turn are stronger than those supported by coercion. This logic is particularly important for relations of hierarchy/privilege (see criterion 12). The underlying rationale is that belief, once established, requires relatively few resources to sustain a given social structure; calculation requires more resources in the form of side payments; and coercion requires most resources. In effect, there is a sliding scale from belief, which makes the relevant behaviours largely internally self-enforcing, through to coercion, which requires widespread external enforcement to maintain the relevant behaviour. If the relevant resources are assumed to be in limited supply, then social structures requiring higher resource inputs to sustain will tend to be less stable and have shorter lives. In reality, nearly all social structures will be supported by some complicated mix of these three, putting the emphasis not on pure models but on relative proportions. In part, this criterion links to criterion 2 about the strength/weakness of the units composing GIS, which also depends on a mix of coercion, calculation and belief.

Accurately determining the current and future strength/weakness of GIS in terms of the hierarchy of binding forces would require a separate study. One would have to do a close survey of each PI in the current social structure to get a sense of how it is held in place. It seems likely that many of the current PIs would come out quite well, indicating strength in the GIS. Nationalism, sovereignty, human equality and development, for example, are widely and popularly supported as a matter of belief almost everywhere. Environmental stewardship could join this group. The right to war under specified conditions (e.g., self-defence) and not others (e.g., imperialism) also probably has wide popular support. As argued in Chapter 3, the general public does not, with some exceptions, usually engage much with institutions such as international law, diplomacy and great power management, but these usually find strong support amongst state elites. The market, however, almost certainly has a more mixed profile, being held in place partly by belief, partly by calculation and partly by coercion, and with complex possibilities for the distribution of support and opposition between and amongst people and elites. If these estimates are more or less correct, then much of the social structure of GIS is quite strong. The main question mark is over the market, and whether it will survive the relative decline of the West as its material and ideational backer. Here the emerging line of tension is perhaps state elites who back the market because of its ability to generate wealth and power, and the masses who find decreasing advantage in increasing costs from its operation, though the lines of support and opposition can be much more complex and cross-cutting than this bald statement implies. This general picture of quite broad strength for many PIs, but fragility for a few, seems likely to carry forwards into version 1.2 GIS.

Criterion 12:   Legitimacy of Hierarchy/Privilege

That the hierarchy of binding forces is particularly relevant for HPM structures is indicated by the difference between, on the one hand, a legitimate dynastic structure such as a much-loved monarchy (e.g., Thailand), or a legitimate process of religious succession, such as the papacy, and on the other hand, a warlord type of dictatorship largely held in place by terror and coercion with a narrow base of legitimacy. The same logic applies to international societies. Hierarchical international societies can be strong if the principle on which they are based has widespread legitimacy. This is the kind of argument that Ikenberry (2011) makes when he presents the current liberal order as easy to join and hard to overturn: in other words, strongly supported by belief and calculation. Another example would be the way in which Korea was for long a faithful cultural and political vassal of the classical Chinese-centred world order in East Asia (Swope, 2009). If hierarchical orders do not have that kind of consensual support, then they must be maintained by coercion. Unless coercive resources are extremely one-sided in their distribution, as they were in favour of the Europeans during much of the nineteenth century, then coercive orders are likely to be costly and short-lived. A more recent example would be the Soviet bloc. If China evolves in imperial mode, it is possible we may see another such one-sided coercive order in East Asia. While shared belief in the principles of communism and the leadership of the Communist Party of the Soviet Union did play a significant role, there was also a lot of coercion. Soviet troops had to intervene repeatedly in Eastern Europe, and when this threat was withdrawn, the bloc quickly collapsed, along with the Soviet Union itself.

It is not clear that the distinction between formal and informal, which we developed in part as a way of marking strength and weakness, actually does so. Informal arrangements such as the British constitution can have a lot of strength where they are consensually supported, and formal arrangements, such as colonial rule, might require a good deal of coercion to hold them in place. Other things being equal, though, informality carries the risk of ambiguity in interpretation leading to potential fragmentation.

International societies with strong elements of HPM can therefore be assessed as weak or strong according to their placement on the binding forces spectrum from coercion to belief. By this criterion, contemporary GIS is perhaps weakening as the legitimacy of US and Western leadership declines. But this is happening at the same time as the HPM generally is losing weight in the contemporary GIS because of the diffusion of power, wealth and cultural legitimacy. If we are right in our sense of what version 1.2 GIS will look like, then the specifically HPM issue of strength/weakness is likely to play more strongly at the regional level than at the global one.

4   Conclusions

The main conclusion about the models is that the social structure of GIS has always been far from simple, and that it is getting more complicated as all four models come into play in defining it. There are numerous multifacetted interaction effects between the models that this book has only very provisionally started to address. A second conclusion is that the LUM indeed looms large in the picture. The present GIS is to a large degree defined by segmentary differentiation. Yet 'older' forms, hierarchical (HPM) and functional (FDM) differentiation, are becoming more visible again, as is the more 'recent' geographical differentiation form (RSM). A potential shift from one predominant model to another would arguably mark the change from a GIS version 1.2 to 2.0.

The most obvious conclusion about the question of whether an international society can be assessed as weak or strong, or weakening or strengthening, is that it is an extremely complicated question! The source of this complexity is the complexity of GIS itself, where many different factors bearing on weakness and strength are in play at the same time, and they are not all pulling in the same direction. The discussion can be summed up in static and dynamic terms: how weak or strong is contemporary GIS now; and in what direction are the criteria pointing for version 1.2 GIS? Within those two headings, we can differentiate where the criteria are clearly for stronger, where they are unclear or indeterminate and where they are clearly for weaker.

Static View

Clearly Strong
>   State members
>   Number of primary institutions
>   Disputes over primary institutions
>   Regional international societies
>   Hierarchy of binding forces
>   Core meaning of primary institutions

Indeterminate
>   Types of unit
>   Shared practices within primary institutions
>   Solidarism/pluralism
>   Legitimacy of hierarchy/privilege
>   Cultural cohesion

Clearly Weak
>   Weak/strong states
>   Contradictions amongst primary institutions

Dynamic View

Clearly for Stronger
>   Number of primary institutions

Indeterminate
>   Disputes over primary institutions
>   Shared practices within primary institutions
>   Solidarism/pluralism
>   Legitimacy of hierarchy/privilege
>   Regional international societies

Clearly for Weaker
Cultural cohesion

Change Unlikely
State members
Weak/strong states
Types of unit
Contradictions amongst primary institutions
Hierarchy of binding forces
Core meaning of primary institutions

One conclusion from this is that contemporary international society is quite strong, albeit with some significant weak points and some areas of uncertainty. Only one criterion points towards a clearly weaker GIS in the dynamic view, and that one depends on whether deep pluralism becomes embedded or not. Geographical differentiation in the form of regional or subglobal challenges to other parts of GIS is probably the best candidate for promoting social disintegration under present conditions and may combine with all the other criteria listed as indeterminate under the dynamic view. But there is no guarantee that geographical differentiation will lead to weakening, rather than, say, a new and robust form of pluralism causing strengthening. We think we have gone to considerable lengths to identify potential sources of, and paths for, change. One can hardly argue that we have been unduly biased towards the status quo. However, on our analysis, the status quo in the form of the static view has a lot of things going for it and only a few consistent problems. And these problems, weak states and contradictions among primary institutions, are indeed consistent. The number of weak states in GIS has remained fairly constant in recent years, and contradictions among primary institutions have neither significantly increased or decreased. As we have stressed in this chapter, there are several potential game changers lurking in the background, for example the formal integration of the transnational domain, but these scenarios do not appear likely in the short to medium term.

Another conclusion is that there will be substantial continuity between versions 1.1 and 1.2, with version 1.2 remaining quite robust despite the big changes in the distribution of power, legitimacy and cultural authority. Because of the many criteria for strength and weakness that are in play, it becomes a distinct possibility that GIS changes shape and/or form without necessarily becoming, in aggregate, noticeably stronger or weaker. The balance and composition of the factors may change in ways that more or less cancel out, and precise measurement is not really possible. This is, of course, frustrating from an analytical perspective. Ditto from the perspective of the policy maker and the concerned citizen who would prefer firm predictions about what the future might bring. However, with this aggregation of models and criteria, we have, for the first time, a clearer idea about the relevant questions to ask when addressing the issue of social cohesion on a global scale. And this is a profoundly important issue. A social collapse on the scale of the disintegration of the Roman world in antiquity does not seem to be on the horizon, but it is an ever-present possibility that should be on the minds of IR scholars and the wider public.

In the next and final chapter, we will discuss some of the many implications that result from these arguments, particularly for ES and IR theory, and openings for future research.

Part III

Conclusions

8   Conclusions

In Chapter 1, we set ourselves a number of aims with this book, and now we will review how well or badly we fulfilled these, and what research agenda emerges as a result. With respect to the latter, we will in particular discuss the implications for ES and IR theory and the links to other social science disciplines, notably sociology.

1   How Well Did We Fulfil Our Aims?

One of the things that we have sought to achieve has been to add to the consciousness within IR that much of its theory is abstracted from (mainly Western) history, and that IR theory and world history are in important ways co-constitutive. Amongst the most conspicuous examples of this is the tendency to view GIS as 'Western-global' and the Western parts as more solidarist (often implying more developed, benign, civilized), and any attempts to upset this order as inherently dangerous. We have fundamentally qualified this understanding by unsettling the metaphorical epicentre of 'the global', located in the West, and pushed its boundaries outwards, so that the global now refers to the composite of all global social relations (an intuitively banal but profound analytical move) and does not implicitly or explicitly privilege one part of these. What provoked this change of perspective for us was mainly the question of how to differentiate 'the regional' and 'the subglobal' from the rest of what was going on in GIS: *what* exactly was it that these phenomena were supposed to be differentiated from? Having reviewed the ES literature in this area, it became clear to us that there was an unhelpful propensity towards equating the West with the global, and making this the benchmark against which regional or subglobal differentiation should be judged. The Western interpretation of sovereignty, to give an example, was assumed to be the authoritative one, and non-Western interpretations as deviations from the ideal. Taking this argument further, we might also point to the conventional IR (and particularly realist) inclination to idealize anarchy and bipolarity, rather than seeing these as contingent outcomes of a very malleable international society expansion process. Our discussion in Chapter 2 was partly meant to stress the open-endedness of the expansion story, but also to emphasize (not essentialize) some of the structural legacies that did eventually result from it: the types of state present in GIS; the enduring privilege and hierarchy issues; and, indeed, the regional differentiation of GIS. Once we started to address these structural legacies in a more detached fashion as elements pointing towards (but not equal to) potential models of GIS, we were onto the overall contribution of this book: a new framework for analysis of GIS. This framework is certainly still mainly abstracted from Western history, but we have arguably gone further than most ES and IR scholars in our attempt to incorporate the story of the non-West in our theory.[1] We hope that others, particularly those whose cultural and historical backgrounds lie outside the Western core, will develop this perspective further.

Where we have perhaps not gone far enough in our abstraction efforts is with respect to the pluralist–solidarist debate. Let us be clear from the outset that this is not just a debate of relevance to nerdy ES scholars but one that speaks to enduring concerns of the wider IR discipline: the relative presence, and substance, of cooperation and conflict, and order and justice, between states. The way we have dealt with this debate here has been to frame it as a quintessentially normative debate about two principles that are both contested and tied together. This debate is rooted in the West and in the expansion story. The debate reflects the hard-learned lesson (recall the Thirty Years' War) that it pays off to respect difference, but also the aspiration for unity and the project of convergence around more specific values such as human rights, the market and democracy in the present era of history. The normative content of this debate changes with time and circumstance, but its essential dualism remains the same (see Buzan, 2014a).

For us, there is a temptation to abstract this debate into analytical concepts that may be applicable to not just Western international society but also the non-West and international societies in the more distant past. In fact, this is what Buzan (2004a) attempted with his pluralist–solidarist spectrum of international societies, ranging from from 'asocial' and 'power political' at the pluralist end, through 'coexistence' and 'cooperative', to 'convergence' and 'confederative' at the solidarist end. However, we are still struggling with the question of whether what we associate with the solidarist end of the spectrum is a general form of social structure or rather just a normative (Western) ideal and have

---

[1] For a similar, but in a sense more radical, approach to this, see Schouenborg (2017).

tended to take the latter view. This question became very present in our minds when we had to address it in the context of another question: whether solidarism could be equated with a stronger/thicker international society and pluralism with a weaker/thinner one. Observing the recent and more distant past, this equation did not necessarily appear to hold. It is hard to identify clear examples of confederative international societies, and extensive cooperation indeed seems to be only a feature of some parts of GIS post-1945. By contrast, there are examples of more power political international societies in the past (mediaeval Europe, ancient Greece, China of the warring states period, parts of precolonial Polynesia, etc.) that displayed substantial and sustained interaction between the units and had a range of primary institutions that proved quite enduring. How can we not label the latter strong/thick social structures? We may also recall here the observation in Chapter 5 that seemingly very oppressive privilege–equality nexuses can be profoundly stable, especially when supported by belief.

Maintaining solidarism's association with strong/thick will require us to make the seemingly illogical move of assessing social structures in most of recorded history as weak since supposedly solidarist structures are so rare and mainly contemporary. We hesitate to go down that path. As discussed in previous chapters, to us, an intuitive definition of strong/thick appears to be the volume, scale and range of social interactions and functions shared, as well as the relative absence of fragmentation of primary institutions (including regionally and subglobally). According to this standard many societies in the past were strong/thick, including some that were indeed very uncooperative and conflictual. Schouenborg (2017), for example, has documented in some detail how such uncooperative and conflictual societies can have quite elaborate primary institutions in several distinct functional spheres. Consider the Mongols, a quintessential warrior society, that nevertheless displayed institutions well beyond the functional sphere of warfare. In fact, it had a very complex political economy revolving around the production and exchange of silk, with a range of primary institutions. Some of these practices were directly tied to war and plunder, and yet others appeared more cooperative (Schouenborg, 2017: 107–13). Of course, this economic system was not as complex as twenty-first century finance capitalism. But it would seem counterintuitive to deem it less strong on that basis.

A potential objection to the line of argument developed in the preceding is that many societies may indeed have been strong/thick in the past, but that solidarist societies today are *even* stronger/thicker. Following this reasoning, one might argue that power political societies (according to

Buzan's understanding) may have quite elaborate rules about conflict, but that those rules will be in a narrow band. Building further on this argument, one might say that cooperation will inevitably involve a broader range of issues and thus naturally result in a larger volume of primary institutions around these. However, a war society need not only be focused on war, as just discussed in relation to the Mongols. There may also be institutions related to predatory trade or predatory environmental practices, and even predatory diplomacy (deceiving and isolating enemies). Arguably, in principle, for every imaginable instance of institutionalization around cooperation, in whatever functional sphere, it is possible to conceive an inverse example of institutionalization around conflict. To use an analogy, crime can be viewed as a one-to-one institutionalized way of getting around the cooperative rules established by society. For every rule or norm, there is a potential counter rule or norm. We do recognize that in practice, a lot of institutional rule breaking is premised on the prior establishment of cooperative rules. The complex ways of getting around WTO rules in trade would not exist if the WTO regime had not been created in the first place. However, does that fundamentally challenge the argument that conflictual social structures can be just as elaborate as cooperative ones? We are not so sure about this. And even if it is true that there are more issue areas and rules in play in cooperative societies, what prevents those from being signs of institutional fragmentation rather than the uniformity we tend to associate with societal strength? These questions need more debate.

Another potential objection: it may initially appear as if written laws (often implicitly associated with cooperation), with their many articles and paragraphs and so on, are indeed very complex/thick. However, we wonder whether they are in fact more complex/thick than the subtle unwritten norms of some uncooperative and conflictual societies. Also, the great historical expansion of law in society seems to be associated with modernity and the increasing division of labour, thus relating this argument back to the one concerning the functional differentiation model, and how solidarism and strength/thickness might only be intensely correlated in that particular model.

And to dispel a third potential objection, or rather misinterpretation, we do not think of strength/thickness as coordination of specific policies or effective alliances against common enemies – in other words, collective action. To again bring up the example of the fascist international society (Schouenborg, 2012), it displayed relatively little of these things. However, it did represent a fairly stable consensus around a set of primary institutions.

Anticipating some of the discussion in one of the following sections on the link to sociology, there is a pronounced tendency when thinking about social cohesion to project one's own normative values into the concept. Today, in Europe, the concept of social cohesion has come to be associated with economic equity and social rights, amongst other things, in political discourse. Yet in North America, the same concept refers instead to multiculturalism and diversity (Koff, 2013: 48–9). Perhaps we just need to reconcile ourselves to the conclusion that pluralism and solidarism are inherently normative concepts that do not lend themselves to inclusion in neutral social structural theory. The one potential exception to this point, from our perspective, is when we are dealing with the likely consequences for one or more of our models of pursuing certain normative values in an international society. As we have discussed in previous chapters, the extensive integration implied in convergence and confederation (both normative values in the Western tradition) would seem to suggest a natural momentum towards further division of labour and hence further functional differentiation. However, this is a hypothesis that should be explored. If the hypothesis is true, that means that solidarist PIs seem likely to strengthen the FDM dimension of an international society, as we also noted in one of the previous paragraphs. Moreover, we have argued that the inherent logic of convergence in the LUM would similarly mean that solidarist PIs would strengthen this dimension of an international society. But pluralism–solidarism do not seem to have a bearing on the social cohesion question with respect to the other two dimensions covered by our models. The strength/weakness criteria elaborated for the RSM and HPM are not dependent on the pluralist or solidarist content of PIs. The pluralist–solidarist debate thus occupies a marginal position in the ES social structural framework we have arrived at in this book.

Let us stress, though, that we do not think that we have conclusively settled this issue of strength/weakness, thickness/thinness and pluralism–solidarism. As should be clear from our discussion, this is an immensely complicated topic, and at most we claim to have brought it into sharp enough focus to trigger a useful debate. We hope that our discussion appeals to analytical and normative ES scholars alike. Analytical scholars should by definition be interested in the development of a sounder taxonomy. And normative scholars should benefit from having a clearer idea about what is in front of them, and whether this structure is getting weaker or stronger, as a point of departure for debating their ethical ideals and how to achieve them.

Another general aim of ours has been to get a better handle on what it actually is that we (ES scholars and the wider IR discipline) refer to when we invoke the idea of international society at the global level, and the question of whether that society is getting weaker or stronger. These are issues that also occupied the minds of the classical ES scholars in the context of decolonization and declining British influence in international affairs, but they seem to have become all the more urgent today as the whole West is going into relative decline. We have taken a modelling approach to this and have attempted to abstract from the structural legacies that we detected in the expansion story, as well as from our knowledge of differentiation theory in sociology. That resulted in the four models that have formed the core of this book. Now, one might object that the act of abstracting from the expansion story leaves us open to the same charge of Westcentrism that we have critiqued elsewhere. However, that would be to overlook some important characteristics of what we are doing. We emphatically do not attempt to idealize any of these structural legacies in a normative fashion, but rather use them as a jumping-off point for identifying ideal-typical social structural principles that can be applied transhistorically and cross-culturally. For example, we do not come out and say that a like-units anarchy is the optimal way of arranging international relations or anything of that sort. We are saying instead that the like-units principle is a structural element of international relations that may be more or less present, and in a mix with the remaining three principles captured by our four models. Have we missed any important structural legacies in our modelling? We don't think so, because our models cover thoroughly the more stratificatory forms of international society that dominated much of the history of civilization across the world. It is now for others to assess this and see whether our new framework is as comprehensive as we think it is. Also, our identification of the core principle in each model is subject to debate. We certainly struggled with untangling the different principles of the RSM and HPM. Nevertheless, what we end up with is a radically new framework for analysis of international society at the global level. It arguably allows us, for the first time, to analyse the parts that make up this social whole in a comprehensive and systematic fashion.

A second thing that this framework allows us to do is to address the question of whether the social whole of GIS is getting weaker or stronger. Although far from being absent from previous ES scholarship, this question has nevertheless not received any sustained or systematic attention. Ours is, as far as we are aware, the first attempt to think through systematically the criteria that might be used for such an assessment. Altogether, we have derived twelve criteria from the four models and applied them to contemporary GIS. As we discussed in the previous chapter, this resulted in the conclusion that GIS is fairly strong at present, albeit with some significant weak points and some areas of uncertainty (this could come as a surprise to many in the context of the doom and gloom that dominated the international public discourse following the admittedly very important political events of 2016!). It is appropriate here to reiterate the point made in Chapter 3 that what we have attempted has been a form of reconnaissance or scoping exercise, aimed at doing an initial, and inevitably somewhat rough and impressionistic, survey of the landscape of international society as seen through the lens of differentiation theory. The purpose has been to open up and problematize this topic for more detailed theoretical and empirical analysis in the future. With that important caveat in mind, our assessment of the strength/weakness of GIS and the criteria with which we have approached this are highly provisional. Moreover, we have come to realize that some of the criteria for assessing strength/weakness appear to cut both ways, which further complicates analysis. And to the probable dismay of many of our methods-conscious colleagues in IR and beyond, the different criteria do not seem to lend themselves to precise measurement. All this said, we think we have managed to establish a baseline for a future debate that may very well include questions such as these: Are there more potential criteria by which strength/weakness might be assessed? Are some of the twelve criteria formulated by us problematic? Do the criteria, despite our best efforts, still reflect a lingering Westcentrism? What is the balance between the criteria, i.e., are some more important than others? Related to the latter, what is the balance between the three types of criteria (units, structure, binding forces)? These are just some of the obvious questions that readily occur to us. And, of course, in our framework the strength/weakness criteria are derived from our four models. Add or subtract a model, or change the configuration within, and this will have repercussions for how we approach the strength/weakness question.

We thus believe that we have fulfilled our taxonomical aim of providing a set of conceptual tools for engaging the problem of international society at the global level. We have done this in part by retelling the expansion story in a way that pays much more attention to those who were expanded on, and not just those doing the expanding. This perspective tells us a lot about the structure of the world we are now in. However, large questions remain that are equally of a taxonomical nature, and where our choices are, at the very least, debatable. For example, we have chosen to integrate the three domains (interstate, transnational and interhuman) into all four models. We think it makes sense, but it could be argued that the domains are structural legacies in their own right and thus deserving of being thought of as independent models. Arguing in the other direction, another potential objection is that there is a sense in which the interstate domain overlaps with the like-units model. Both are concerned with the morphology of states. Should they be fused into one? However, defending our position, the transnational domain, for example, seems to be so tightly integrated with several of our models, notably FDM and HPM, that it would be hard to configure them without that domain. And pursuing the interhuman domain as an independent model would probably take us too far away from the subject area of IR that we still believe rightly to be the substance of interactions between corporate social actors, and particularly states in the contemporary era of history (see Schouenborg, 2017). To conclude, we think we have fulfilled the aims we set ourselves, but at the same time stress that, more than anything, this should be considered an opening for further debate. This is precisely the point we want to take up in the following two sections, where we look in more detail at, first, the implications for ES and IR theory, and second, for sociology and the social sciences more broadly.

2   Implications for ES and IR Theory

It seems appropriate to start this discussion with the three concepts that arguably stand at the centre of the ES tradition: international system, international society and world society. Most of what we have said in previous chapters has related directly to international society, not to the other two concepts. The reason for bypassing international system was discussed early on and needs no extensive treatment here. Our basic view is that there is no purchase in distinguishing between (international) system and society. Any kind of interaction between corporate social actors will involve social content, and thus the mechanical, machinelike understanding of IR implied in the system concept is at root misleading. Even the mechanical, billiard-ball anarchical system portrayed by some realists depends on the prior social agreement on the constitutive rule of sovereignty (Onuf, 2002: 228). World society, by contrast, has been a kind of silent passenger on the theoretical journey in this book. We have made mention of the concept in passing several times but not subjected it to any sustained discussion. This might have come as a surprise given Buzan's (2004a) earlier work in this area. To be honest, this neglect of world society, if you will, was not a conscious choice of ours. Rather, it seems to have come about as a consequence of our conscious and direct pursuit of global international society and models for differentiating this particular social structure. That said, the conclusions we have reached do appear to have implications for world society, and, equally, world society may have implications for how we think about the social cohesion of international society. For the purpose of reflecting on these implications, we will draw on Buzan's (2018a) understanding of world society as containing three distinct meanings: normative, political and integrative. Since these labels are new, they deserve a little elaboration.

Normative world society, according to Buzan, suggests a collective identity that acts as the moral referent for the political and normative aspirations of the society of states. In traditional ES scholarship, this collective identity has mainly been approached in cosmopolitan fashion as the largest one imaginable: humankind. However, as Buzan stresses, there is in principle no reason why other more limited group identities should be excluded from this understanding of world society; any kind of group identity is potentially fit for motivating political and normative action. National identity is a prime example of such a limited identity, as are different regional and civilizational identities such as European, Scandinavian and Confucian. In this *normative* understanding of world society, group identity is just that: a normative referent. The group does not have to have organization or even internal consciousness of being a group; it need not exist, other than in the minds of those who make normative and political claims on behalf of it. Definite organizational form, by contrast, is the core characteristic of *political* world society. Here Buzan is trying to capture all those actors outside the society of states – in other words, non-state actors – that have organizational capacity to engage with and potentially influence the society of states. This applies to corporate social actors ranging from the antislavery movement to Amnesty International, as well as to individual human beings as activists, who can also act in this non-state political capacity. In short, then, normative world society is about collective identity, and political world society about NSAs. Normative world society is the ideational resource on which political world society draws to lobby the society of states. Combining these two understandings with Buzan's three domains (interhuman, transnational and interstate), *integrated* world society becomes a suggestive template for a possible future world political structure whereby NSAs (including individuals) have obtained a degree of equal standing and rights vis-à-vis states. It would not necessarily be a world government, but it could take that form, and could draw legitimacy from the normative ideal of representing all of humankind on a planetary scale, both as humankind and as an array of subglobal collective identity groupings.

What are the implications for world society of our analysis in this book? First, we have reconfirmed some of the conclusions already present in the world society literature. Partly this is because we drew extensively on this literature in making our own arguments. For example, we have confirmed that NSAs have become more prominent in and consequential for international society over the past 150 years or so. They have grown in numbers and have been able to shape and influence political agendas in international society. In turn, GIS, particularly the liberal and Western parts of it, has conferred legitimacy onto NSAs by delegating responsibilities to them and by integrating them into collective decision-making, making them partners in global governance. We have also confirmed that NSAs are still formally subordinated to states and are likely to remain so for the foreseeable future. Yet we have made some partly novel observations too. We have put forward functional differentiation as a key driver of the expansion of political world society, which can be related to the creation of modern states and societies in the nineteenth century, a transformation of world historical magnitude (see Buzan and Lawson, 2015a). This functional differentiation is likely to continue. Presently, we do not see much scope for rolling this development back. Trump and his followers, as well as kindred populist movements across the West and beyond, are no doubt clamouring for a return to a golden and venerated past. However, we find it highly implausible that such backward-looking movements can overturn the partly market-driven functional differentiation in contemporary societies. The arguable beacons of functional differentiation, modern cities, which are projected to grow at a rapid pace in the twenty-first century, will work against such movements. So will the many other vested interests that have a political and economic stake in the present globalized order. Even at a popular level, it would seem that people, by and large, accept a substantial degree of functional differentiation as a natural part of modern life. For these reasons, barring some cataclysmic, game-changing crisis, functional differentiation will continue and will only take new forms within the confines of potential future protectionist trade policies. And if functional differentiation continues, so will the expansion of political world society. That is our hypothesis.

Our book may also offer new tools for analysing political world society. The HPM and the concept of privilege–equality nexi holds forth the promise of more fine-grained pictures of the complicated relationships between NSAs and states that appear likely in the future. The FDM opens up space for NSAs and the logic that drives their rise. Perhaps these tools can take us beyond what is, for some purposes, an unhelpful dichotomy in ES debates between the ideal of an integrated world society and the present situation where NSAs are formally subordinated to states. As pointed out in previous chapters, history suggests that there are many different solutions to marrying the principles of equality and privilege in politics (and other functional spheres) that may obtain a great deal of belief-based acceptance. For example, delegation of responsibility over some functional tasks to NSAs, say, development assistance, may indeed go very far. It is easy to think of cases where private development agencies are in practice working alongside public agencies as equals or even crowding the latter out. Haiti springs readily to mind.

There are equally some logical and obvious connections when trying to think through the implications of world society for our argument. Focusing on normative world society, one cannot help but recall Wight's (1977: 33) assertion: 'We must assume that a states-system will not come into being without a degree of cultural unity among its members.' One question that follows from this is whether an encompassing group identity is a sign of a strong international society. To provide the obvious example, is the strength of GIS dependent on the idea of humankind as a normative world society referent? Maybe. However, as mentioned previously, Buzan (2018a) also allows for the presence of more limited regional or subglobal group identities as normative world society referents. Perhaps these can mutually reinforce one another through a logic of deep or embedded pluralism and together provide for the same 'level' of international society strength. The obvious example here is how nations as particularistic normative world society referents are sufficiently broadly accepted across the globe to constitute nationalism as a key primary institution of GIS. Yet it is certainly possible to imagine group identities pulling in the other direction, fragmenting the social fabric of GIS. The revolutionary challenges posed by communism, fascism and so on are cases in point. All this runs in close to parallel to what we argued in respect to the RSM in previous chapters. Again, we hope that these insights help to problematize the weak/strong question in an interesting and useful way.

There is also the highly interesting question of whether international society *itself* can fulfil the role of a normative world society referent and how this plays into the question of weakness/strength. To the extent that international society represents a group identity with certain definite and identifiable characteristics, it does have this quality. Moreover, the integrity and safety of this group identity have been used over and over again down through the centuries as a normative justification for action by statesmen and NSAs alike: from the ambition to reestablish the tranquillity and repose of Europe in the course of the Thirty Years' War, to justifying the different coalitions against revolutionary France and Napoleon in the late eighteenth and early nineteenth centuries. A potential spin on this is how a past political society can act as the normative referent for a present or future one. Examples are again readily forthcoming. Think only of the place of the Roman Empire in the mythology of Western international society before and after it became global, or the past Sino-centric Empire in East Asia as a normative referent for present Chinese political aspirations. Do such normative usages of international society suggest strength or weakness?

Lastly, we will briefly touch upon the 'nuclear option' of fusing international and world society conceptually. Without using the specific terms, this is in fact what Schouenborg (2017: 15) is suggesting when he argues that there is presently already only *one* global society. This is not the same as Buzan's integrated world society, discussed previously, which depends on the meeting of fairly strict criteria about reducing or eliminating the hierarchy amongst the different types of unit in play. This understanding takes the simpler view that GIS is already a single society because individuals, NSAs and states are all interacting with each other in a fairly intense way, and that inevitably social institutions are involved in this. This society has two different dimensions: one pertaining to its first-order elements (individuals) and one to its second-order elements (corporate social actors or polities).[2] The latter can include anything from families, through bowling teams, to states. However, while society has these two dimensions, it is nevertheless essentially indivisible; it is one. A major benefit of this approach is that it takes us consciously away from the traditional reification of the state in IR and ES theory that follows naturally from the division between international society (states) and world society (non-state). This latter division seems to be an accident of modern Western history and thus not appropriate for transhistorical and cross-cultural theory (if that is indeed our ambition with social theory). This is a quite radical proposal that will probably struggle with attracting followers within the ES and beyond. However, it is a proposal with a distinct logic to it that, at a minimum, deserves consideration by historically minded scholars.

Primary institutions, and less so secondary institutions, have been central to the argument developed in this book. Primary institutions have acted as the key empirical referents for the different models and informed much of our thinking about the strength/weakness question. We have not pursued the kind of typological work that characterized some of our previous separate engagements with institutions (Buzan, 2004a; 2014a; Schouenborg, 2011; 2017; see also Wilson, 2012), but rather approached primary institutions as, to an extent, theoretically

---

[2] For discussion about the distinction between individuals and corporate actors, and within the latter between state and non-state, see Buzan (2004a: 91–7, 118–27).

unproblematic. Yet primary institutions *are* problematic. They are hard to pin down as discrete phenomena, and they obviously change over time. They can be evolved through incremental adaptation between the corporate social actors involved and their surrounding environment, and they can be imposed or adopted more rapidly by new or present members of society as a consequence of coercion, calculation or belief. Moreover, they display complex and open-ended interaction effects. That is, they shape and condition one another in ways that we (the ES and IR) are still only in the early stages of exploring. This should be a priority for future research. Nevertheless, a tentative and by no means uncontested consensus is beginning to emerge within the ES about a list of global primary institutions: sovereignty, territoriality, diplomacy, international law, nationalism, human equality, development, the market, great power management, the balance of power and war. This is complemented by a shorter list of possibly emerging primary institutions that remain contested by different sections of GIS. Democracy is much advocated by liberals as an emerging global primary institution, but in fact seems to have fought to a draw with authoritarianism and is therefore an institution only for a certain subset of states. Likewise, human rights are promoted by liberals as a universal value, but remain hotly, deeply and widely contested as to whether its focus should be more on political and social rights or more on economic, development and survival ones. Environmental stewardship is more of a shared fate issue, and arguably (Falkner and Buzan, 2017) with the Paris agreement of 2015 it has arrived as a global primary institution despite the continuing opposition of climate change deniers. Our analysis in this book can be seen as an attempt to strengthen this consensus, while we, of course, welcome further research and debate.

As of now, relatively little effort has been dedicated to thinking through the problem of what the primary institutions of world society look like. However, new work on this is beginning to emerge. For example, in a recent paper, Thomas Davies (2017) has argued that there are analogous institutions in world society to those found in international society. Intriguingly, he finds that NSAs can be demonstrated to operate with a whole host of primary institutions. The society of NSAs has membership criteria that fulfil the same function as that of sovereignty in international society. They also seem to engage in practices that are really similar, in basic form at least, to diplomacy, international law, the balance of power, war, territoriality and great power management. Environmental stewardship and human rights are equally present. Davies does not reflect much on whether there are any primary institutions that are unique to world society, meaning dissimilar to those found in international society, and moreover gives little attention to 'uncivil society', but he does succeed in jump-starting debate in this area. Buzan (2018a) has also started to address this issue in the context of discerning the different meanings of world society discussed in this book. Here he argues that 'collective identity' is the core primary institution of normative world society and that 'advocacy' stands at the centre of political world society. Furthermore, he has begun the taxonomical exercise of trying to define in more detail the institutional interplay between world society and international society. The models developed in this book can easily provide the signposts for taking this research further. The LUM can be used to explore the extent to which NSAs share a basic morphology related to the institutional composition of the transnational domain, and similarities and contrasts with the actor-likeness present in the society of states. The RSM will allow for studies of the subglobal and regional distribution of primary institutions in world society. The HPM can focus attention on the hierarchical organization of NSAs and the ways in which this is expressed in primary institutions and conditioned by broader general status roles such as race, gender, class and civilization. And lastly, the FDM can throw light on the increasing and multifacetted division of labour between NSAs and states, and the primary institutions that have likely emerged as a result. Our hunch is that all of this will produce new and longer lists of primary institutions, which in turn will provide the justification for theorizing institutions in more detail. That might take us back to our aforementioned separate typologies of primary institutions (Buzan, 2004a; 2014a; Schouenborg, 2011; 2017).

Secondary institutions have featured far less prominently in this book. Yet they do deserve more attention going forward. Recall from the definition given in Chapter 1 that secondary institutions are purposefully designed functional organizations. So far, they have mainly been understood as IGOs. It is not inconceivable that the relationship between primary and secondary institutions holds some potential for unlocking the secrets of social cohesion in international society. Secondary institutions in the form of IGOs both express primary institutions (in their constitutional documents) and reproduce and develop them (in their practices and rhetoric). New important ES work on this relationship is already in the pipeline (Knudsen and Navari, forthcoming; see also Spandler, 2015). Buzan (2018a) has recently offered the idea that NSAs can be thought of as the secondary institutions of world society, and that on this basis states themselves might also be a form of secondary institution. NSAs fit pretty clearly within the idea of purposefully designed functional organizations. On balance, as lobbying outfits NSAs will tend to have more actor quality than IGOs, many of which are mainly forums with not much actor quality (Buzan and Little, 2000: 266–7). Only a few IGOs, such as the EU and the World Bank, have serious actor quality beyond the collective will of their members. So, both NSAs and IGOs are a mix of forums and actors.

Whether or not states can or should be considered as secondary institutions is more problematic and requires more thought. States fit the definition inasmuch as they are organizations rather than just principles or practices, and also because they have functional purposes. But states are generally not purposefully designed in the way that NSAs and IGOs are. More like primary institutions, and in tandem with them, states have mostly evolved. They are the organizational expressions and reproducers of primary institutions, initially of sovereignty and territoriality, and from the nineteenth century, also of nationalism. Thinking along these lines opens up some radical possibilities. It could bring the LUM into play in a much more profound way as the main vehicle for exploring the morphology of states, IGOs and NSAs alike. Framing secondary institutions in this way, as including entities with actor qualities, can put this debate on a whole new footing and connect it to another prominent debate within IR, the one concerning the agent–structure problem (see in particular Wight, 2006). Following this framing, agents would refer to secondary institutions and structure to primary institutions. As we read this debate, it has mainly been focused on the issues of change and causality, and not least ontology and epistemology, but it could also offer potential insights into the social cohesion question: whether certain relations between agents and structures provide for a stronger or weaker international society? Building a bridge between these two IR debates could thus be a way of further unpacking the social cohesion question in the future.

One of our overall aims with this book has been to provide a set of systematic criteria for comparative and evolutionary studies of historical international societies, and we believe that the four models and the strength/weakness criteria accomplish that. They also permit us to take existing historically focused ES debates in new directions. For example, Watson's (1992) pendulum model of change and his typology of international societies might be combined with our HPM. This could lead to studies of, say, how historical suzerain international societies were underpinned by different general status roles such as race, gender, class, etc.; how historical dominion international societies might have displayed something similar to great power management today; or how hegemonic international societies approached the privileging of some collective social actors over others. Such studies may illuminate past social arrangements but can also help us understand the potential for change in our present global international society by pushing the boundaries of the imaginable.

Sticking with the theme of hierarchy, the HPM may have two additional benefits. First, the model may take the debate about hierarchy in the ES to full maturity. As we discussed in previous chapters, contributions to this debate have proliferated in recent years and gone well beyond the important and pioneering works by Gong (1984) and Keene (2002). But ours is the first model that systematically integrates what we see as the three main areas of discussion: (1) the privileged position of some states vis-à-vis other states; (2) the privileged position of states vis-à-vis both non-state actors and individuals; and (3) the privileged position of broader, general status roles. And the model moreover introduces the important concept of privilege–equality nexuses that can tie the three together in different and complex ways. With this, a strong foundation for taking this debate forward has been built. The second benefit follows from the first. It is our impression that the wider discipline of IR at times views the ES as a conservative and antiquated holdout of the British imperial tradition, with all the normative baggage that entails (see, for example, Callahan, 2004). This may be true to an extent, but to us the ES has always first and foremost been an attempt, drawing on insights from history, law, philosophy and sociology, to grapple with some rather open-ended questions concerning the shape and logics of the 'social whole' that we have come to label global international society. The initial questions asked by the classical ES were therefore bound to be subject to revision and updating. With the HPM, we have done so with respect to the arguable core of the British, and all other, imperial traditions: hierarchy. Going forward, we hope that this can revitalize ES theory and provide a bridge to other growing constituencies within the IR discipline, notably those interested in postcolonialism, history and theory.

In the preceding, we have made different observations about the implications for central ES concepts and debates, and now we will turn to a set of more specific issues and hypotheses that have emerged in the course of the discussion in this book.

First there is the idea of *sectoral* international societies advanced by Stroikos (2015). He develops this in relation to nuclear issues and space, but it is an idea with wider implications. As previously noted, it served as one of several inspirations for our FDM. To us, there is no doubt that functional differentiation, as implied in sectoral division, is an important principle in contemporary GIS. However, the question is whether it is presently so important that it makes sense to speak about separate sectoral international societies with specific primary institutions, as we do with reference to regional international societies. Stroikos suggests that there are technology-driven international societies. For example, he argues that there is a space-faring international society (as in extraterrestrial space) and an international cybersociety. Such arguments are convincing up to a point. Yet we do not think differentiation has progressed far enough to warrant such labels. We have discussed the issue of space (sea, air, extraterrestrial space and cyberspace) in depth in previous chapters, and one of the conclusions was that while the logics involved challenged the traditional territorial framing of international society, these logics had not yet fundamentally undermined this framing nor constituted competing international societies. For example, we have not witnessed large-scale permanent colonization of sea space, and sailors and houseboat inhabitants do not usually claim to be members of a separate international society. The sectoral nuclear society proposed by Stroikos is not space-bound but rather exclusively based on technology: the national ability to harness nuclear power. To be sure, he can demonstrate that a lot of international law, diplomacy, great power management and so on is dedicated to this specific issue area, but it still feels wrong to label this a separate international society. That said, when we speak about regional international societies, we do not demand that these are fully separate societies either; we are quite comfortable with speaking about degrees of differentiation within GIS. That would seem to count in favour of Stroikos' argument. We do not propose to settle this debate here but merely note that it is up to future research to determine more clearly the levels of differentiation possible in international society, be that functional, geographical, hierarchical or segmentary.

In Chapter 7, as part of our problematizing of the weakness/strength question, we asked whether a move towards formalizing NSA status within GIS would strengthen it. Counting in favour of the strengthening view would be the increased legitimacy derived from formally recognizing actors already involved in international public policy, as well as the likely benefits of increased coordination and legal standing. However, it is relatively easy to think of scenarios where these benefits could be undone or where they would instead promote weakening. The integration of NSAs could undermine the legitimacy of states as the privileged actors in the present international order, and potentially, further down the line, lead to the unravelling of the states-system. Furthermore, a formal, recognized role does not always lead to more coordination, but could equally lead to more obstruction, particularly if NSAs achieved the legal means to do so in international courts. More broadly, decision-making with multiple actors would be complex and potentially ineffectual. However, we may be suffering from a number of biases in making these reflections. One such bias concerns the very idea of the beneficial nature of effective decision-making and its link to societal strength. If a social system is faced with a tangible threat – say, climate change – that is likely to result in this social system's collapse if unmet, then effective decision-making would seem to be a requirement. Yet if we instead adopt our general notion of strength/thickness as the volume, scale and range of social interactions and functions shared, as well as the relative absence of PI fragmentation (including regionally and subglobally), then that would in principle be possible with quite dysfunctional decision-making at the international level. Not necessarily likely, but possible. We may also overestimate the consequences of decision-making complexity and underestimate the means to counter this. The EU is a good case study of how multiple actors – state, supranational and subnational – get quite a few things done within a complex institutional framework. Barbara Koremenos (2016) similarly teaches us how states of widely varying sizes and capacities on a day-to-day basis succeed in designing complex legal regimes to provide for effective international action in different functional spheres: security, the economy, the environment, etc. Such legal regimes could arguably be constructed for the inclusion of NSAs as well. And as we have pointed out previously, there are also several historical examples of complex decision-making with multiple actors from which to draw lessons. All this seems to merit further research and is an area where the ES might rekindle its old connection to international law.

The issue of whether, in general, informality produces weakness and formality strength is related to the preceding discussion. We have argued that, other things being equal, informality breeds ambiguity and conflicts over interpretation, thus potentially leading to the fragmentation of the institutions of international society. That would be a clear weakening scenario. Nevertheless, we have discussed several examples of how informality might produce the opposite effect in practice. The British constitutional system, or the lack thereof, is a case in point. We realize that in engaging in this debate, we have perhaps opened up a Pandora's box of problems. It seems to be a debate with an extensive root network across the social sciences. We are, for example, reminded about Durkheim's (2013) observation that social violation in 'primitive' mechanic societies, supposedly informal, was followed by prompt and instinctive sanction. Whereas in 'advanced' organic societies, supposedly formal, the same violation would be subject to a potentially drawn-out and fraught legal process. Which of the two is indicative of the strongest society? It will take a most intrepid scholar (or group of scholars) to get to the bottom of this. We hope someone out there is willing to rise to the challenge.

Lastly, there is the issue of binding forces. More research is called for to assess their presence and role in GIS, not least in terms of the strength/ weakness question. The way we have empirically approached binding forces in this book has been highly impressionistic. Schouenborg (2013) is slightly more systematic and detailed in his analysis of the binding forces in the Scandinavian regional international society. Yet this is, to our knowledge, the only other large-scale attempt at applying the concept of binding forces in ES scholarship. Here we would like to invite innovation on two fronts. First, we would just encourage more empirical studies of individual binding forces and individual primary institutions. For example, what is the role of coercion as a binding force in contemporary GIS? Or which mix of binding forces supports, say, the market, human rights, international law or diplomacy? Taking this further, it would be beneficial to have more comparative studies of the binding forces supporting regional or subglobal international societies as those conducted by Schouenborg (2013: 50–69). This would naturally appear to suggest innovation on a second front, namely how to methodologically assess the presence of the different binding forces. Schouenborg (2013: 40–9) has presented certain overall criteria, but a lot more work can potentially be put into this. We do not anticipate one magic formula – a research framework that will offer a cast-iron approach to identifying binding forces for methodologically frustrated graduate students and the like. The difficulties surrounding the application of other central ES concepts such as primary institutions, pluralism and solidarism, and indeed international society, should caution against such simplistic hopes. Rather, what we foresee is the potential for multiple angles of attack, employing multiple empirical methods.

3   Links to Debates in Other Disciplines

Sociologists are probably the scholars that have thought the hardest about the problem of social cohesion, given that they are obviously interested in what it is that holds (domestic) society together (for one overview, see Friedkin, 2004). Some of the issues raised in this literature might initially appear less relevant to our discussion in this book. For example, the issue of membership competition with other societies does not seem to match the conditions in contemporary international society: there are presently no alternative societies to join. However, when thought about more carefully, the issue of membership is, of course, relevant. In theory, states could opt to exit the UN and choose to disregard the primary institutions of international society more broadly, potentially setting up their own competing 'clubs'. The Soviet bloc did, of course, represent a kind of alternative, and as the United States under Trump turns away from global leadership, there is speculation as to whether China will try to create an alternative. And arguably some so-called rogue states have had some of their membership privileges of international society suspended. Moreover, the issue of formal membership of NSAs of international society has certainly been a topic of discussion in this book.

Meanwhile, sociologists are not the only ones who have been interested in social cohesion. Indeed, the concept has attracted attention from a diverse set of academic disciplines (see Green and Janmaat, 2011) and have been used actively by national and international policy makers as well as IGOs. As a result, it seems, the concept suffers from stretching, fragmentation and outright normative agendas. As noted in a previous section, social cohesion may refer to multiculturalism and diversity in a North American context, while in Europe it can signify economic equity and social rights in political discourse (Koff, 2013: 48–9). Green and Janmaat (2011: 6) have done a comprehensive survey of these meanings in academia and the policy community and argue that the concept is often associated with the following characteristics (social attitudes and behaviours):

- Shared values and goals (such as liberty, democracy, meritocracy, equality, etc.)
- A sense of belonging and common identity (including national and other forms of identity)
- Tolerance and respect for other individuals and cultures
- Interpersonal and institutional trust
- Civic cooperation
- Active civic participation
- Law-abiding behaviour (low crime rates)

Moreover, again according to Green and Janmaat (2011: 6), the literature views certain social institutions as a prerequisite for social cohesion:

- Institution for the sharing of risk and providing social protection (the welfare state)
- Redistributive mechanisms (such as taxes) to foster equality or equality of opportunity
- Conflict resolution mechanisms

The two authors eventually arrive at their own definition that sees social cohesion as referring to 'the property by which whole societies, and the individuals within them, are bound together through the action of specific attitudes, behaviours, rules and institutions which rely on consensus rather than pure coercion' (Green and Janmaat, 2011: 18). We agree with the first part of this definition, but of course see coercion as something that can, usually in combinations with calculation and belief, produce cohesion as well. On the same page, they indicate that intergroup harmony is part of this togetherness, something that we have strongly contested in this book. To us, societies that display, or even celebrate, large-scale violent conflict can be enduring, stable and strong. Nor, according to our understanding, do such societies have to be characterized by interpersonal and inter-group trust or cooperation. The crucial issue is consensus around social institutions, amongst which can be some that are premised on conflict, such as the institution of war in contemporary international society. To that extent, we probably agree with Friedkin's (2004: 410) sociological definition:

Groups are cohesive when group-level conditions are producing positive membership attitudes and behaviors and when group members' interpersonal interactions are operating to maintain these group-level conditions. Thus, cohesive groups are self-maintaining with respect to the production of strong membership attractions and attachments.

It thus seems as if there is a certain resonance between the understanding of social cohesion in international society set out in this book and those found in cognate disciplines. However, given our more expansive time frame, covering the expansion of international society, as well as touch-ing upon societies in the more distant past, we are perhaps less prone to read into the concept of social cohesion the characteristics of the present era of history, and particularly the normative values associated with modern liberal (welfare) democracies. It also appears as if we have gone quite far in formulating criteria for assessing strength/weakness based on our four models. Here sociologists and others might take something from this book that they can build on. More broadly, the dialogue about social cohesion might help to bridge the always somewhat artificial boundary between IR and its cognate disciplines.

Another bridge that is worth crossing is to the literature that deals with societal collapse. In this book, we have mainly contemplated scenarios in which GIS goes through different forms of transformation. Yet we have also been open to the idea that different factors (a game-changing war, changes in the planetary environment, technological innovation, etc.) might produce a more profound unravelling of GIS. Interestingly, Bull (1977: 12–13) also briefly touched upon this issue in his discussion of Heeren and the nature of order. In that context, it seems obvious to pursue the link to the literature that has explored this phenomenon in the past. Most readers are probably familiar with Jared Diamond's popular book *Collapse: How Societies Choose to Fail or Succeed* (Diamond, 2005). It has received a lot of attention and critique, but also, it seems, propelled debates forward, particularly in archaeology. There is now a large literature on environmental determinism (what Diamond is often accused of) and on other factors contributing to collapse and the timing of it (quick versus slow) (e.g., Tainter, 1988; Lawler, 2010; McAnany and Yoffee, 2010; Butzer, 2012; Middleton, 2012; Cline, 2014; Johnson, 2017; Storey and Storey, 2017).

One might object that the scope conditions are too different. Diamond, for example, mainly deals with the collapse of small island societies such as Easter Island in the Pacific. Can this be meaningfully compared to GIS? The same applies to the admittedly larger Maya civilization, which has also received attention from Diamond and others. Another potential objection is that these historical societies are simply too different from the market-integrated and functionally differentiated GIS that we observe today. These points should be considered carefully. Yet our basic assumption is that it is possible and valuable to compare across time and space. 'Societies' is probably a classification more like fruit than like apples: one needs to keep aware of differences, and to proceed with caution, in making comparisons, but there are nonetheless significant shared features across a more general category such as fruit or society. There is a parallel here to our discussion of classification systems in earlier chapters. In fact, one of our ambitions with this book has been to provide a theoretical framework that can, metaphorically speaking, travel back into the past. Now, having that as our starting premise, what are the most obvious and significant connections that can made between this literature and our book?

First, most contributions to the collapse literature appear to be concerned with the issue of explanation: what causes collapse? Diamond's book (2005) and his 'five-point framework' can again be used as an example. He argues that five factors affect the process of collapse: (1) environmental damage; (2) climate change; (3) hostile neighbours; (4) friendly trade partners; and (5) society's response to environmental problems. In a more recent contribution, Johnson (2017) adopts a similar framework (environment, agriculture, trade, society and catastrophes) but puts particular emphasis on the idea of social hubris as the thing that prevents societies from successfully responding to external or internal problems. By social hubris, he means 'excessive pride or arrogance ... that causes people to ignore evidence and prevents proactive adaptation' (Johnson, 2017: 1–2). Our framework is not an explanatory framework. We do not explain *why* international society has changed over time, only *how* it has changed. What we offer is a set of models for thinking about social structural composition and transformation. However, those interested in explanatory theory may take inspiration from what is offered here. Scholars in the collapse tradition may find parts of our framework compelling, since they have tended to undertheorize, it seems to us, the social dimension of collapse (some may retort that we have overtheorized it!). In the same way, ES and IR scholars interested in large-scale explanation may attempt to combine some of the insights of the collapse literature with our framework to construct new theories of international political change. To give but one example, can any of the factors mentioned by Diamond and Johnson be connected to, say, the evolution of the HPM dimension of GIS?

Second, the collapse literature may help us think through more carefully different collapse scenarios. Very interestingly, one of the issues that the literature has debated at length is the momentum of collapse: quick versus slow (see, for example, Lawler, 2010; Storey and Storey, 2017). The very word 'collapse' seems to imply abrupt or sudden change. But contributors to this debate have suggested that the unravelling of societies can occur over longer time periods. Storey and Storey (2017), for example, in their comparative study of the 'slow collapse' of Maya civilization and ancient Rome, argue that the process can unfold over a couple or several centuries. Allowing for the distinct possibility that change happens faster in contemporary GIS, this is nevertheless a fascinating scenario to contemplate. Could it be that regional differentiation in international society would gather momentum slowly and only result in the complete disintegration of primary institutions at the global level after, say, a century? Or will the movement of people away from some areas of the planet that are becoming gradually uninhabitable due to global warming take place over fifty years or two hundred years? And what would the latter do to the institutions of international society, notably sovereignty and territoriality?

Another fascinating issue discussed in this literature is the variable impact of collapse on elites and commoners. Many have noted the disconnect between the two. In Johnson's (2017: 8) words: 'For the most part, elite and large-scale components of a society are the hardest hit, while ordinary citizens tend to muddle through transitions and adapt to a new normal.' There are intriguing examples of how more mundane aspects of culture are carried forward in the wake of a collapse. For instance, archaeologists have discovered villages in northeastern England that held on to the traditions of the Roman Empire (language, kitchenware, construction methods) after it had retreated south, while neighbouring villages quickly adopted new cultural practices (Lawler, 2010: 907). In the same way, one might imagine that the potential collapse of international society need not be catastrophic for the planet's inhabitants. They would probably be subject to all sorts of disruptions and changes, but people might not be dying in the streets as is sometimes suggested in apocalyptic scenarios. The issue of elites and commoners also speaks to our discussion in previous chapters about the depth of international society, or how rooted international society is in global collective consciousness, beyond the ruling echelons. For example, people at large may have a rudimentary understanding of some of the principles of diplomacy or great power management, but these primary institutions are mainly carried forward by a global political elite. Take away or fragment this elite, and international society will unravel, so the logic must go. Following on from this, elites are probably also where we should first look for signs of impending collapse. This is the direction in which Johnson (2017) appears to be pushing us when he suggests that we should focus in particular on elite social hubris as a facilitating factor for collapse. We hope it is therefore clear that this literature is pregnant with implications for thinking about contemporary GIS and where it might be heading in the future, as well as offers insights into the social cohesion or strength/weakness question.

4   Conclusions

We have claimed this book to be a new framework for analysis for global international society. Five concrete accomplishments justify that claim:

- Both in our historical account and in the setting out and integration of the four models, we think we have made substantial progress towards both identifying what the subject is when we talk about 'global international society' and delinking that idea from its close association with a Westcentric interpretation of 'global'. We are confident that our four models capture a very wide range of both historical and possible future forms of international society.
- We think that our four models have both exposed the ironic hegemony of 'like-units' thinking in the ES that was bemoaned by Wight and Watson and opened clear analytic pathways to thinking not only about hierarchy and privilege, but also functional differentiation. By delinking GIS from the West, we have also cleared away a big obstacle to thinking about regional and subglobal international society.
- We think we have opened up and problematized the vital, but neglected, question of how to assess whether an international society is strong or weak, and strengthening or weakening. That said, we are highly conscious that we started from a low base – little more than a

periodic concern over this question without any systematic investigation about how to answer it in any authoritative way. We hope to have at least provided the basis for a debate about what needs to be taken into account to make such judgements. We are fully aware that this is a very complicated question with many variables in play, and that some of the variables themselves work in ambiguous ways. There is scope here both for more theoretical and conceptual work and for empirical studies.

- We think we have opened up and problematized an important but neglected aspect of the solidarist/pluralist debate by addressing the confusion between these two normative ideas on the one hand, and whether international societies are thick or thin, and weak or strong, on the other. Our main interest is to construct more objective ways of assessing weakness and strength and to rely less on criteria drawn from explicitly normative agendas. We think we have made some progress down this path, though we have by no means entirely disentangled the two. We hope that opening up this line of thinking will make it both easier and more necessary for those in the normative debates to think about the consequences for international society of what they advocate.

- We have not focused particularly on the world society issue in this book, but as suggested in this chapter, our analytical framework opens up a variety of pathways for thinking about how international and world society are differentiated, and in what ways they can be, or arguably have to be, recombined.

- We hope that our new framework for analysing GIS takes forward a variety of debates in and around the ES. There is certainly room to contest some of what we have done. There is also a lot of opportunity for additional research in some of the areas and questions that we have opened up. However readers may respond, we are absolutely confident that the ES in particular and IR and some other social sciences more generally need to get to grips better than they have so far done both with the structure and evolution of GIS, and with assessing what makes international society stronger or weaker.

Bibliography

Aalberts, Tanja E. (2014) 'Rethinking the Principle of (Sovereign) Equality as a Standard of Civilisation', *Millennium: Journal of International Studies*, 42:3, 767–89.

Acharya, Amitav (2004) 'How Ideas Spread: Whose Norms Matter? Norm Localization and Institutional Change in Asian Regionalism', *International Organization*, 58:2, 239–75.

— (2011) 'Norm Subsidiarity and Regional Orders: Sovereignty, Regionalism, and Rule-Making in the Third World', *International Studies Quarterly*, 55:1, 95–123.

— (2014) *The End of American World Order*, Cambridge: Polity.

Acharya, Amitav and Barry Buzan (2019) *Towards a Global International Relations: Reflections on IR at 100*, Cambridge University Press.

Albert, Mathias (1999) 'Observing World Politics: Luhmann's Systems Theory of Society and International Relations', *Millennium: Journal of International Studies*, 28:2, 239–65.

Albert, Mathias and Barry Buzan (2011) 'Securitization, Sectors and Functional Differentiation', *Security Dialogue, Special Issue*, 42:4–5, 413–25.

Albert, Mathias, Barry Buzan and Michael Zürn (eds.) (2013) *Bringing Sociology to International Relations: World Politics as Differentiation Theory*, Cambridge: Cambridge University Press.

Amin, Samir (1976) *Unequal Development: An Essay on the Social Formations of Peripheral Capitalism*, New York: Monthly Review Press.

Appadurai, Arjun (1996) *Modernity at Large: Cultural Dimensions of Globalization*, Minneapolis and London: University of Minnesota Press.

— (2013) *The Future as Cultural Fact: Essays on the Global Condition*, London and Brooklyn: Verso.

Armstrong, David (1993) *Revolution and World Order: The Revolutionary State in International Society*, Oxford and New York: Clarendon Press.

— (1998) 'Globalization and the Social State', *Review of International Studies*, 24:4, 461–78.

— (1999) 'Law, Justice and the Idea of a World Society', *International Affairs*, 75:3, 547–61.

Ayoob, Mohammed (1999) 'From Regional System to Regional Society: Exploring Key Variables in the Construction of Regional Order', *Australian Journal of International Affairs*, 53:3, 247–60.

(2010) 'Making Sense of Global Tensions: Dominant and Subaltern Conceptions of Order and Justice in the International System', *International Studies*,
47:2–4, 129–41.

Bain, William (2003) *Between Anarchy and Society: Trusteeship and the Obligations
of Power*, Oxford: Oxford University Press.

(2014) 'The Pluralist-Solidarist Debate in the English School', in Cornelia
Navari and Daniel M. Green (eds.) *Guide to the English School in International
Studies*, Chichester: Wiley-Blackwell, 159–70.

Barnett, Michael N. and Martha Finnemore (1999) 'The Politics, Power, and
Pathologies of International Organizations', *International Organization*, 53:4,
699–732.

Bell, Duncan (2013) 'Race and International Relations: Introduction', *Cambridge
Review of International Affairs*, 26:1, 1–4.

Bentley, Jerry H. (1993) *Old World Encounters: Cross-Cultural Contacts and
Exchanges in Pre-Modern Times*, Oxford: Oxford University Press.

Blanchard, Eric M. (2011) 'Why Is There No Gender in the English School?',
Review of International Studies, 37:2, 855–79.

Bloomfield, Alan (2016) 'Norm Antipreneurs and Theorising Resistance to
Normative Change', *Review of International Studies*, 42:2, 310–33.

Bloomfield, Alan and Shirley V. Scott (eds.) (2017) *Norm Antipreneurs and the
Politics of Resistance to Global Normative Change*, Abingdon and New York:
Routledge.

Boli, John and George M. Thomas (eds.) (1999) *Constructing World Culture:
International Nongovernmental Organizations since 1875*, Stanford: Stanford
University Press.

Bowden, Brett (2009) *The Empire of Civilization: The Evolution of an Imperial Idea*,
Chicago: University of Chicago Press. Kindle edn.

(2014) 'To Rethink Standards of Civilisation, Start with the End', *Millennium:
Journal of International Studies*, 42:3, 614–31.

Brooks, Stephen G., G. John Ikenberry and William Wohlforth (2012–13) 'Don't
Come Home, America: The Case against Retrenchment', *International
Security*, 37:3, 7–51.

Brown, L. C. (1984) *International Politics and the Middle East*, London: I. B.
Tauris.

Bukovansky, Mlada (2002) *Legitimacy and Power Politics: The American and
French Revolutions in International Political Culture*, Princeton: Princeton
University Press.

Bukovansky, Mlada, Ian Clark, Robyn Eckersley, Richard MacKay Price,
Christian Reus-Smit and Nicholas J. Wheeler (2012) *Special Responsibilities: Global Problems and American Power*, Cambridge: Cambridge University Press.

Bull, Hedley (1977) *The Anarchical Society*, London: Macmillan.

(1980) 'The Great Irresponsibles? The United States, the Soviet Union,
and World Order', *International Journal: Canada's Journal of Global Policy
Analysis*, 35:3, 437–47.

(1982) 'The West and South Africa', *Daedalus*, 101:2, 255–70.

(1984a) 'The Revolt against the West', in Hedley Bull and Adam Watson (eds.) *The Expansion of International Society*, Oxford: Oxford University Press, 217–28.

(1984b) *Justice in International Relations*, Hagey Lectures, Ontario: University of Waterloo.

(1990) 'The Importance of Grotius in the Study of International Relations', in Hedley Bull, Benedict Kingsbury and Adam Roberts (eds.) *Hugo Grotius and International Relations*, Oxford: Clarendon, 65–93.

Bull, Hedley and Adam Watson (eds.) (1984a) *The Expansion of International Society*, Oxford: Oxford University Press.

(1984b) 'Introduction', in Hedley Bull and Adam Watson (eds.) *The Expansion of International Society*, Oxford: Oxford University Press, 1–9.

Butterfield, Herbert and Martin Wight (1966) 'Preface', in Herbert Butterfield and Martin Wight (eds.) *Diplomatic Investigations: Essays in the Theory of International Politics*, London: George Allen & Unwin, 11–13.

Butzer, Karl W. (2012) 'Collapse, Environment, and Society', *Proceedings of the National Academy of Sciences*, 109:10, 3632–9.

Buzan, Barry (1991 [1983]) *People, States & Fear: An Agenda for International Security Studies in the Post–Cold War Era*, 2nd edition, Colchester: ECPR Press.

(1993) 'From International System to International Society: Structural Realism and Regime Theory Meet the English School', *International Organization* 47:3, 327–52.

(2004a) *From International to World Society? English School Theory and the Social Structure of Globalisation*, Cambridge: Cambridge University Press.

(2004b) '"Civil" and "Uncivil" in World Society', in Stefano Guzzini and Dietrich Jung (eds.) *Contemporary Security Analysis and Copenhagen Peace Research*, London: Routledge, 94–105.

(2005) 'The Challenge of International Political Economy and Globalization', in Alex J. Bellamy (ed.) *International Society and Its Critics*, Oxford: Oxford University Press, 115–33.

(2006) 'Will the "Global War on Terrorism" Be the New Cold War?', *International Affairs*, 82:6, 1101–18.

(2010a) 'Culture and International Society', *International Affairs*, 86:1, 1–25.

(2010b) 'China in International Society: Is "Peaceful Rise" Possible?', *Chinese Journal of International Politics*, 3:1, 5–36.

(2012) 'How Regions Were Made, and the Legacies of That Process for World Politics', in T. V. Paul (ed.) *International Relations Theory and Regional Transformation*, Cambridge: Cambridge University Press, 22–46.

(2014a) *An Introduction to the English School of International Relations*, Cambridge: Polity Press.

(2014b) 'The "Standard of Civilization" as an English School Concept', *Millennium: Journal of International Studies*, 42:3, 576–94.

(2017) 'Universal Sovereignty', in Tim Dunne and Christian Reus-Smit (eds.) *The Globalisation of International Society*, Oxford: Oxford University Press, 227–47.

(2018a) 'Revisiting *World Society*', *International Politics*, 55:1, 125–40.

(2018b) 'China's Rise in English School Perspective', *International Relations of the Asia-Pacific*, 18:3.

Buzan, Barry, Charles Jones and Richard Little (1993) *The Logic of Anarchy: Neorealism to Structural Realism*, New York: Columbia University Press.

Buzan, Barry, Ole Wæver and Jaap de Wilde (1998) *Security: A New Framework for Analysis*, Boulder.: Lynne Rienner.

Buzan, Barry and Richard Little (2000) *International Systems in World History: Remaking the Study of International Relations*, Oxford: Oxford University Press.

Buzan, Barry and Ole Wæver (2003) *Regions and Powers*, Cambridge: Cambridge University Press.

Buzan, Barry and Ana Gonzalez-Pelaez (eds.) (2009) *International Society and the Middle East*, Basingstoke: Palgrave.

(2009) 'Introduction: Watson and World History', in Adam Watson (ed.) *The Evolution of International Society*, reissued with a new introduction, London: Routledge, ix–xxxv.

Buzan, Barry and Mathias Albert (2010) 'Differentiation: A Sociological Approach to International Relations Theory', *European Journal of International Relations*, 16:3, 315–37.

(2014) 'The Historical Expansion of International Society,' in Cornelia Navari and Daniel M. Green (eds.) *Guide to the English School in International Studies*, Chichester: Wiley-Blackwell, 59–75.

Buzan, Barry and Yongjin Zhang (2014) 'Introduction: Interrogating Regional International Society in East Asia', in Barry Buzan and Yongjin Zhang (eds.) *Contesting International Society in East Asia*, Cambridge: Cambridge University Press, 1–28.

Buzan, Barry and George Lawson (2014a) 'Rethinking Benchmark Dates in International Relations', *European Journal of International Relations*, 20:2, 437–62.

(2014b) 'Capitalism and the Emergent World Order', *International Affairs*, 90:1, 71–91.

(2015a) *The Global Transformation: History, Modernity and the Making of International Relations*, Cambridge: Cambridge University Press.

(2015b) 'Twentieth Century Benchmark Dates in International Relations: The Three World Wars in Historical Perspective', *International Security Studies (Beijing)*, 1:1, 39–58.

(2016) 'The Impact of the "Global Transformation" on Uneven and Combined Development', in Alexander Anievas and Kamran Matin (eds.) *Historical Sociology and World History: Uneven and Combined Development over the Longue Durée*, London: Rowman & Littlefield, 171–84.

(2018) 'The English School: History and Primary Institutions as Empirical IR Theory?', in William R. Thompson (ed.) *The Oxford Encyclopedia of Empirical International Relations Theories*, New York: Oxford University Press.

Callahan, William A. (2004) 'Nationalising International Theory: Race, Class and the English School', *Global Society*, 18:4, 305–23.

(2009) 'Chinese Visions of World Order: Post-hegemonic or a New Hegemony?', *International Studies Review*, 10:4, 749–61.

Cantir, Cristian (2016) 'World Society, International Society and the Periphery: British Abolitionists and the Post-Slave State of Haiti in the Early Nineteenth Century', *Cambridge Review of International Affairs*, 29:2, 660–76.

Carr, E. H. (1946) *The Twenty Year's Crisis 1919–1939: An Introduction to the Study of International Relations*, 2nd edition, London: Macmillan.

Castells, Manuel (1996) *The Rise of the Network Society, Volume I. The Information Age: Economy, Society, and Culture*, Oxford: Blackwell.

(1997) *The Power of Identity, Volume II. The Information Age: Economy, Society and Culture*, Oxford: Blackwell.

(1998) *End of Millennium, Volume III. The Information Age: Economy, Society and Culture*, Oxford: Blackwell.

Cerny, Phil (1993) '"Plurilateralism": Structural Differentiation and Functional Conflict in the Post-Cold War World Order', *Millennium: Journal of International Studies*, 22:1, 27–51.

Charnovitz, Steve (2006) 'Nongovernmental Organizations and International Law', *American Journal of International Law*, 100:2, 348–72.

Chase-Dunn, Christopher and Thomas D. Hall (1997) *Rise and Demise: Comparing World-Systems*, Boulder: Westview Press.

Chen, Yudan (2015) 'Chinese Notions of Sovereignty', in Jamie Gaskarth (ed.) *China, India and the Future of International Society*, London: Rowman and Littlefield, 39–52.

Clapton, William (2014) *Risk and Hierarchy in International Society: Liberal Interventionism in the Post–Cold War Era*, Basingstoke: Palgrave Macmillan.

Clark, Ian (1989) *The Hierarchy of States: Reform and Resistance in the International Order*, Cambridge: Cambridge University Press.

(2005) *Legitimacy in International Society*, Oxford: Oxford University Press.

(2007) *International Legitimacy and World Society*, Oxford: Oxford University Press.

(2009a) 'Democracy in International Society: Promotion or Exclusion?', *Millennium: Journal of International Studies*, 37:3, 563–81.

(2009b) 'Towards an English School Theory of Hegemony', *European Journal of International Relations*, 15:2, 203–28.

(2011) *Hegemony in International Society*, Oxford: Oxford University Press.

(2013) *The Vulnerable in International Society*, Oxford: Oxford University Press.

Cline, Eric E. (2014) *1177 B.C.: The Year Civilization Collapsed*, Princeton: Princeton University Press.

Cochran, Molly (2009) 'Charting the Ethics of the English School: What "Good" Is There in a Middle-Ground Ethics?', *International Studies Quarterly*, 53:1, 203–25.

Cohen, Raymond, and Raymond Westbrook (eds.) (2002) *Amarna Diplomacy: The Beginnings of International Relations*, Baltimore: Johns Hopkins University Press.

Collier, Paul (2008) *The Bottom Billion: Why the Poorest Countries Are Failing and What Can Be Done about It*, Oxford: Oxford University Press.

Cooper, Robert (1996) *The Postmodern State and the World Order*, London: Demos, Paper no. 19.

Costa-Buranelli, Filippo (2015) '"Do You Know What I Mean?" "Not Exactly": English School, Global International Society and the Polysemy of Institutions', *Global Discourse*, 5:3, 499–514.

Cui, Shunji (2014)《人的发展与人的尊严：再思人的安全概念》 [Human Development and Human Dignity: Rethinking the Concept of Human Security], *Journal of International Security Studies*, 32:1, 63–77.

Cui, Shunji and Barry Buzan (2016) 'Great Power Management in International Society', *Chinese Journal of International Politics*, 9:2, 181–210.

Davies, Thomas (2013) *NGOs: A New History of Transnational Civil Society*, London: Hurst.

(2017) 'Institutions of World Society: Parallels with the International Society of States', paper presented at the International Studies Association's Annual Convention in Baltimore.

Der Derian, James (2003) 'The Question of Information Technology', *Millennium: Journal of International Studies*, 32:3, 441–56.

Deudney, Daniel (forthcoming) *Dark Skies*, Princeton: Princeton University Press.

Deutsch, Karl W., Sidney A. Burrell, Robert A. Kann, Maurice Lee Jr, Martin Lichtenman, Raymond E. Lindgren, Francis L. Loewenheim and Richard W. Van Wagenen (1957) *Political Community and the North Atlantic Area*, Princeton: Princeton University Press.

Diamond, Jared (1998) *Guns, Germs and Steel: The Fates of Human Societies*, London: Vintage.

(2005) *Collapse: How Societies Choose to Fail or Succeed*, New York: Viking Penguin.

Diez, Thomas (2000) 'Cracks in the System, Or Why Would I Need Luhmann to Analyze International Relations', Draft paper for the European Consortium for Political Research (ECPR) workshop on 'Modern Systems Theory and International Society', Copenhagen: COPRI.

Diez, Thomas and Richard Whitman (2002) 'Analysing European Integration, Reflecting on the English School: Scenarios for an Encounter', *Journal of Common Market Studies*, 40:1, 43–67.

Diez, Thomas, Ian Manners and Richard G. Whitman (2011) 'The Changing Nature of International Institutions in Europe: The Challenge of the European Union', *European Integration*, 33:2, 117–38.

Donelan, Michael D. (ed.) (1978) *Reason of States: Study in International Political Theory*, London and Boston: Allen & Unwin.

Donnelly, Jack (1998) 'Human Rights: A New Standard of Civilization?', *International Affairs*, 74:1, 1–23.

(2006) 'Sovereign Inequalities and Hierarchy in Anarchy: American Power and International Society', *European Journal of International Relations*, 12:2, 139–70.

(2007) 'The Relative Universality of Human Rights', *Human Rights Quarterly*, 29:2, 281–306.

(2009) 'Rethinking Political Structures: From "Ordering Principles" to "Vertical Differentiation" – and Beyond', *International Theory*, 1:1, 49–86.

(2012) 'The Elements of the Structures of International Systems', *International Organization*, 66:4, 609–43.

Dunne, Tim (2003) 'Society and Hierarchy in International Relations', *International Relations*, 17:3, 303–20.

Dunne, Tim and Chris Reus-Smit (2017) *The Globalization of International Society*, Oxford: Oxford University Press.

Durkheim, Émile (translated by George Simpson) (2013 [1893]) *The Division of Labor in Society*, Overland Park: Digireads.com Publishing.

Elden, Stuart (2013) *The Birth of Territory*, Chicago and London: University of Chicago Press.

European Commission (2016) '"One of Us" Citizens' Initiative'. Available at: http://ec.europa.eu/citizens-initiative/public/initiatives/successful/details/2012/000005 (accessed 4 January 2016).

Fairbank, John King (1968) *The Chinese World Order*, Cambridge, MA: Harvard University Press.

Falkner, Robert (2016) 'The Paris Agreement and the New Logic of International Climate Politics', *International Affairs*, 92:5, 1107–25.

Falkner, Robert and Barry Buzan (2017) 'The Emergence of Environmental Stewardship as a Primary Institution of Global International Society', *European Journal of International Relations*, online first.

Fazal, Tanisha M. (2007) *State Death: The Politics and Geography of Conquest, Occupation, and Annexation*, Princeton: Princeton University Press.

Ferguson, Niel (2004) *Empire: How Britain Made the Modern World*, London: Penguin.

Ferguson, Yale and Richard Mansbach (1996), *Polities: Authority, Identities and Change*, Columbia: University of South Carolina Press.

Finnemore, Martha and Kathryn Sikkink (1998) 'International Norm Dynamics and Political Change', *International Organization*, 52:4, 887–917.

Flockhart, Trine (2016) 'The Coming Multi-Order World', *Contemporary Security Policy*, 37:1, 3–30.

Frank, André Gunder (1967) *Capitalism and Underdevelopment in Latin America: Historical Studies of Chile and Brazil*. New York: Monthly Review Press.

Freedom House (2015) 'Freedom in the World 2015'. Available at: https://freedomhouse.org/report/freedom-world/freedom-world-2015#.VfvIu5ezk84 (accessed 18 September 2015).

Friedkin, Noah. E. (2004) 'Social Cohesion', *Annual Review of Sociology*, 28, 409–25.

Fund for Peace (2016) 'Fragile States Index 2016'. Available at: http://fsi.fundforpeace.org/rankings-2016 (accessed 22 December 2016).

Galtung, Johan (1971) 'A Theory of Structural Imperialism', *Journal of Peace Research*, 8:2, 81–118.

Geldenhuys, Deon (2009) *Contested States in World Politics*, Basingstoke: Palgrave Macmillan.

Gellner, Ernest (1983) *Nations and Nationalism*, Oxford: Blackwell.

Gilpin, Robert (1981) *War and Change in World Politics*, Cambridge: Cambridge University Press.

(1987) *The Political Economy of International Relations*, Princeton: Princeton University Press.

Goldsmith, Jack L. and Tim Wu (2006) *Who Controls the Internet? Illusions of a Borderless World*, Oxford: Oxford University Press.

Gong, Gerritt W. (1984) *The Standard of 'Civilization' in International Society*, Oxford: Clarendon Press.

Gonzalez-Pelaez, Ana (2009) 'The Primary Institutions of the Middle Eastern Regional Interstate Society', in Barry Buzan and Ana Gonzalez-Pelaez (eds.) *International Society and the Middle East*, Basingstoke: Palgrave, 92–116.

Gray, Jack (2002) *Rebellions and Revolutions: China from the 1800s to 2000*, Oxford: Oxford University Press.

Green, Andy and Jan Germen Janmaat (2011) *Regimes of Social Cohesion: Societies and the Crisis of Globalization*, Basingstoke: Palgrave Macmillan.

Grimm, Sonja, Nicolas Lemay-Hébert and Olivier Nay (2014) '"Fragile States": Introducing a Political Concept', *Third World Quarterly*, 35:2, 197–209.

Haldén, Peter (2011) 'Republican Continuities in the Vienna Order and the German Confederation 1815–1866', *European Journal of International Relations*, 19:2, 281–304.

Hall, Thomas D., P. Nick Kardulius and Christopher Chase-Dunn (2011) 'World-Systems Analysis and Archaeology: Continuing the Dialogue', *Journal of Archaeological Research*, 19:3, 233–79.

Harris, Stuart (2014) *China's Foreign Policy*, Cambridge: Polity.

Headrick, Daniel R. (2010) *Power over Peoples: Technology, Environments and Western Imperialism*, Princeton: Princeton University Press.

Held, David, Anthony G. McGrew, David Goldblatt and Jonathan Perraton (1999) *Global Transformations: Politics, Economics, and Culture*, Stanford: Stanford University Press.

Herbst, Jeffrey (2000) *States and Power in Africa: Comparative Lessons in Authority and Control*, Princeton: Princeton University Press.

Hobson, Christopher (2008) 'Democracy as Civilisation', *Global Society*, 22:1, 75–95.

Hobson, John (2004) *The Eastern Origins of Western Civilization*, Cambridge: Cambridge University Press.

Hobson, John M. and J. C. Sharman (2005) 'The Enduring Place of Hierarchy in World Politics: Tracing the Social Logics of Hierarchy and Political Change', *European Journal of International Relations*, 11:1, 63–98.

Holbraad, Carsten (1984) *Middle Powers in International Politics*, London: Macmillan.

Holsti, Kalevi J. (1991) *Peace and War: Armed Conflicts and International Order 1648–1989*, Cambridge: Cambridge University Press.

(2004) *Taming the Sovereigns: Institutional Change in International Politics*, Cambridge: Cambridge University Press.

Hoover, Joe (2015) 'The Human Right to Housing and Community Empowerment: Home Occupation, Eviction Defence and Community Land Trusts', *Third World Quarterly*, 36:6, 1092–109.

Howard, Michael (1976) *War in European History*, Oxford: Oxford University Press.

(1984) 'The Military Factor in European Expansion', in Hedley Bull and Adam Watson (eds.) *The Expansion of International Society*, Oxford: Oxford University Press, 33–42.

(2008) 'Lost Friend', in Coral Bell and Meredith Thatcher (eds.) *Remembering Hedley*, Canberra: ANU Press, 127–9.

Huntington, Samuel P. (1991) *The Third Wave: Democratization in the Late 20th Century*, Norman: University of Oklahoma Press.

(1993) 'The Clash of Civilizations?', *Foreign Affairs*, 72:3, 22–49.

(1996) *The Clash of Civilizations: And the Remaking of World Order*, New York: Simon and Schuster.

Hurrell, Andrew (1995) 'Regionalism in Theoretical Perspective', in Louise Fawcett and Andrew Hurrell (eds.) *Regionalism in World Politics*, Oxford: Oxford University Press, 37–73.

(2007a) 'One World? Many Worlds? The Place of Regions in the Study of International Society', *International Affairs*, 83:1, 127–46.

(2007b) *On Global Order: Power, Values and the Constitution of International Society*, Oxford: Oxford University Press.

Ikenberry, G. John (2009) 'Liberal Internationalism 3.0: America and the Dilemmas of Liberal World Order', *Perspectives on Politics*, 7:1, 71–87.

(2011) *Liberal Leviathan: The Origins, Crisis, and Transformation of the American World Order*, Princeton: Princeton University Press.

Jackson, Robert (1999) 'Introduction: Sovereignty at the Millennium', *Political Studies*, 47:3, 423–30.

Jackson, Robert H. (1990) *Quasi-States, Sovereignty, International Relations and the Third World*, Cambridge: Cambridge University Press.

(2000) *The Global Covenant: Human Conduct in a World of States*, Oxford: Oxford University Press.

James, C. L. R. (2001) *The Black Jacobins: Toussaint L'ouverture and the San Domingo Revolution*, London: Penguin.

Jansen, Marius B. (2000) *The Making of Modern Japan*, Cambridge, MA: Belknap Press.

Johnson, Scott A. J. (2017) *Why Did Ancient Civilizations Fail?*, New York and Abingdon: Routledge.

Jones, Charles A. (2006) 'War in the Twenty-First Century: An Institution in Crisis', in Richard Little and John Williams (eds.) *The Anarchical Society in a Globalized World*, Basingstoke: Palgrave, 162–88.

(2007) *American Civilization*, London: Institute for the Study of the Americas.

Kang, David (2003) 'Getting Asia Wrong: The Need for New Analytical Frameworks', *International Security*, 27:4, 57–85.

(2003–4) 'Hierarchy, Balancing and Empirical Puzzles in Asian International Relations', *International Security*, 28:3, 165–80.

(2005) 'Why China's Rise Will Be Peaceful: Hierarchy and Stability in the East Asian Region', *Perspectives on Politics*, 3:3, 551–4. [page references are to the online version, which goes from 1–6].

Karns, Margaret P. and Karen A. Mingst (2010) *International Organizations: The Politics and Processes of Global Governance*, 2nd edition, Boulder: Lynne Rienner.

Katzenstein, Peter J. (2005) *A World of Regions: Asia and Europe in the American Imperium*. Ithaca and London: Cornell University Press.

Keal, Paul (2003) *European Conquest and the Rights of Indigenous Peoples: The Moral Backwardness of International Society*, Cambridge: Cambridge University Press.

Keck, Margaret E. and Kathryn Sikkink (1998) *Activists beyond Borders: Advocacy Networks in International Politics*, Ithaca: Cornell University Press.

Keene, Edward (2002) *Beyond the Anarchical Society: Grotius, Colonialism and Order in World Politics*, Cambridge: Cambridge University Press.

(2009) 'International Society as an Ideal Type', in Cornelia Navari (ed.) *Theorising International Society: English School Methods*, Basingstoke: Palgrave Macmillan, 104–24.

(2013) 'The Naming of Powers', *Cooperation and Conflict*, 48:2, 268–82.

(2014) 'The Standard of "Civilisation", the Expansion Thesis and the 19th-Century International Social Space', *Millennium: Journal of International Studies*, 42:3, 651–73.

Keohane, Robert O. (1984) *After Hegemony: Cooperation and Discord in the World Political Economy*, Princeton: Princeton University Press.

Kettell, Steven and Alex Sutton (2013) 'New Imperialism: Toward a Holistic Approach', *International Studies Review*, 15:2, 243–58.

Kingsbury, Benedict (1999) 'Sovereignty and Inequality', in Andrew Hurrell and Ngaire Woods (eds.) *Inequality, Globalization, and World Politics*, Oxford: Oxford University Press, 66–94.

Kirby, Paul and Laura J. Shepherd (2016) 'Reintroducing Women, Peace and Security', *International Affairs*, 92:2, 249–54.

Knudsen, Tonny Brems and Cornelia Navari (eds.) (forthcoming) *International Organization in the Anarchical Society: The Institutional Structure of World Order*, Palgrave.

Koff, Harlan (2013) 'Comparing the "A, B, Cs" of Social Cohesion across World Regions: Association, Belonging and Change', in Candice Moore (ed.) *Regional Integration and Social Cohesion*, Bruxelles: P. I. E. Peter Lang, 41–72.

Koremenos, Barbara (2016) *The Continent of International Law: Explaining Agreement Design*, Cambridge: Cambridge University Press.

Kozyrev, Vitaly (2016) 'Harmonizing 'Responsibility to Protect': China's Vision of a Post-Sovereign World', *International Relations*, 30:3, 328–45.

Kupchan, Charles A. (1998) 'After Pax Americana: Benign Power, Regional Integration, and the Sources of Stable Multipolarity', *International Security*, 23:2, 40–79.

(2002) *The End of the American Era: US Foreign Policy and the Geopolitics of the Twenty-First Century*, New York: Alfred Knopf.

(2012) *No One's World: The West, the Rising Rest, and the Coming Global Turn*, New York: Oxford University Press.

(2014) 'The Normative Foundations of Hegemony and the Coming Challenge to Pax Americana', *Security Studies*, 23:2, 219–57.

Lach, Donald F. (1965, 1970, 1993) *Asia in the Making of Europe*, Vols. 1–3, Chicago: University of Chicago Press.

Lake, David A. (2009) *Hierarchy in International Relations*, Ithaca: Cornell University Press.

Lasmar, Jorge M., Danny Zahreddine and Delber Andrade Gribel Lage (2015) 'Understanding Regional and Global Diffusion in International Law: The Case for a Non-Monolithic Approach to Institutions', *Global Discourse*, 5:3, 470–96.

Lawler, Andrew (2010) 'Collapse? What Collapse? Societal Change Revisited', *Science*, 330:6006, 907–9.

Linklater, Andrew (2016) *Violence and Civilization in the Western States-Systems*, Cambridge: Cambridge University Press.

Little, Richard (2007) *The Balance of Power in International Relations: Metaphors, Myths and Models*, Cambridge: Cambridge University Press.

Lövbrand, Eva and Johannes Stripple (2006) 'The Climate as Political Space: On the Territorialisation of the Global Carbon Cycle', *Review of International Studies*, 32:2, 217–35.

Mackintosh-Smith, Tim (2002) *The Travels of Ibn Battutah*, London: Picador.

Mann, Michael (1986) *The Sources of Social Power, Volume 1: A History of Power from the Beginning to AD 1760*, Cambridge: Cambridge University Press.

(1993) *The Sources of Social Power, Volume 2: The Rise of Classes and Nation-States, 1760–1914*, Cambridge: Cambridge University Press.

(2012) *The Sources of Social Power, Volume 3: Global Empires and Revolution, 1890–1945*, Cambridge: Cambridge University Press.

(2013) *The Sources of Social Power, Volume 4: Globalizations, 1945–2011*, Cambridge: Cambridge University Press.

March, James G. and Johan P. Olsen (1998) 'The Institutional Dynamics of International Political Orders', *International Organization*, 52:4, 943–69.

Mathews, Jessica T. (1997) 'Power Shift', *Foreign Affairs*, 76:1, 50–66.

Mayall, James (1990) *Nationalism and International Society*, Cambridge: Cambridge University Press.

(2000) 'Democracy and International Society', *International Affairs*, 76:1, 61–76.

McAnany, Patricia A. and Norman Yoffee (eds.) (2010) *Questioning Collapse: Human Resilience, Ecological Vulnerability, and the Aftermath of Empire*, Cambridge: Cambridge University Press.

Merke, Federico (2011) 'The Primary Institutions of Latin American Regional Interstate Society', Paper for IDEAS Latin America Programme, LSE, 27 January 2011.

(2015) 'Neither Balance nor Bandwagon: South American International Society Meets Brazil's Rising Power', *International Politics*, 52:2, 178–92.

Meyer, John W. (2010) 'World Society, Institutional Theories, and the Actor', *Annual Review of Sociology*, 36, 1–20.

Meyer, John W., John Boli, George M. Thomas and Francisco O. Ramirez (1997) 'World Society and the Nation-State', *American Journal of Sociology*, 103:1, 144–81.

Middleton, Guy D. (2012) 'Nothing Lasts Forever: Environmental Discourses on the Collapse of Past Societies', *Journal of Archaeological Research*, 20:3, 257–307.

Migdal, Joel S. (1988) *Strong Societies and Weak States*, Princeton: Princeton University Press.

Morris, Ian (2014) *War! What Is It Good For? Conflict and the Progress of Civilization from Primates to Robots*, reprint edition, New York: Farrar, Straus and Giroux.

Mueller, Milton L. (2010) *Networks and States: The Global Politics of Internet Governance*, Cambridge, MA and London: MIT Press.

Murphy, R. Taggart (2014) *Japan and the Shackles of the Past*, Oxford: Oxford University Press.

Nandy, Ashis (1983) *The Intimate Enemy: Loss and Recovery of Self under Colonialism*, New Delhi: Oxford University Press.

Navari, Cornelia (ed.) (1991) *Condition of States: A Study in International Political Theory*, Milton Keynes and Philadelphia: Open University Press.

—— (2007) 'States and State Systems: Democratic, Westphalian or Both?', *Review of International Studies*, 33:4, 577–95.

—— (2016) 'Primary and Secondary Institutions: Quo Vadit?', *Cooperation and Conflict*, 51:1, 121–7.

—— (2018) 'Two Roads to World Society: Meyer's "World Polity" and Buzan's "World Society"', *International Politics*, 55:1, 11–25.

Noortmann, Math, Bas Arts and Bob Reinalda (2001) 'The Quest for Unity in Empirical and Conceptual Complexity', in Math Noortmann, Bas Arts and Bob Reinalda (eds.) *Non-State Actors in International Relations*, Aldershot: Ashgate, 299–307.

North, Douglass C., John Joseph Wallis and Barry R. Weingast (2009) *Violence and Social Orders: A Conceptual Framework for Interpreting Recorded Human History*, Cambridge: Cambridge University Press.

Nye, Joseph S. (2014) 'The Regime Complex for Managing Global Cyber Activities', Global Commission on Internet Governance Paper Series, no. 1, Waterloo and London: Centre for International Governance (CIGI) and Chatham House.

Onapajo, Hakeem and Christopher Isike (2016) 'The Global Politics of Gay Rights: The Straining Relations between the West and Africa', *Journal of Global Analysis*, 6:1, 21–45.

Onuf, Nicholas (2002) 'Institutions, Intentions and International Relations', *Review of International Studies*, 28:2, 211–28.

Paine, S. C. M. (2003) *The Sino-Japanese War of 1894–5: Perceptions, Power and Primacy*, New York: Cambridge University Press.

—— (2012) *The Wars for Asia 1911–1949*, New York: Cambridge University Press.

—— (2017) *The Japanese Empire: Grand Strategy from the Meiji Restoration to the Pacific War*, New York: Cambridge University Press.

Parent, Joseph M. (2011) *Uniting States: Voluntary Union in World Politics*, Oxford and New York: Oxford University Press.

Paul, T. V. (2010) 'State Capacity and South Asia's Perennial Insecurity Problems', in T.V. Paul (ed.) *South Asian's Weak States: Understanding the Regional Insecurity Predicament*, Stanford: Stanford University Press, 3–27.

Pearcey, Mark (2015) 'Sovereignty, Identity, and Indigenous-State Relations at the Beginning of the Twentieth Century: A Case of Exclusion by Inclusion', *International Studies Review*, 17:3, 441–54.

Pejcinovic, Lacy (2013) *War in International Society*, Abingdon and New York: Routledge.

Pella Jr, John Anthony (2013) 'Thinking Outside International Society: A Discussion of the Possibilities for English School Conceptions of World Society', *Millennium: Journal of International Studies*, 42:1, 65–77.

(2015a) *Africa and the Expansion of International Society: Surrendering the Savannah*, Abingdon and New York: Routledge.

(2015b) 'World Society, International Society and the Colonization of Africa', *Cambridge Review of International Affairs*, 28:2, 210–28.

Phillips, Andrew (2012) 'Saving Civilization from Empire: Belligerency, Pacifism and the Two Faces of Civilization during the Second Opium War', *European Journal of International Relations*, 18:1, 5–27.

Phillips, Andrew and J. C. Sharman (2015) *International Order in Diversity: War, Trade and Rule in the Indian Ocean*, Cambridge: Cambridge University Press.

Philpott, Daniel (2001) *Revolutions in Sovereignty: How Ideas Shaped Modern International Relations*, Princeton: Princeton University Press.

Pieke, Frank N. (2016) *Knowing China: A Twenty-First Century Guide*, Cambridge: Cambridge University Press.

Pieterse, Jan Nederveen (2003) *Globalization and Culture: Global Mélange*, London: Rowman & Littlefield.

(2011) 'Global Multiculture: Cultures, Transnational Culture, Deep Culture', in Claudio Baraldi, Andrea Borsari and Augusto Carli (eds.) *Hybrids, Differences, Visions: On the Study of Culture*, Aurora: Davies Group, 81–96.

Piketty, Thomas (2014) *Capital in the Twenty-First Century*, Cambridge, MA: Harvard University Press.

Pines, Yuri (2012) *The Everlasting Empire: The Political Culture of Ancient China and Its Imperial Legacy*, Princeton: Princeton University Press.

Pouliot, Vincent (2014) 'Setting Status in Stone: The Negotiation of International Institutional Privileges', in T. V. Paul, Deborah Welch Larson and William C. Wohlforth (eds.) *Status in World Politics*, Cambridge: Cambridge University Press, 192–215.

Poulsen, Lauge N. Skovgaard and Emma Aisbett (2013). 'When the Claim Hits: Bilateral Investment Treaties and Bounded Rational Learning', *World Politics*, 65:2, 273–313.

Quayle, Linda (2013) *Southeast Asia and the English School of International Relations: A Region-Theory Dialogue*, Basingstoke: Palgrave Macmillan.

Ralph, Jason (2007) *Defending the Society of States: Why America Opposes the International Criminal Court and Its Vision of World Society*, Oxford and New York: Oxford University Press.

Ren, Xiao (2015) 'Human Security in Practice: The Chinese Experience', JICA-RI Working Paper, No.92, March.

Reus-Smit, Christian (1999) *The Moral Purpose of the State: Culture, Social Identity, and Institutional Rationality in International Relations*, Princeton: Princeton University Press.

(2011) 'Struggles for Individual Rights and the Expansion of the International System', *International Organization*, 65:2, 207–42.

Reynolds, Glenn Harlan (2004) 'Space Law in the 21st Century: Some Thoughts in Response to the Bush Administration's Space Initiative', *Journal of Air Law and Commerce*, 69, 413–23.

Riemer, Andrea K. and Yannis A. Stivachtis (eds.) (2002) *Understanding EU's Mediterranean Enlargement: The English School and the Expansion of Regional International Societies*, Frankfurt: Peter Lang.

Risse-Kappen, Thomas (1995) 'Bringing Transnational Relations Back In: Introduction', in Thomas Risse-Kappen (ed.) *Bringing Transnational Relations Back In: Non-State Actors, Domestic Structures and International Institutions*, Cambridge: Cambridge University Press, 3–33.

Risse, Thomas (2002) 'Transnational Actors and World Politics', in Walter Carlsnaes, Thomas Risse and Beth A. Simmons (eds.) *Handbook of International Relations*, London: Sage, 255–74.

Risse, Thomas, Stephen C. Ropp and Kathryn Sikkink (1999) *The Power of Human Rights: International Norms and Domestic Change*, Cambridge: Cambridge University Press.

Rosenau, James N. and Ernst-Otto Czempiel (eds.) (1992) *Governance without Government: Order and Change in World Politics*, Cambridge: Cambridge University Press.

Rosenberg, Justin (1994) *The Empire of Civil Society*, London: Verso.

(2013) 'Kenneth Waltz and Leon Trotsky: Anarchy in the Mirror of Uneven and Combined Development', *International Politics*, 50:2, 183–230.

(2016) 'International Relations in the Prison of Political Science', *International Relations*, 30:2, 127–53.

Rostow, W. W. (1960) *The Stages of Economic Growth: A Non-Communist Manifesto*, Cambridge: Cambridge University Press.

Roughead, Gary (2015) 'In the Race for Arctic Energy, the U.S. and Russia Are Polar Opposites', *Wall Street Journal*. Available at: www.wsj.com/art icles/in-the-race-for-arctic-energy-the-u-s-and-russia-are-polar-opposites-1440542608 (accessed 28 August 2015).

Ruggie, John (1983) 'Continuity and Transformation in the World Polity: Towards a Neo-Realist Synthesis', *World Politics*, 35:2, 261–85.

(1993) 'Territoriality and Beyond: Problematizing Modernity in International Relations', *International Organization*, 47:1, 139–74.

Sassen, Saskia (2008) *Territory, Authority, Rights: From Medieval to Global Assemblages*, Princeton: Princeton University Press.

Schell, Orville and John Delury (2013) *Wealth and Power: China's Long March to the Twenty-First Century*, London: Little, Brown.

Schouenborg, Laust (2011) 'A New Institutionalism? The English School as International Sociological Theory', *International Relations*, 25:1, 26–44.

(2012) 'Exploring Westphalia's Blind Spots: Exceptionalism Meets the English School', *Geopolitics*, 17:1, 130–52.

(2013) *The Scandinavian International Society: Primary Institutions and Binding Forces, 1815–2010*, Abingdon and New York: Routledge.

(2017) *International Institutions in World History: Divorcing International Relations Theory from the State and Stage Models*, Abingdon and New York: Routledge.

Schulz, Carsten-Andreas (2014) 'Civilisation, Barbarism and the Making of Latin America's Place in 19th-Century International Society', *Millennium: Journal of International Studies*, 42:3, 837–59.

Scott, James C. (1999) *Seeing Like a State: How Certain Schemes to Improve the Human Condition Have Failed*, New Haven: Yale University Press.

Shimazu, Naoko (1998) *Japan, Race and Equality: The Racial Equality Proposal of 1919*, London: Routledge.

Simpson, Gerry (2004) *Great Powers and Outlaw States: Unequal Sovereigns in the International Legal Order*, Cambridge: Cambridge University Press.

Sjoberg, Laura (2012) 'Gender, Structure, and War: What Waltz Couldn't See', *International Theory*, 4:1, 1–38.

Smith, Gayle (2014) 'Hailing the Contributions of the Private and Non-Profit Sectors to the Ebola Fight', White House, 6 November 2014. Available at: www.whitehouse.gov/blog/2014/11/06/hailing-contributions-private-and-non-profit-sectors-ebola-fight (accessed 17 March 2018).

Sørensen, Georg (2001) *Changes in Statehood: The Transformation of International Relations*, Basingstoke: Palgrave.

Spandler, Kilian (2015) 'The Political International Society: Change in Primary and Secondary Institutions', *Review of International Studies*, 41:3, 601–22.

Spruyt, Hendrik (1994) *The Sovereign State and Its Competitors: An Analysis of Systems Change*, Princeton: Princeton University Press.

Stern, Philip J. (2011) *The Company-State: Corporate Sovereignty and the Early Modern Foundations of the British Empire in India*, Oxford: Oxford University Press.

Stivachtis, Yannis A. (2003) 'Europe and the Growth of International Society: Anarchy More Than Culture', *Global Dialogue*, 5:3/4, 87–99.

——— (2006) 'Democracy, the Highest Stage of "Civilised" Statehood', *Global Dialogue*, 8:3/4, 101–12.

——— (2010) 'International Society: Global/Regional Dimensions and Geographic Expansion', in Robert A. Denemark (ed.) *The International Studies Encyclopedia*, Blackwell Publishing for International Studies Association (ISA).

——— (2014) 'European Union and World Order: An English School Approach', *Estudos Internacionais*, 2:2, 321–41.

——— (2015) 'Interrogating Regional International Societies, Questioning the Global International Society', *Global Discourse*, 5:3, 327–40.

Storey, Rebecca and Glenn R. Storey (2017) *Rome and the Classic Maya: Comparing the Slow Collapse of Civilizations*, New York and Abingdon: Routledge.

Strandsbjerg, Jeppe (2012) 'Cartopolitics, Geopolitics and Boundaries in the Arctic', *Geopolitics*, 17:4, 818–42.

Strauss, Michael J. (2013) 'Boundaries in the Sky and a Theory of Three-Dimensional States', *Journal of Borderlands Studies*, 28:3, 369–82.

Stroikos, Dimitrios (2015) 'Failure and Denial in International Society: Modernity, Technology and the Global Nuclear Order', paper for *Millennium* Conference, LSE, October.

Suzuki, Shogo (2009) *Civilization and Empire: China and Japan's Encounter with European International Society*, London: Routledge.

Suzuki, Shogo, Yongjin Zhang and Joel Quirk (eds.) (2014) *International Orders in the Early Modern World: Before the Rise of the West*, London: Routledge.

Swope, Kenneth M. (2009) *A Dragon's Head and a Serpent's Tail: Ming China and the First Great East Asian War*, Kindle editon, Norman: University of Oklahoma Press.

Tainter, Joseph (1988) *The Collapse of Complex Societies*, Cambridge: Cambridge University Press.

Tilly, Charles (1990) *Coercion, Capital and European States AD 990–1990*, Oxford: Basil Blackwell.

Towns, Ann E. (2009) 'The Status of Women as a Standard of "Civilization"', *European Journal of International Relations*, 15:4, 681–706.

———— (2010) *Women and States: Norms and Hierarchies in International Society*, Cambridge: Cambridge University Press.

———— (2012) 'Norms and Social Hierarchies: Understanding International Policy Diffusion "from Below"', *International Organization*, 66:2, 179–209.

True, Jacqui (2005) 'Feminism', in Alex J. Bellamy (ed.) *International Society and Its Critics*, Oxford: Oxford University Press, 151–62.

United Nations (2013) *International Migration Report 2013*, New York: United Nations, Department of Economic and Social Affairs.

United Nations Department of Economic and Social Affairs (2015) 'World Population Projected to Reach 9.7 Billion by 2050'. Available at: www.un.org/en/development/desa/news/population/2015-report.html (accessed 14 November 2016).

United Nations High Commissioner for Refugees (UNHCR) (2015) *World at War: UNHCR Global Trends – Forced Displacement 2014*, Geneva: UNHCR.

Vatican (2015) 'Population', Available at: www.vaticanstate.va/content/vatican state/en/stato-e-governo/note-generali/popolazione.html (accessed 31 August 2015) (appears in ch. 2).

Vincent, R. John (1984) 'Racial Equality', in Hedley Bull and Adam Watson (eds.) *The Expansion of International Society*, Oxford: Oxford University Press, 239–54.

———— (1986), *Human Rights and International Relations: Issues and Responses*, Cambridge: Cambridge University Press.

Walker, William (2012) *A Perpetual Menace: Nuclear Weapons and International Order*, Abingdon and New York: Routledge.

Wallerstein, Immanuel (1974) *The Modern World-System*, New York: Academic Press.

———— (2004) *World-Systems Analysis: An Introduction*. Durham: Duke University Press.

Wang, Qiu-bin (2007) 'The Northeast Asia Regional International Society: From the English School Perspective', *Jilin University Journal Social Sciences Edition*, 2, 59–65.

Watson, Adam (1964) *The War of Goldsmith's Daughter*, London: Chatto & Windus.

———— (1984) 'European International Society and Its Expansion', in Hedley Bull and Adam Watson (eds.) *The Expansion of International Society*, Oxford: Oxford University Press, 13–32.

(1992) *The Evolution of International Society*, London: Routledge.

(1997) *The Limits of Independence: Relations between States in the Modern World*, London: Routledge.

(2001) 'Foreword' to 'Forum on the English School', *Review of International Studies*, 27:3, 467–70.

Waltz, Kenneth N. (1979) *Theory of International Politics*, Reading: Addison-Wesley.

Weiss, Thomas G. (2013) *Global Governance: Why? What? Whither?*, Cambridge: Polity Press.

Wendt, Alexander (1999) *Social Theory of International Politics*, Cambridge: Cambridge University Press.

Wheeler, Nicholas J. (2000) *Saving Strangers: Humanitarian Intervention in International Society*, Oxford: Oxford University Press.

Wiener, Antje (2004) 'Contested Compliance: Interventions on the Normative Structure of World Politics', *European Journal of International Relations*, 10:2, 189–234.

(2014) *A Theory of Contestation*, Heidelberg: Springer.

Wight, Colin (2006) *Agents, Structures and International Relations: Politics as Ontology*, Cambridge and New York: Cambridge University Press.

Wight, Martin (1960) 'Why Is There No International Theory?', *International Relations*, 2:1, 35–48.

(1977) *Systems of States*, Leicester: Leicester University Press.

Wight, Martin (edited by Gabriele Wight and Brian Porter) (1991) *International Theory: The Three Traditions*, Leicester: Leicester University Press.

Williams, John (2011) 'Structure, Norms and Normative Theory in a Re-Defined English School: Accepting Buzan's Challenge', *Review of International Studies*, 37:3, 1235–53.

Wilson, Peter (2012) 'The English School Meets the Chicago School: The Case for a Grounded Theory of International Institutions', *International Studies Review*, 14:4, 567–90.

Womack, Brantly (2014) 'China's Future in a Multinodal World Order', *Pacific Affairs*, 87:2, 265–84.

World Society Research Group (WSRG) (1995) 'In Search of World Society', Darmstadt/Frankfurt/M.: World Society Research Group Working paper no. 1. Updated version (2000) 'Introduction: World Society', in Mathias Albert, Lothar Brock and Klaus Dieter Wolf (eds.) *Civilizing World Politics. Society and Community Beyond the State*, Lanham: Rowman & Littlefield, 1–17.

Young, Crawford (1994) *The African Colonial State in Comparative Perspective*, New Haven: Yale University Press.

Yurdusev, Nuri (2009) 'The Middle East Encounter with the Expansion of European International Society', in Barry Buzan and Ana Gonzalez-Pelaez (eds.) *International Society and the Middle East*, Basingstoke: Palgrave, 70–91.

Zakaria, Fareed (2009) *The Post-American World and the Rise of the Rest*, London: Penguin.

Zarakol, Ayşe (2011) *After Defeat: How the East Learned to Live with the West*, Cambridge: Cambridge University Press.

Zhang, Feng (2009) 'Rethinking the "Tribute System": Broadening the Conceptual Horizon of Historical East Asian Politics', *Chinese Journal of International Politics*, 2:4, 545–74.

Zhang, Yongjin (1991) 'China's Entry into International Society: Beyond the Standard of "Civilization"', *Review of International Studies*, 17:1, 3–16.

(1998) *China in International Society since 1949*, Basingstoke: Macmillan.

(2001) 'System, Empire and State in Chinese International Relations', in Michael Cox, Tim Dunne, and Ken Booth (eds.) *Empires, Systems and States: Great Transformations in International Politics*, Cambridge University Press, 43–63.

(2014) 'The Standard of "Civilisation" Redux: Towards the Expansion of International Society 3.0?" *Millennium: Journal of International Studies*, 42:3, 674–96.

Zhang, Yongjin and Barry Buzan (2012) 'The Tributary System as International Society in Theory and Practice', *Chinese Journal of International Politics*, 5:1, 3–36.

Zürn, Michael, Barry Buzan and Mathias Albert (2013) 'Conclusion: Differentiation Theory and World Politics', in Mathias Albert, Barry Buzan and Michael Zürn (eds.) *Bringing Sociology to International Relations: World Politics as Differentiation Theory*, Cambridge: Cambridge University Press, 228–45.

Scholar Index

Subject Index

absent states, 58–59
advocacy, by primary institutions, 26
AIDB. *See* Asian Infrastructure
  Development Bank
Amnesty International, 167
anti-globalization, 148
Asian Infrastructure Development Bank
  (AIDB), 167
assessment, of GIS, 10
Australia
  in HPM, 127
  in repopulation submodel, 52
authoritarianism, 67
  in China, 67
  in FDM, 175–76
  NSAs under, 199
  in Russia, 67

belief criterion, in LUM, 91, 95
British Exit (Brexit), 67–68
Buddhism, 41
Bush, George W., 91

Canada
  in HPM, 127
  in repopulation submodel, 51
capitalism
  global, 171
  neoliberal, 66–67
    challenges to, 67–68
CARE. *See* Cooperative for Assistance and
  Relief Everywhere
CCP. *See* Chinese Communist Party
Chavez, Hugo, 91
China
  authoritarianism in, 67
  cyberspace and, territoriality of, 107
  economic capabilities of, 63
  in encounter/reform submodel, 56–57
  in HPM, 126, 140–41
  as hybrid of modernity, 69
Chinese Communist Party (CCP), 92

Christianity
  Islam and, 40–41, 45
  modernity and, 170
  in RSM, 106–7
Citizens' Initiative, 115
coercion, 38
  in European expansion, 42
coexistence type, of international
  society, 81
cohesion. *See* social cohesion
Cold War, 126
*Collapse: How Societies Choose to Fail or
  Succeed* (Diamond), 239–40
collapsed states, 58–59
collective identity, in interhuman
  domains, 26
colonial states, in sub-Saharan Africa, 59
colonialism
  HPM and, 145–47
  stratificatory differentiation and, 23
colonization/decolonization submodel, 44,
  53–56
  in Middle East, 53
  Ottoman Empire, 55
  regional differentiation in, 54–55
  in sub-Saharan Africa, 53–54
Concert of Europe, 125
Conference on Security and Cooperation
  in Europe (CSCE), 69
Confucianism, 41
Congress of Vienna, 125
consensual agreement, among GIS
  members, 85–86
constructivism
  ES and, 7–8
  GIS and, 8
convergence type, of international
  society, 81
cooperation type, of international
  society, 81
Cooperative for Assistance and Relief
  Everywhere (CARE), 167